Dick, 4/7/07

Thanks for all you taught me. Keep accelerating Webster!

Dan Coughlin

ACCELERATE

20 PRACTICAL LESSONS TO BOOST BUSINESS MOMENTUM

DAN COUGHLIN

Editorial Director: Jennifer Farthing
Acquisitions Editor: Shannon Berning
Production Editor: Samantha Raue
Production Artist: Todd Bowman
Cover Designer: Gail Chandler

Published by Kaplan Publishing,
a division of Kaplan, Inc.

Printed in the United States of America

May 2007

07 08 09 10 9 8 7 6 5 4 3 2 1

Library of Congress Cataloging-in-Publication Data
Coughlin, Dan, 1962-
Accelerate : 20 practical lessons to boost business momentum / Dan Coughlin.
p. cm.
ISBN-13: 978-1-4195-9372-7
ISBN-10: 1-4195-9372-2
1. Organizational effectiveness. 2. Business planning. 3. Leadership. I. Title. II. Title: 20 practical lessons to boost business momentum. III. Title: Twenty practical lessons to boost business momentum.
HD58.9.C6744 2007
658–dc22 2006100856

For information about ordering Kaplan Publishing books at special quantity discounts, please call 1-800-KAP-ITEM or write to Kaplan Publishing, 888 Seventh Ave., 22nd Floor, New York, NY 10106.

This book is dedicated to the three greatest treasures in my life, Barb, Sarah, and Ben.

Contents

Acknowledgments vii
Introduction: The Education of an Executive Coach ix

PART ONE
ACCELERATE YOUR INDIVIDUAL RESULTS

1. ENHANCE PERSONAL EFFECTIVENESS 3
"I Could Do So Much More for This Company."

2. UTILIZE PRIORITY MANAGEMENT 27
"And Exactly When Am I Going to Have Time to Do That?"

3. AVOID DISASTROUS COMMUNICATION 41
"You Said What to Whom?"

4. PROVIDE LEADERSHIP 53
"My Boss Tells Me I'm a Mood-Ring Leader."

5. KICK START CREATIVITY 69
"People Don't Pay Me to Sit Around and Think."

PART TWO
ACCELERATE YOUR STAFF'S RESULTS

6. IDENTIFY REASONS FOR LACK OF UNITY 79
"You Call That a Team?"

7. STRENGTHEN TEAMWORK 89
"We Just Sit Wherever We Want."

8. EMBRACE COLLABORATION 109
"What Do You Mean It's Not Enough to Be Right?"

9. EXPEDITE EXECUTION 115
"We Could Get More Done If We Had More Time."

10. MANAGE CHANGE 125
"When Are All These Changes Going to Stop?"

PART THREE
ACCELERATE YOUR ORGANIZATION'S RESULTS

11. ESTABLISH YOUR LEADERSHIP COUNCIL 135
"How Do I Get My Leadership Council to, You Know, Lead?"

12. ACKNOWLEDGE THE MISTAKES OF STRATEGIC PLANNING 147
"Are We Doing Enough?"

13. GAIN STRATEGIC FOCUS 157
"Let's Just Pick One Thing and Do It Really Well."

14. USE TALENT MANAGEMENT 189
"Where Do We Find the Right People?"

15. INCREASE INNOVATION 201
"We've Got to Find Ways to Grow the Business Now."

PART FOUR
ACCELERATE YOUR IMPACT ON CONSUMERS

16. STUDY BUSINESS RESEARCH 217
"Our Customers Just Didn't Do What They Were Supposed to Do."

17. DELIVER CONVENIENCE 231
"You Can Do What with Your iPod?"

18. OPERATE IN THE CREATIVITY AGE 237
"You Haven't Lived Until You've Been Googled."

19. CLARIFY CONSUMER DEMANDS 243
"I Want It Now at a Lower Price with Better Service."

20. BUILD THE BRAND 255
"Will This Be Good for Our Brand?"

Appendix: Tools to Accelerate 271
About the Author 281
Index 283

Acknowledgments

Thanks so much to the following people:

Jeff Herman, my literary agent, who has continued to believe in my work. Every author should have an advocate like Jeff.

Jennifer Farthing, Shannon Berning, Brigit Dermott, Samantha Raue, Kelly Barrales-Saylor, and the whole team at Kaplan Publishing for being such tremendous partners. I appreciate every little detail of what they've done for this book.

Sam Horn, who taught me how to embrace the responsibility of the blank page and create an approach to writing a book that I could really get excited about.

Jill Wettstein, my graphic artist, who designed all the process visuals in this book by taking my limited drawings and bringing them to life.

Mark French, Rainey Foster, Matt Jones and the whole team at Leading Authorities for being such wonderful and fun partners. I've thoroughly enjoyed the adventure we continue to experience together.

Jason Jennings for taking the time to teach me about the life of an author.

The more than one hundred people I've had the honor of working with as their executive coach. You've taught me so much about business and life, and I appreciate it greatly.

Dr. Gary Clark and Dr. Alan Weiss, who have been my two primary mentors over the past ten years. They both taught me a great deal about the life of a business and the business of a life, and I appreciate every insight they offered to me.

Gene and Laura Coughlin, my parents, who embody the American Dream. It was their vision, focus, sacrifice, and sustained effort that turned dreams into realities for all six of their children.

My wife, Barb, and our two children, Sarah and Ben, who make life an adventure every day. Together we create a very fun environment where all of us can live, grow, learn, and express ourselves.

Thank you all from the bottom of my heart!

THE EDUCATION OF AN EXECUTIVE COACH

In October 1996, I met with a regional director of operations at McDonald's Corporation to discuss putting on four half-day workshops on leadership and teamwork for a group of his department heads. A month later, he was promoted, and I thought my first chance to work with a major corporate client was going to disappear before I even started. Fortunately, two months later, his replacement brought me in to complete the project.

In July 1997, I followed up with my original contact and offered to go over the material in the workshops on a one to one basis as a thank you for bringing me into McDonald's. He then asked if I would serve as his executive coach. Little did I know how that moment would change my life.

My first executive coaching relationship at McDonald's evolved into me working with more than 50 individuals at McDonald's. In addition to the director of operations, I worked with restaurant managers who ran a single restaurant and area supervisors who were responsible for 15 restaurants. I would ride with them and observe them in the restaurants and in meetings and offer my insights.

After proving that I could add value that drove real business results, I worked with regional and divisional executives responsible for a billion dollars or more of the business. The challenges for these executives ranged from overseeing the performance of 500 McDonald's restaurants to interacting with McDonald's owner/operators to communicating with their bosses back in the Oak Brook world headquarters to managing a staff of 65 employees.

And then this thing really started to spread.

Here's a typical month of how I interacted with my clients.

Early in the month, I worked with an operations team within McDonald's to clarify its specific goals, tactics, and planned activities for an upcoming initiative. Later in the month, I did a workshop on innovation for a group of McDonald's marketing people as well as their advertising agencies. In between those two events I interviewed ten people at the Coca-Cola Company in preparation for a workshop on teamwork for a cross-functional team within Coca-Cola made up of people from operations, marketing, and account services.

The next day, I rode all day with a truck driver for Cassens Transport to better understand the challenges that drivers and union members face. A few weeks after that experience, I facilitated a series of discussions between 80 truck drivers and the top management of the company.

At the end of the month, I provided a coaching session for a senior-level executive at ANDEO Nalco Chemical, a large chemical company working in the paper treatment industry. He was in charge of the pulp and paper division, and we discussed the impact the internet was having on the paper industry. The day after that I met with the CEO of a newly founded biotech company and we discussed how to create an effective board made up of scientists, private investors, and management personnel. The next day I spent several hours observing the head of operations at a large Marriott hotel and then shared my observations of his performance with him.

This variety of events with various organizations has gone on continuously for ten years.

I've watched and offered my input on a variety of projects. I coached the top two executives in one McDonald's region for a period of seven years as they generated the longest consecutive streak of positive annual comp sales growth of any McDonald's region in the country. I worked very closely with the director of new business development at GSD&M, a national advertising agency, during the entire five-month, three-phase winning pitch for the $100 million BMW account. Since I know nothing about advertising, my role was to observe her in action, give her feedback, and collaborate with her on how to effectively influence a variety of key moments.

I worked for a year with the vice president of ticket sales for the St. Louis Cardinals as he and his team broke the all-time record for preseason ticket sales. I worked with the leaders of Mackey Mitchell & Associates, the architectural firm, as they prepared the winning presentation for redesigning the University of Notre Dame's campus.

I coached the vice president of risk management for Marriott USA. He was responsible for all the insurance claims filed at all the Marriott branded hotels across the United States, which represented about $6 billion in hotel revenues. Anything from sexual harassment to a guest slipping on a wet floor to Hurricane Katrina was his responsibility. He had teams of 30 to 35 people set up in five offices spread across the United States. I sat silently through a three-day meeting with his direct reports and watched the human dynamics involved in running such a complicated situation. Then I gave everyone feedback.

Over the years, at any given moment I would be coaching a group of people responsible for anywhere from $2 to 5 billion worth of revenues. My clients included division vice presidents for the Coca-Cola Company, a national manager for Toyota, the president of a billion-dollar construction company, and the division president for a billion-dollar chemical company. Through it all, not only was I observing the people I coached, but I also saw hundreds of other executives and managers interact in very diverse, real-life business situations. Each of these clients added their wisdom to my continually expanding knowledge of what makes managers successful.

As you might expect, my role with these executives has been much like that of a business quarterback coach. I held many sessions with them behind closed doors and over the phone to prepare for important meetings and critical decisions. The topics included key personnel moves, strategic maneuvers, critical communications, developing innovative approaches for creating improvements throughout their business units, adjusting to massive changes in market trends, dealing with difficult people, managing the flow of talent, and a host of unexpected crises both locally and nationally.

I would sit for hours and hours observing an executive in situations ranging from huge conferences to private strategic planning sessions. We would then discuss what had just happened and identify what worked well and what could have made the scenario more effective in terms of moving the business forward. Many times, I was asked to facilitate difficult meetings on hot topics with the manager's direct reports and colleagues. I soaked up every observation, every conversation, and every process being used. I filtered every piece of input through the screen of what was actually improving important business results and what was not.

Meanwhile, I continued to do keynotes and workshops for a variety of organizations. In preparing for every presentation, I would interview 10 to 15 people in the organization to learn more about their industry, the opportunities they faced, and the dangers they dealt with. In this manner, I learned about companies like AT&T, which was SBC at that time; Eli Lilly; Boeing; and Albertsons.

Oftentimes I would spend entire days next to employees in these corporations while they did their normal day-to-day work in order to learn their business from an internal perspective. I spent a day working as a crew member at McDonald's and several days riding with department heads from over a dozen different functions; two days at Marriott next to the concierge, the housekeepers, the people at the front desk, the people in the kitchen, and the valet drivers; and four days with sales managers at Toyota Financial Services, meeting with a variety of people at Toyota dealerships in four different cities.

Another added bonus in my development occurred when the managers I coached told me about the books and magazines they were reading. Every time something was recommended to me, I read it. Without realizing it, I was becoming a warehouse for ideas on what I came to call "the discipline of business acceleration," which is the field of study of how businesses generate significant, sustainable, and profitable growth.

I've now provided over 1,500 executive coaching sessions for more than 100 managers in over 20 industries, and invested more than 3,000 hours on-site observing executives and managers in their jobs. With each interaction, I picked up one more insight into what it takes to successfully run a business unit. You might be surprised how often success came down to doing and saying the little things.

The biggest lesson I've learned is the managers who are most successful in terms of accelerating their organization's desired short-term and long-term business results are very practical.

Here is a brief summary of some common traits of these practical managers.

They simplify their businesses rather than making them more complicated. They work with their staffs and business partners to clarify the two to three most important business outcomes for their organizations to achieve. They collaborate with people from various functions to identify what needs to be done and how it will be accomplished to achieve the desired results for both the short term and the long term. They ask difficult questions and listen for the answers. They follow up with people to ensure that commitments are being kept, and they provide positive or negative consequences depending on the situation.

These practical managers remind everyone in their organizations of the importance of really understanding consumer needs and demands. They focus the people in their organizations on executing the few items that are critical to driving the desired outcomes. They are relentless about getting people in their organizations who think clearly, communicate effectively, and get things done. They are equally relentless about letting go of employees who are rude, constantly theoretical, and don't accomplish what needs to happen.

They maintain lives outside of their business lives. They realize that burnout is a real issue that needs to be carefully avoided. They also carve out time away from their families, employees, and customers just to think about the key issues that will move their organizations forward. In all situations, they avoid business rhetoric and management buzzwords.

Most importantly, they don't try to be someone they're not. They know what they're good at doing and what they're passionate about doing. Then they spend the vast majority of their time leveraging their strengths and passions in ways that generate better sustainable results for both their organizations and their customers.

This book provides in detail what I have learned about how to be a practical manager from the extraordinary group of teachers I've had the honor of working with as an executive coach. I hope the ideas in it will help you to accelerate the achievement of your most important business outcomes. I hope it helps you to accelerate your career, as well. Throughout this book, I will share with you what I've learned in trying to find the answer to these four major questions:

1. What makes a manager effective in terms of his or her individual performance?
2. What makes a manager effective in terms of improving a group's performance?
3. What makes a manager effective in terms of improving an organization's performance?
4. What can be learned from consumers and how can those lessons be used to improve the future performance of an organization?

In this book, I share a couple dozen stories from my executive coaching sessions. All the dialogue in the stories is based on actual experiences, but I have changed the identity of the individuals in the stories.

A few years ago, I taught an MBA class on managerial leadership. The department head wanted me to focus almost solely on business theories. I did it his way for two weeks, and then I tossed out the theories and gave the students practical advice based on real business situations. Interestingly, things went much better when the students got information they could actually use. Instead of receiving a diploma, my goal is for you to gain something from this book that could be more useful: practical ideas on how to generate better sustainable results in your most important business outcomes.

Part One

ACCELERATE YOUR INDIVIDUAL RESULTS

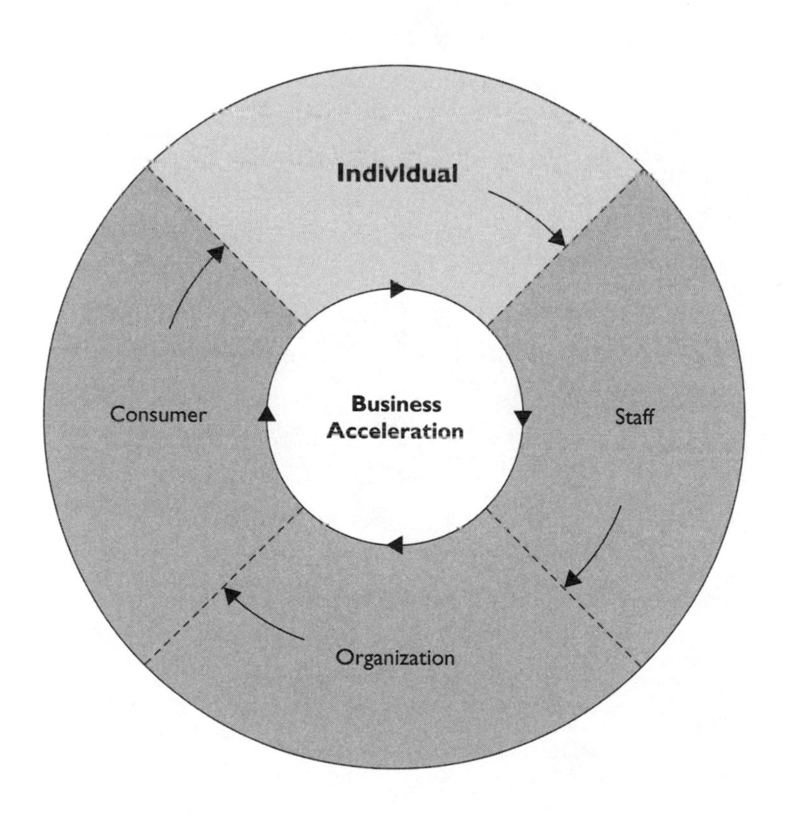

Chapter

1

ENHANCE PERSONAL EFFECTIVENESS

"I Could Do So Much More for This Company."

Joe was frustrated.

He had been with his company for 14 years. He was well thought of by upper management, had a very strong work ethic, and was labeled as having high potential for an upper management position. He had recently been promoted to run an important business unit. I was hired as an executive coach to work with him toward increasing the profitable growth of the business unit.

Joe and I hit it off, and we made strong progress with enhancing the performance of the business unit. Then one day he started our meeting by saying, "Dan, I'm frustrated. I could do so much more for this company, but they want me to do everything the way the guy before me did it. It worked for him, but I don't want to do it that way. I've challenged my boss a few times, and he just tells me to stick with what has worked in the past. What do you think I should do?"

I said, "Joe, it's up to you. You can do it the way the guy before you did it and be mediocre at best, or you can take a chance, do it your way, and possibly achieve greatness. But you are not going to achieve greatness by trying to do it in a way that you're not good at and you're not passionate about."

In the end, Joe applied his strengths and his passions toward improving the desired business outcomes. At first, he didn't do well at all. He learned some things, made some adjustments, and ended up being seen as one of the best executives in the division. He was promoted twice and was offered a variety of other promotions.

This story is not at all unique. Over and over again, executives come to a fork in the road where they have to choose between either managing the way their bosses want them to manage, or stepping back and figuring out how to apply their strengths and passions in a way that will improve the desired outcomes.

In order to improve your effectiveness as an individual, let's start at the very beginning. Take out your business card and scratch out your title. That's right, just scratch it out. As you go through this book, you will realize how useless your title really is. If you just received that title, I apologize, but it still needs to go.

During one memorable stretch, I coached three people who were each responsible for managing a billion-dollar business unit. They worked for the same company and had the same title: *regional vice president.* It made for a great case study of what makes a person successful as an individual inside of a large organization. All three of these people were very successful in their jobs and in moving the business forward.

Two were women and one was a man. One was very tall, and two were of average height. Two were white and one was black. At that time, one was 49, one was 41, one was 35, and they all had two children under the age of 10. One was very process oriented, one was a charismatic and dynamic public speaker, and one was very empathetic and a great listener.

One was a brand new regional VP, one was in the second year of being a VP, and one was in the sixth year of being a VP. One was in charge of a region that had had five straight good years, another was in charge of a region that was just starting to improve after several poor years, and the third one was put in charge of a region that was in a significant slump.

The question that kept running through my mind was, "What made each of these diverse individuals so successful?" It wasn't their title because other people with the same title had failed miserably. It wasn't their personality or leadership style because each of them had a different personality and a different style. It wasn't their tenure or age or gender or race or height or public speaking ability.

So what was it? I kept driving myself to find some commonality between these three people. And then one day on a trip home from Austin, Texas, while visiting another client, it hit me. What made these people successful, and for that matter, what all people who achieve long-term success have in common, was their ability to use what they were good at and passionate about in a way that drove better sustainable business results for their organization.

The person who was good at process development created processes that lasted long after someone else took over the position. The dynamic speaker leveraged that skill and got people so fired up about the business that they kept raising the performance bar. The great listener was able to build relationships and pull people together who had never wanted to work together in the past.

While each person had strengths and passions that were different from the other two, they were all successful because they each put his or her own strength and passion in a position to make a difference. This is the key point I want to drive home in this chapter.

THE FIVE ESSENTIALS OF PERSONAL EFFECTIVENESS

As a manager, you're empowered to make decisions that affect your customers, your organization, various internal groups, and a lot of individuals. Having the title of manager won't help you make successful decisions.

This book is about what it takes to be an effective manager. There are a lot of management essentials, but the least important one is your title. In my opinion, only one title matters: value-adder. Value is anything that increases the chances that other people will achieve what they want to achieve. Your job is to be a value-adder.

In a world where whole industries can be turned upside-down in a moment's notice through a technological change, your title could be gone in a minute anyway. Why not hang on to a label that has some staying power?

The best place to start the discussion of what it takes to manage business acceleration is with what it takes to be personally effective. In my opinion, managers who accelerate the sustainable achievement of high priority desired business outcomes have five characteristics:

1. They understand their greatest value.
2. They operate at the intersection of greatness.
3. They behave with discipline.
4. They act with integrity.
5. They maintain the capacity to fail.

UNDERSTAND YOUR GREATEST VALUE

The value you bring to a situation is a combination of your strengths and your passions as seen in Figure 1.1.

People in Quadrant I are doing things they are not very good at and for which they have very little passion. My question for people in this quadrant is, "Why?" As in, why are you staying in this job, and why is your boss letting you stay in this job?

I operated in this quadrant when I was an engineering student at Notre Dame. I wasn't very good at it and had no passion for the topic. The dean and I reached a mutual agreement that if I promised never to be an engineer, he would allow me to graduate. However, I

FIGURE 1.1

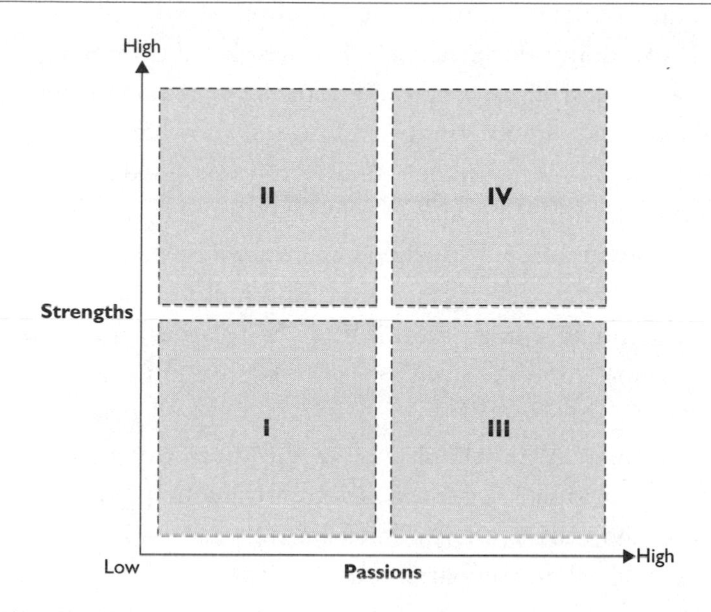

did notice that the best engineering students were competent at the material and passionate about the courses.

People in Quadrant II are functional. They are good at being able to do the work, but they have no passion for it. They're just functional.

When I graduated from college, I was looking for a way to make a living, and several people said, "You were good at math in high school. Why don't you be a math teacher?" I said okay and got on with it. I was a functional math teacher. I could explain algebra and geometry in a way that students could understand. The problem was I simply didn't care about the Pythagorean theorem, the quadratic formula, or the fact that two triangles are congruent if two sides and the included angle of one triangle are equal to two sides and the included angle of another triangle. I was functional, but being functional is not a person's greatest value.

While I was a teacher, I had the opportunity to work with some extraordinary teachers, several of whom received national recognition for their teaching abilities. They were doing work that they were passionate about and highly skilled at doing.

Are you doing work that you are merely functional at, but not passionate about? If you are, you'll never be a great manager.

People in Quadrant III are energized. They have great passion for the work, but unfortunately, they're not very good at it.

At 24 years old, I became one of the youngest NCAA Division I head coaches in the country when I was named the head soccer coach at DePaul University. I was energized and had unlimited energy for recruiting and coaching and meeting with players on an individual basis. No one outworked me or poured more enthusiasm into his work than I did.

Unfortunately, I quickly found out why there are very few 24-year-old NCAA Division I head coaches. Most are simply not ready for the job. I had tons of energy, but I wasn't very good at college soccer coaching. When compared with other head coaches, I was not as competent in terms of game strategy, player development, recruiting, and scheduling, which basically covers the whole job description. At 27 years old, I was one of the youngest former NCAA Division I head coaches in the country. Being energized does not automatically equate to adding great value.

The best managers operate in Quadrant IV where they deliver their greatest value. They know their strengths, they know their passions, and they spend the vast majority of their day doing things they are good at and passionate about. For some, this means preparing every detail of an important upcoming meeting so well they literally don't even have to be at the meeting for it to run smoothly. For others, it means crafting a speech to a large audience so well that the message resonates long after the presentation and continually drives improvements in behaviors and results.

Here is the key point: great managers do not all have the same skills or passions. However, they all know their own greatest skills and passions, and they spend the largest chunk of their time putting those assets into action.

They also know what they are not good at and not passionate about, and they spend as little time as possible deploying their weaknesses or doing things they don't care about.

After ten years of teaching high school and coaching, I stepped back and said to myself, "This career thing isn't going very well. I have to figure out another way to approach it." So I took out a piece of paper and wrote down my strengths. They are:

- The ability to simplify the complicated.
- The ability to listen well and be able to connect what someone said today with what they said six months ago.
- The ability to explain ideas in a way that people at different levels in different organizations and in different functions can understand them.
- The ability to collaborate well with people in developing better ideas than either of us had to start with.
- The ability to communicate with candor and let people know in private conversations and in a calm, professional manner what I see as their strengths and weaknesses.

Then I flipped the page over and wrote down my passions:

- I love to learn what makes other people successful.
- I really, really love to work with other people to achieve whatever they want to achieve.

With those strengths and passions in mind, I very slowly began to move forward and eventually made my way to that fateful day in 1997. As you may have noticed, there is nothing exceptional about these strengths and passions. The reason why they are so useful to me is because they are *my* strengths and passions. These are my tools for moving results forward. What are yours?

WHAT IS YOUR GPA?

Your GPA is the combination of what you're good and passionate at doing. The key to your success as a manager is to use your strengths and passions as often as you can. What is your highest GPA? What is it that you do better than anything else that you do, and what is it that you are more passionate about doing than anything else? When you know the answers to those questions, you are on your way toward being more effective as a manager and as an employee.

I encourage you to take out a sheet of paper and write down your greatest strengths, regardless of the area of your life where you've used them, and your greatest passions, which are the things that turn you on the most. You might be thinking, "Isn't this self-evident? Doesn't everyone know that they do their best work when they're doing something they love to do and that they are good at doing?"

I used to think that. Then I started working with real-life executives and managers, and what I found was a different reality. The vast majority of them were doing things they felt needed to be done to secure their income or please their boss. Instead of doing things as a manager that they were passionate about and good at, they focused maniacally on some competency their boss wanted improved.

With person after person, I practically had to brainwash them into realizing they were always going to be mediocre if they spent the vast majority of their time trying to improve their weaknesses and impress their boss. As Peter Drucker wrote in his classic book, *The Effective Executive,* "The effective executive makes strength productive. He knows that one cannot build on weakness. To achieve results, one has to use all the available strengths. Those strengths are the true opportunities."

One of my first steps as an executive coach is to ask two questions, "What are you good at? What are you passionate about?" That's where effectiveness begins. It's not hard to answer these questions, but you do have to step off the train of constant activities, take out a sheet of paper, and write down your answers.

When you are done, you will more clearly see the greatest value you have to offer an organization. Don't wait until it's too late. Once a year I speak to a group of executives who are between jobs. It's amazing to me how willing people are to do these basic exercises when they are desperately trying to find a job, but they aren't willing to do them when they are working like squirrels storing nuts for the winter.

The best time to leverage your strengths and your passions is when you have a good job and some say over your daily activities. In order to do that, you have to actually know those strengths and passions. Your strengths and passions do not have to be some phenomenal and rare entity, but they do have to be yours.

REVIEW PAST SUCCESSES, PREVIEW FUTURE SUCCESSES

Another way to understand your greatest value is to review your past success stories and preview your future success stories. This simple paradigm is seen in Figure 1.2.

Recall a time in your life when you achieved something you thought you could not achieve or other people thought you could not achieve. What was your goal, what were the obstacles you had to overcome, how did you persevere, what lessons did you learn from going through that experience, and how did it feel when you actually achieved the goal? Write down your answers.

This story of a past success will remind you that you've been down this road before. It will show you that you can persevere in your current situation and give you clues on how you can achieve your desired outcomes for this year. Far too often, I've seen managers race from one project to another without ever taking the time to reflect on past successes and how they were achieved.

FIGURE 1.2

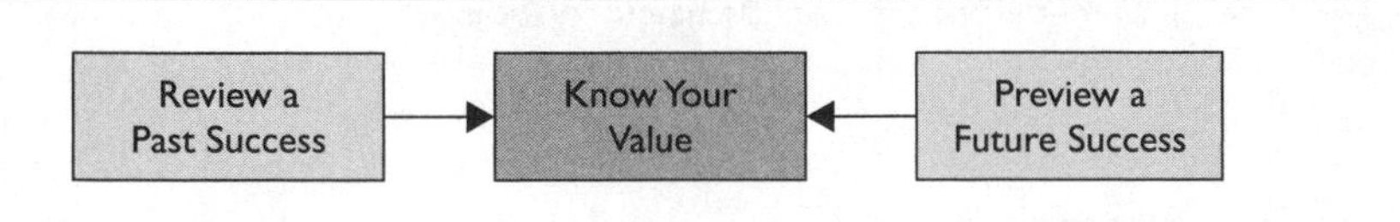

Now preview a future success. What do you want to achieve? What stands in your way and how will you persevere? Most important, what lessons from your past experiences do you need to apply in your current situation in order to achieve success?

I have seen over and over how people move forward with greater confidence and efficiency when they see the desired result clearly. Some people call this visionary leadership. I call it seeing the end game before you start moving. Call it what you want, and get on with it.

Acceleration Case Study

I once gave a seminar in Atlanta for a hundred sales and marketing professionals from Marriott International. During an exercise on recalling past success stories, I partnered with a young man and asked him for one of his stories. He told me he had won a state high school wrestling championship.

I said that must have been pretty rewarding. He then said, "Well, I was born without a left foot, so I had to learn how to gain leverage with just one foot." He went on to say, "Sometimes I run into tough challenges with my clients today, and so I always think about how I had to be creative in wrestling and continue to persevere."

He made me realize that all of us have powerful success stories in our past. We just need to make the time to draw those stories out and leverage them for future success.

At a seminar for a group of federal employees who were about to potentially lose their jobs when their office closed down in six months, I met a woman who told me her success story was passing a swimming class in high school. I asked what it was like. She said, "Well, they threw me in the deep end and told me to swim. Since I had no choice, I survived and swam out. It's like my career right now. I will survive and find another job." Do you see now the power of your past success stories? But you have to take time to recall them before they will be useful for you.

As with all the ideas in this book, I hope you will apply them not only for yourself, but also with the people who report to you. Ask them to write down their strengths, their passions, and their past success stories. Listen to their answers. Challenge them to spend as much of their working day as possible deploying their strengths and passions. And then ask them to visualize their future success stories.

There was a time in my life when I pooh-poohed the importance of these exercises. I thought they were good with younger people, but I felt certain they were too basic for highly successful managers. I was wrong.

Yes, they are basic exercises, but no, they are not too basic for managers, even those people who run business units of a billion dollars or more. Actually, they're more important for managers with huge responsibilities because many of them, maybe you included, never step off the train to reflect on these questions. Instead they're in constant motion. If you want the train to go faster, step off of it, reflect on important questions, clarify your answers, and then step back on the train.

OPERATE AT THE INTERSECTION OF GREATNESS

The intersection of greatness is the point where the manager's greatest value intersects with her organization's most important desired business outcomes and her client's most important business outcomes. This narrow area of pure value added is shown in Figure 1.3.

The executives who thrive operate right at this intersection. By her own evaluation, Meg Whitman, CEO of eBay, is a bit frumpy, but she gets the job done. She gets the job done because she operates in a way that leverages her strengths and passions in guiding and coaching people toward democratizing auctions. She helps to create millions of entrepreneurs.

In his early days at the Walt Disney Company, then-CEO Michael Eisner was able to generate enormous value by applying his passion

FIGURE 1.3

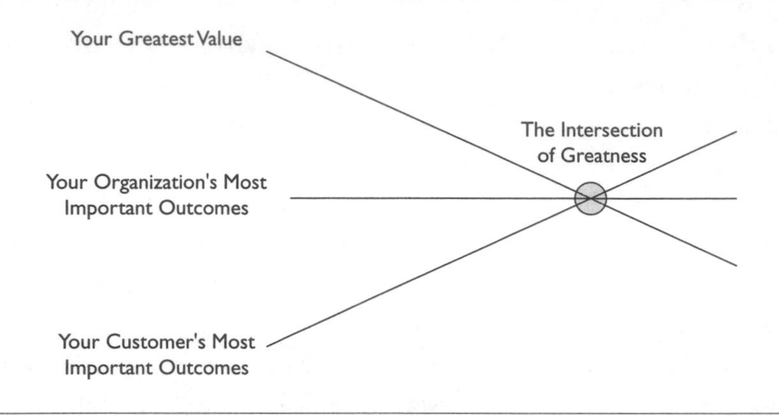

and talent for developing good stories and converting them into a series of mega-hits that revitalized the Disney brand and launched a whole new generation of children hooked on Walt Disney. It was only when he got away from his specific greatest value and started micro-managing every aspect of Disney that his problems blossomed.

In essence, this is what career acceleration is all about. Be a value-adder by helping other people to achieve what they want. Of course, the best way to be a value-adder is to add your greatest value, which is the combination of your strengths and your passions, in a way that helps both your organization and your organization's customers succeed.

Once, while sitting in an audience of about 5,000 people, I wrote down a question on an index card that was forwarded to Bill Gates. The question was, "What does it take to be world-class in any field?" He rocked back and forth, smiled, and said the first key is you have to do something you love doing. He said he always loved writing software as a grade school and high school student. Clearly, he went on to find the intersection of greatness.

Martha Stewart always had a passion for raising the bar on all things domestic, and in her heyday she built an amazing business centered on that passion and her perseverance. Admired and reviled, Jack Welch clearly had a passion for confronting people in order to improve performance, and he led GE to unprecedented heights.

An Acceleration Exercise on Personal Effectiveness

In order to clarify your own intersection of greatness, answer these five questions:

1. What is my greatest value? In other words, what am I both good at and passionate about doing?
2. What is one high priority business outcome that my organization wants to achieve this year?
3. What is one high priority outcome that one of my customers wants to achieve?
4. Which of my strengths and passions can I use in my next interaction with my customer?
5. How will I use those strengths and passions to help my customer achieve his desired outcome, and help my organization achieve its desired outcome?

Finding the answer to the fifth question makes all the difference in a person's career.

It takes time and patience to put yourself in a position to leverage your strengths and passions in a way that drives critical outcomes for your organization and your clients, but the first step is to answer the five questions in this acceleration exercise.

BEHAVE WITH DISCIPLINE

That sounds like something your mother might say, but sustainable success as a manager does sometimes come down to things your mom might say. Remember, I'm talking about the essentials of optimizing your own effectiveness. Dressing a certain way, looking a certain way, and talking a certain way are not essentials, but maintaining discipline is essential. Discipline is one of the common threads that must be woven into the entire fabric of your responsibilities as an executive.

Ten Areas Where Discipline Is Truly Essential

1. Maintain confidentiality. Managers are like bartenders. They hear a lot of private information, and in most cases, it had better stay with them. If a person comes to you to vent about her boss or the new policy, let her vent. Listen intently, try to offer some practical value to her, and then keep the session to yourself, unless she wants you to share it with someone else.

Keeping information confidential is one way to build trust. Now, there are two obvious times when you should not keep information confidential. First, when the person tells you he or she is stealing from the company, cheating the customers, or lying to the public. Then you blow the whistle loud and hard. Second, when you or someone you know is being sexually or verbally harassed. Let the appropriate people know what is happening right away.

2. Communicate with respect. Being a manager is hard work. You've got those endless meetings, constant travel, and enormous pressures to deal with. Oftentimes, you'll be worn down and tired in the office. Unfortunately, that still doesn't mean you can go off on another person.

As the senior executive in the group, your every word will be heard and your every action will be watched. More than anything it means you must communicate with respect to each person. You don't have to be Mr. Happy, but you do have to be respectful and treat people with dignity. This requires a daily dose of discipline that you can't fake.

3. Give candid feedback. It's hard work to have tough conversations with people. It's a whole lot easier to skip giving another person honest feedback, but all that does is exacerbate the problem in the future.

Keep in mind that staying disciplined on the little things includes making time to meet with the other person in private, discussing (in private) the behavior and decision making the person displayed, and listening to his perspective. If you do that consistently and see it as being in the best interests of the other person, it becomes easier to do.

4. Be punctual. Nobody will tell you, but every time you show up late for a meeting you throw off everyone else's day. Acting like you have the power to be late while everyone else needs to be on time is not about your title, it's about your ego. It also sends the message that other people can be late for other meetings. That builds a culture that accepts lateness.

Here's how this works: be on time. It's not complicated, it builds trust with employees, and it builds a culture that gets things done on time.

5. Minimize schedule changes. I'm stunned by how often executives cancel meetings of groups of 20 or more people with one or two days notice. If you find yourself regularly changing your schedule, and even more important, other people's schedules, you have a problem with a lack of discipline when it comes to organizing your time and staying on track. That is going to affect your relationship with your peers and staff members.

Unless it's a crisis that must be handled immediately, don't jerk people's schedules around. For that matter, if you keep the scheduled activities on target when your group or organization is facing a crisis, you send the message that you're remaining calm in the midst of the chaos. In doing so, you subliminally reassure other people that everything will be okay.

6. Operate within the strategy. Since the senior executive is the final decision-maker in the group, she can make a call on switching tactics or adding planned activities and that decision will be upheld. Unfortunately, this can ruin momentum.

Any major initiative takes some time to develop and make an impact. When the undisciplined executive makes changes on a regular basis, he wipes out the capacity for synergy and for people to build on each other's efforts. I think in many ways this was the downfall of Carly Fiorina at Hewlett-Packard. She seemed to change the focus of the company on a regular basis.

7. Let go of poor performers. This is one of the hardest jobs for any manager. Many times managers have worked in an organization for 15 to 25 years, have become good friends with their employees, and their children have developed friendships with the employee's children. However, some of those employees have begun to drift off in terms of performance. Either they can't or won't learn to use the new technologies or raise the bar in terms of their performance to add value commensurate with their increased paycheck. This creates an awful situation for the manager as well as the employee.

It may seem easier in the short term for the manager to avoid the situation and not confront his friend, who also happens to report to him. This is when the manager needs to stay disciplined, keep in mind what is best for the group and organization and customers, confront the person as early as possible and let him know he needs to improve his performance, and, ultimately, let him go if he doesn't improve. If the manager doesn't do this, the issue gets bigger and bigger, his employees stop respecting him, and he ends up with a host of poor performers.

8. Take care of your health. As a busy and successful manager, you can make a strong argument that you simply do not have the time to work out or eat properly. In my executive coaching sessions, I've heard this argument over and over with some people. My point to these people is that it's fine in the short term not to exercise, but over the long term, your lack of energy will affect every aspect of your personal and professional life.

You can't just catch up on exercise in one weekend. It does take discipline to work out three times a week. It means you have to carve out the time and do it. It's been my experience that roughly 90 percent of the time, the fastest rising executives who sustain their career over the long term are those who stay in very good shape.

Dr. Richard Meyers, the long-time president of Webster University with over 100 campuses around the world, told me that regular exercise is a must for a senior-level executive. He felt there is no other way that executives can remain effective over the long term.

One executive I worked with got up each day at 4:30 AM to work out for 45 minutes. She had two young children, a great marriage, was enormously effective in her job, and was constantly up for meaningful promotions. She attributed her increased energy to a great deal of her success. Maybe that's too much of a commitment for many of us, but I do encourage you to exercise at least twice a week for 40 minutes.

9. Follow through on commitments. An executive's job is to make decisions and influence people in a way that his behaviors will support those decisions and improve results for the organization. In order to influence people, they must trust you. When you do what you said you would do, you increase trust.

This includes a hundred little things like showing up on time, returning phone calls that you committed to make, meeting with a person you said you would meet with, and fulfilling your promises to audiences large and small. Simply doing what you said you would do demonstrates tremendous self-discipline.

10. Say no. Having said all of this, perhaps the most important area of discipline is not in something you do, but rather in lots of things you don't. Saying no requires self-discipline. Knowing you can't do everything well helps you remember the importance of saying no more often than saying yes. Remember, and I'll come back to this in the next chapter, acceleration is the art of sacrifice.

Acceleration Case Study

I met a CEO of a $1.5 billion company who told me he was on 15 boards. At first, I thought he meant he had served on 15 boards over the course of his career. I came to find out he meant he was serving on 15 boards at that moment.

I thought to myself, "Either, A, he has an addiction problem; B, he has an ego problem; C, he loves to promote himself and his company because there's no way he's adding real value to 15 boards at the same time; or D, he can't say no to anyone." In the end, it may have been a little of all of those reasons, but he certainly was not being an effective executive for his company and an effective board member for 15 organizations all at the same time.

Six Steps to Strengthen Your Self-Discipline

For the most part, I suggest people make far fewer commitments and follow through on a much higher percentage of them. Following through on your commitments is a powerful way to strengthen your self-esteem and to build strong relationships with other people. Others know they can count on you and in turn will give you greater opportunities to make a contribution.

When speaking to a group of students at the University of Washington, Warren Buffett said, "The chains of habit are too light to be felt until they are too heavy to be broken." In other words, you decide on your habits and then they determine your long-term success. While talent, knowledge, experiences, connections, and creativity are all valuable, self-discipline is one of the fundamental keys to long-term success. Self-discipline allows you to follow through on your commitments to both other people and yourself. The following six steps will help you strengthen your self-discipline.

1. Clarify your commitment to another person. When you make a commitment, be absolutely clear about what you plan to do: write the commitment down and state it to another person. This statement establishes the first strand of commitment. Without this step, it becomes far too easy to let it go and rationalize your way out of doing it.

2. Identify the benefits of actually doing what you said you would do. Writing your commitments down and describing them to another person is only the first step toward establishing true commitment and increasing self-discipline. At this point, you may have compliance, but not commitment. In other words, you may say that you are going to do it, but there may be no real intention of following through.

To increase your commitment, answer this question, "What are the benefits if I actually follow through and do what I said I would do?" Take out a sheet of paper and write down your answers. Try to think of as many benefits as you can, for both yourself and other people, if you follow through on your commitment. Now that single strand of commitment is starting to be reinforced with each additional benefit that you identify.

3. Identify the negative consequences of not doing what you said you would do. Sometimes you will be more inspired to act by realizing the downside of not keeping your commitment than by the upside of doing it. So, make a list of all the negative consequences to yourself and others if you don't do anything. Again, you are strengthening your commitment to taking action.

In order to see the downside of not following through, answer this question, "What are the negative consequences if I do not follow through?" This may seem like unnecessary grunt work, but I believe that without taking the time to reinforce your commitments, you may let some things go. They just won't seem as important two days after you made the commitment.

4. Identify why you believe you can do it. To increase your belief that you will follow through, answer this question, "Why do I believe I can do it?" Make a list of all the reasons you think you can successfully execute what you have promised. Recall past success stories, identify why you are passionate about this topic, and zero in on why you will follow through.

Many times people will see the value of doing something and the downside of not doing it, but they will not move into action because subconsciously they do not believe they really can do it. It is very important to consciously identify why you believe you will be able do what you have committed to do.

5. Read over your answers every day. The whole point of answering these questions is to increase the level of *mental* commitment that you are making to the action you have promised to do. Unless you are mentally committed, then there is a very good chance you will fail to follow through. Through daily reinforcement of your answers, you will continually strengthen within yourself the importance of meeting your commitments.

6. Focus on repetitions. The final step is to repeat steps one through five over and over again. One repetition does not equate to strengthened self-discipline. Only when all five steps are repeated over and over again does it eventually become a habit. At first, the habit is too light to be felt, but over time, it will become too strong to be broken.

As you apply these six steps in one area of your life, you will soon find they can be repeated over and over again in other areas as well.

ACT WITH INTEGRITY

I have yet to find the organization that doesn't have integrity listed as one of their core values. The word is plastered in brochures, on wall plaques, in new employee orientation packets, and on corporate Web sites everywhere you turn.

Apparently everyone is in agreement on the importance of the word "integrity," including several prominent executives who went to jail. If everyone agrees that integrity is one of the critical pieces of long-term success, why do I bother mentioning it as one of the five essentials of personal effectiveness for practical managers? The reason is because the walk does not always match the talk.

Integrity is one of the easiest business concepts to explain. It means do the right thing. All right, let me spell that out a little more clearly. It means never lie, never cheat, and always tell the truth. Never lie about your performance. If you blew it and it cost your organization a fortune, don't lie about your results. Don't cheat on your travel expenses or any other little bonus or fringe benefit you think you deserve. If you know you did something wrong or that someone else did something wrong, tell the truth. Don't wait until someone asks, just tell the truth. As I said, this is not a hard one to explain.

One client taught me the all-time classic definition of integrity. He said integrity is doing the right thing even when no one else will ever know. That's powerful. That goes way beyond concerns about corporate governance, fear of whistle blowers, and anxiety over the media.

When you have that kind of integrity, you have a solid foundation. In a changing economy, and trust me when I say we're in a changing economy, anyone can lose his or her job. If you maintain your integrity and the dignity that goes along with it, you will always be able to make a comeback. If you lose your integrity and your dignity, you're done. Acting with integrity is at the very heart of understanding your greatest value and operating at the intersection of greatness.

MAINTAIN THE CAPACITY TO FAIL

I don't know how people survive without reading books. I know I couldn't. My love affair with books can be traced back to my oldest brother, Kevin, who is such a prolific reader he makes me look like a kindergartener, and to the St. Louis Public Library.

When I was growing up in the late 1960s and early 1970s, the St. Louis Public Library provided this incredible service known as the Bookmobile. Every two weeks this brown library on wheels that looked like a miniature mobile home would pull into the parking lot of my grade school. Every time I stepped into that small library, I was taken to another world.

Up until I was 11 years old, 98 percent of my life was spent within a six-block radius of my house. It was three blocks to my grade school, and three more blocks to Shiloh Park, where we played soccer, baseball, and basketball. All my friends lived within those six blocks. But when I stepped into that Bookmobile, I was suddenly with Thomas Edison, Jackie Robinson, Teddy Roosevelt, Marie Antoinette, Martin Luther King, Jr., Madame Curie, and Kareem Abdul-Jabbar. I would check out the maximum number of books allowed, read a book a night, and repeat the process two weeks later.

I haven't changed. I still read book after book after book. Biographies and autobiographies are still my favorites. As I said earlier, one of my passions is to learn what makes other people successful. I'm much more interested in their journey up the ladder of success than I am in their stay at the top. By far, the most common lesson taught in each of these books was that every person maintained the capacity to fail on the road to incredible success.

The most powerful story was the most surprising: *The Other Side of Me,* the autobiography of Sidney Sheldon. Sheldon has sold more than 300 million copies of his books. I assumed falsely that he never had a tough day in his life. The truth is he wrote his first book at the age of 53, and it "only" sold 17,000 copies in the first two years. He spent more on publicity than the book earned for him.

His second book, *The Other Side of Midnight,* he wrote at the age of 56, and it became a runaway international bestseller. He didn't expect it to be a bestseller. He was simply putting value in the marketplace to see what might happen. All 18 of his books have been on the *New York Times* Bestseller list. He also created and wrote the television shows *I Dream of Jeannie, The Patty Duke Show,* and *Hart to Hart.*

Along the way he experienced huge failures, as did every other person I studied. The first movie he produced, *Dream Wife,* starring Cary Grant, received such poor reviews that MGM did not even promote it and it died an early death. He quit MGM shortly after that experience. Two of his first four Broadway plays flopped, badly. He lost his job, as did all the others I read about, at the age of 40 and had to sell his home and move to a small apartment. He succeeded, like all the others, because he maintained the capacity to fail.

When a person tells me she can't afford to fail in a certain project she is working on, I know she is in big trouble. If you can't allow yourself to fail, then you can't allow yourself to achieve greatness. No matter how old you are right now, you must go into every situation with the capacity to fail. If you refuse to fail, then you are stuck in that awful place known as mediocrity.

When it comes to maintaining the capacity to fail as a manager, here are two questions to consider:

1. What project is your group considering doing to grow the business, but is hesitant to do so because it might fail?
2. What are the benefits your organization can achieve if the project is successful?

If the only reason you are not doing the project is the possibility you might fail, then get started now. The benefit of trying will far outweigh the downside of "failing."

RESOURCE RECOMMENDATION

The Other Side of Me by Sidney Sheldon. (The audio version is excellent as well.)

This book is a very quick read with a ton of practical advice. I encourage you to give it a try. It is applicable to all people regardless of their position or responsibilities.

Acceleration Tips

- ✓ Know your strengths. I mean really know what you're good at in all aspects of your life. These strengths are your foundation for adding continually greater value in a professional setting.
- ✓ Know your passions. What turns you on? Give that question considerable time for reflection. It will make all the difference in you helping your organization move forward, and in moving your career forward.
- ✓ Do your work in a way that leverages your strengths and passions toward accelerating the achievement of some of your organization's highest priority outcomes and some of your customer's highest priority outcomes.
- ✓ Stay disciplined over the long term in the day-to-day stuff. The little things really do add up, and it's this collective impact that makes a manager a positive force.
- ✓ Act with integrity. Everything else falls apart when you lie. Integrity is doing the right thing even when no one else knows what you've done. With integrity, you can always come back in your career. Without it, you may very well be done.
- ✓ Always maintain the capacity to fail. It allows you the freedom to achieve greatness.

Chapter

2

UTILIZE PRIORITY MANAGEMENT

"And Exactly When Am I Going to Have Time to Do That?"

It's not difficult for a successful manager to keep his work and personal life in balance. It's darn near impossible. I call it the work/life balance fallacy.

When I began coaching Julie, a highly successful and fast-rising 39-year-old executive, she told me in our first meeting that she desperately wanted to improve her work/life balance. She had two children at home, and her husband worked an equally time-consuming job. She was constantly working or taking care of her family.

I said, "Julie, you need to do some things just for yourself to recharge your batteries. If you don't, you may very well burn out and that won't help your company, your family, or your career." She looked at me and said, "And exactly when am I going to have time to do that?"

When I asked how many hours she was working, she paused, got very quiet, and said, "Do you mean with travel or without travel?" At that point I knew we were stepping into a sensitive area. She told me when she wasn't traveling, she left home at 7:30 AM and got home at 6:30 PM. That's a 55-hour work week. When she traveled, she was usually gone two nights a week, and that added an additional 26 hours a week away from her home. Add in the two hours of work she did on Saturday and Sunday from her home office, and Julie was working 85 hours each week.

She estimated she slept seven hours a night from 11 PM to 6 AM. That's 49 more hours a week that she's not available for the important people in her life. Now she's up to 129 hours a week when she's not available. That leaves exactly 39 hours a week to be with her family, friends, community groups, possibly go to religious services, attend her children's activities, meet with her kids' teachers, possibly do a hobby, go shopping, get dressed, take showers, go to the bathroom, and brush her teeth.

Toss in a four-day leadership conference or a week-long trip to a special client or the ever popular business trip as a reward for a great year's performance—which ends up being three more days away from her family, and pretty soon we're talking about an even bigger problem. And heaven forbid if she were to actually get sick and have to stay home for a few days. A pile of work would be there when she got back to the office. On top of all that, figure in the concept of the ever-present office, in which she can pick up her e-mail and voicemail from any location at any time.

Now do you see why I call this the work/life balance fallacy?

Julie and I immediately began to map out a plan for her to take back some of her life and channel some of her time into other personally enhancing activities. As she carved out more time for herself, she found that her business results were even higher than before and she had more time for her family.

Julie's story is the norm of the people I've coached, not the exception. I've never come across the manager who is a modern day Ward Cleaver who is home every day by 5 PM. The executives and managers I've interacted with are jumping on planes and checking e-mail and preparing for important meetings and doing research to make important decisions and dealing with important people issues and finding new customers and working to strengthen relationships with current customers. Without parameters, they could work 24/7.

At least 85 percent of my executive coaching clients have expressed a great desire for better work/life balance. In a nutshell, they want to be home more.

As a human being, you have one weapon to get your life in balance. You have the ability to make choices. Sometimes the barrage of activities seem so overwhelming and pervasive, you may feel you have lost the capacity to control your life. Please, for your own sake, shake off the covers of your weekly schedule, get up, and remind yourself that you choose what you do each day.

At the root of personal dignity is the belief that you are in control of your own life and your own destiny. Abraham Maslow wrote about this concept more than 40 years ago in his book *Maslow on Management:* "True self-esteem rests on a feeling of personal dignity, the belief that you are in control of your own decisions and your own destiny."

Many times when I work with a manager, we have to spend a good chunk of time focusing on this issue before we can move on to other "more important" issues like talent management, customer relationships, strategy, branding, and innovation. People don't hire me to get control of their lives, but many times we end up starting there because they feel they've lost control of their schedules, which negatively affects their self-esteem and keeps them from thriving as managers. Here are 20 ideas to help you regain your personal dignity and feel that you are more in control of your schedule and your life.

TWENTY WAYS TO GET CONTROL OF YOUR LIFE

1. Understand the Business Upside of Downtime

If your argument for working so many hours is that's what it takes to succeed, then I want to point out that one key to being a successful manager is having energy. Maintaining your composure, building relationships, staying strategic, being creative, executing tactics, and dealing with crises all require energy.

If your batteries wear out, then you may ruin business results in a flash. By getting away from work, you bring much greater focus and energy to every situation while you're working. Until you buy into this concept, you will continue to push yourself under the belief that the more hours you work, the more you accomplish.

People tell me all the time how ideas come to them when they are not working. Yet some of these people tell me they have to work 60 to 80 hours a week because of the demands of their businesses. They believe they will generate better business results by working more hours. I suggest they will achieve better results if they work fewer hours. When you get away from work, your mind opens up and suddenly a breakthrough idea appears to solve an age-old problem. Consequently, you need to plan time away from your work. Go on a vacation, watch a television show, attend a concert, and have a hobby. Do you see the business upside of downtime?

2. Focus on Priority Management over Time Management

None of us can alter time. We all get 24 hours a day, 7 days a week. However, each of us can select our highest priority business outcome and work to improving it first. Here's a rule of thumb: a priority list can have at most three items on it. Answer this question: what three things can I do today that would have the greatest positive impact on improving my organization's most important desired business outcome? Then do those three things first. In this way, you will generate far better results on the outcomes that really matter than you would by simply scheduling every hour of the day with appointments and meetings.

Notice: three critical activities. That's already a lot to do, but it's a whole lot more focused than attending 20 meetings a week on ten different important projects. Start with the most important desired business outcome and then work backward to build your schedule around the three things that would have the greatest positive impact on this outcome.

Why spend your important time on activities that are not going to impact your organization's three most important business outcomes? Imagine you have three children and your neighbor has three children. If you only have ten hours a week to be with someone's children, are you going to spend the vast majority of your time with the children who matter the most to you or with three other children?

3. Maintain Singular Focus

I once coached the head of the Greek system at a major university. A university's Greek system is a little like a mini-corporation. They are trying to achieve a noble purpose and provide meaningful personal growth opportunities while dealing with a myriad of weekly crises like drunkenness, abusive behavior, poor academic performance, and so on.

He told me several times that he couldn't get anything done because he was dealing with so many things at once. One day we were sitting in a restaurant and there were four paintings on the wall. I looked at him and asked, "Would you rather paint one painting at a time or all four paintings at once?" Without hesitating, he said, "All four paintings." I was stunned and asked, "Why?" He said, "If I'm painting all four paintings at the same time, then I have an excuse for why none of them was turning out very well."

Wow, what a powerful insight. He was subconsciously loading up on activities in order to have a built-in excuse for not really achieving any of those desired outcomes. Before you laugh, ask yourself if you're doing the same thing. Are you going after eight projects at once so that you can tell your boss there was no way to be successful? If you truly want to achieve something, then focus on one desired outcome at a time.

4. Know Thy Time

The great Peter Drucker said to "know thy time" in *The Effective Executive.* He suggested to his readers that for 30 days they should write down what they did every 30 minutes. Then at the end of 30 days, they should examine how they spent their time. Finally, he suggested that going forward his readers should redistribute their time so they spent the largest chunks of their time on the fewest things that would really enhance their organizations. Drucker gave that advice more than 40 years ago, and it's still great advice. Give it a try.

5. Declare What You're Going to Stop Doing

Get in the habit of stating what you are not going to do, and make sure you stop doing it. When I first started in business on my own, I went to lunch two or three times a week with other small business owners. Between travel and eating, I was giving up six hours a week.

After about a year, I looked back and realized the return on my investment of 600 hours was ridiculously small. Now I simply tell other small business owners that I don't meet for lunch anymore, but I'll be glad to talk over the phone for a few minutes. I've saved myself years of wasted time.

6. Work in a Set Timeframe

Select the number of hours you want to work in a week. Since I regularly hear people say they work 65 to 70 hours a week, I'll establish, for the sake of argument, that the desired goal is a 50-hour workweek. You can make it less or more. It's your desired number, not mine.

When the 50 hours are up, you're done for that week. If you use them up by Thursday, you don't get any more. The first time this happens, I can assure you that you will reexamine how you use your hours each day. The only way to make this boundary work is to make it an actual boundary. You get 50 hours total. That's it. No more.

7. Say "No" and "Not Right Now" on a Regular Basis

Here's the piece of advice I give the most often to my clients when they say they are working too many hours. When people interrupt you with a request, say, "I'll be glad to meet with you. However, I can't meet right now. Here are three options on my schedule later in the week. What would work best for you? Also, please send me an e-mail with the specific question you want me to try to answer and anything I should bring to our discussion. That way I can be prepared to help you."

Work hard to move away from answering questions on the spot. When you meet with the person right away, you're doing all the heavy lifting for him. By forcing him to wait and to phrase his question in an e-mail, he will often solve his problem without meeting with you at all. That's a good thing, not a bad thing. The goal is to get him to think for himself. You're not being rude by saying that you can't drop everything on the spot to help him.

The first time I gave this advice was to the head of HR for a $500 million region. She told me she was only sleeping four hours a night, was 35 pounds overweight, had typed up her resignation letter, and was ready to hand it in later in the week. I asked her to describe a typical day. She said she worked until 8 PM, went home to be with her family, got everyone in bed, and then worked from 10 PM until 1 AM every night.

I asked her what her days were like at work. She told me she was constantly interrupted. I asked what she did when someone interrupted her. She told me she would always stop her work and respond to every request as soon as it happened. That's when I gave her the advice of saying "no" and "not right now." Since she had nothing to lose, she gave it a try.

Over the next four months, she lost 40 pounds, went home every day at 6 PM, slept seven hours every night, and was promoted. She had a mountain of talent, but it was going to waste because she was completely wearing out her batteries. When she recharged her batteries and kept them charged, she achieved dramatic improvements in results.

8. Schedule Only 60 Percent of Your Workday

Leave the rest of the time open to talk with people, provide coaching for other people, observe people in action, and so on. Your days will get filled up, but this way you won't be adding stuff on top of an already packed schedule. Once you've scheduled 60 percent of your allotted time, don't schedule any more meetings or activities.

9. Be Reasonable

You choose what you agree to do. That's right, you choose it. The people asking you to do something are not holding a gun to your head, at least not literally. If you told your boss you would travel four days a week for the next 90 days, then you have made a huge commitment. This does not mean you have to agree to be the head of the PTA at your child's grade school. It does not mean you have to agree to head up the fundraiser for your religious group. It does not mean you have to work every Saturday night at the concession stand at your local high school football game.

Conversely, if you've decided to take on a major community project, you can say no to huge projects at work. Of course, that might keep you from getting promoted. But the point is you are in charge, not the person asking. Be reasonable in what you choose to say yes to and you will maintain your life.

10. Be Candid Quickly

Far too much time is wasted avoiding difficult discussions. Early in my coaching career I was coaching a person at a huge company. I desperately wanted to keep that corporation as a client. Consequently, I would avoid telling the person what I thought he was doing wrong because I didn't want to tick him off and lose my best client.

One day he said, "Dan, do you ever think I do something that is not effective?" I said, "Of course, there are times that I think you are not effective." I had fallen directly into his trap.

He paused and said, "Then tell me. You're not adding any value if you don't tell me what you think I can do better." It only took me once to learn my lesson. Now I am always readily honest with the people I am coaching. It takes the pressure off me, and adds value to them more quickly.

I encourage you to do the same. If someone you're managing is behaving in an inappropriate manner, then set up a meeting with the other person behind closed doors or over the phone. Be candid in your evaluation. Do it in a professional way that preserves the other person's dignity, but still be honest with him or her. It will save you time, and it may very well help the other person's career.

11. Leverage Technology versus Losing to Technology

Mobile e-mail devices, cell phones, voicemail boxes, and faxes can eat you alive and ruin your career. Let me say that more strongly. Technology can kill your effectiveness and your efficiency, but only if you let it. Telling people they can contact you at any time and expect an immediate response within five minutes is a surefire way to ruin business relationships. It's completely unrealistic. You will become like the fish in the tank that keeps getting poked by the little kid. You will jump back, return to the glass, and then jump back again.

All those pieces of technology are great if you use them in reasonable (there's that word again) doses. Your job is to add value to customers and employees in a way that generates better results for the customers and better sustainable results for your organization and the people in it. Your job is not to check e-mails seven times daily. Sometimes managers forget that.

Establish a time for checking e-mails, voicemails, faxes, and cell phone messages. Perhaps you check your voicemail and cell phone every 90 minutes. Maybe you check your e-mails and faxes twice a day. Let people know what they can expect from you.

For very important calls, let the other person know that you will leave your cell phone on and you will take his or her call. Then tell the other people you are with that you are only going to be taking one call. Everything else will be going into your voicemail. That way the other people understand why you are talking on your cell phone in the middle of an important meeting.

12. Resolve Emotional Issues after 24 Hours and Before 72 Hours

In a perfect world, people add value to customers and there are no complications. However, those darn human beings do become emotional and issues can flare up on a moment's notice. Rather than trying to squelch emotional fires on the spot, give them 24 hours to burn out a bit. Then meet with the person or the group of individuals to talk through what happened, why it happened, and what can be done about it.

Letting the fire simmer for weeks can be even more deadly than trying to deal with it on the spot. If you don't bring the situation to some type of resolution within 72 hours, you will lose credibility and that will cost you time over the long run.

13. Don't Lock into a Rigid Starting Time or a Permanent Ending Time

A director once told Sidney Sheldon—perhaps the most prolific writer of screenplays, Broadway performances, television shows, and novels in history—that all his writers wrote from 8 AM to 5 PM every day. Sheldon replied that if the director felt this was the way to get good scripts, then he was completely wrong.

Management is an art, not a science. The goal is to generate sustainable improvement in key results. If that means you have to attend a late-night meeting or travel across the country or around the world, then do it. However, that doesn't mean you have to be in the office the next day at 8 AM.

Take time to get on the treadmill, play a racquetball game, have lunch with your spouse, or attend your daughter's dance class. If you think following a rigid schedule is the key to being an effective manager, then, in my opinion, you're completely wrong. Management is about generating output, not about being locked into fixed formations.

14. Partner with Your Administrative Assistant

Meet with your administrative assistant and put in place a few parameters on your schedule.

First, never, ever double book a time period. Someone is going to be upset when you have to cancel or reschedule, and you will be seen as rude. I know it seems inconceivable that someone would double book a block of time, but it happens—a lot. Primarily, it happens because both the manager and the administrative person are keeping the manager's schedule. Select one person to run your calendar.

Double booking also happens because of electronic calendars that allow other people to put their meetings on the manager's schedule and expect the manager to show up. Make it clear to everyone that if you have not personally committed to being at a meeting, they should not expect you to be there.

Second, work with your administrative person to make sure that no meetings are scheduled back to back. Always build in 15 minutes between meetings. Be firm about ending meetings on time. Those 15 minutes are necessary to clear your mind, relax, and prepare for the next meeting.

Finally, don't be a "road victim." If you've traveled three days in a row, then work the fourth day at home in order catch up and be better prepared to meet with your business group the next week. Be sure to run the business unit, and not let the business unit run you.

15. Collaborate with Your Boss

Bosses are wonderful at coming up with ideas on how to improve the business. That's their job. However, bosses are not so wonderful at establishing priorities for activities. That's your job. When your boss comes to you with an offer to take on a new, exciting, and meaningful project, be ready. I suggest you say, "That sounds great. Now, let's review the key business outcomes you want to achieve this year."

After you gain clarity on the desired business outcomes, say, "Okay, so we're trying to achieve these three objectives. Here are the things I'm working on right now plus the new project you just presented. Of these things, which three do you think are the most important in terms of moving our desired business outcomes forward?"

Be patient and repeat the question a few times until the two of you gain clarity on the most important activities. If the new project makes the top three, that's great. Go do it. If it doesn't make the top three, then say, "While that new project is enticing, I'm going to need to stay focused on these other things for now. I'm intrigued by the idea you brought to me, but for now I'm going to have to pass because it won't help us achieve your desired business outcomes as much as these other projects." If you say yes to every good idea, then you are a corporate robot, not an effective manager.

16. Schedule Thinking Time

If I could print out the weekly calendar of every manager I've met, 95 percent of them would be black with ink. Virtually every possible space would be filled in with some activity. It is impossible to accelerate the achievement of your most important business outcomes if you don't take time to think. Schedule when and where you are going to think.

17. Get a Calendar That Works (for You!)

I've seen intelligent, hard-working managers ruin their careers because they couldn't figure out where they were supposed to be at a certain time. They would be late or miss meetings over and over.

The root of the problem was they had four different calendars going at the same time. They had electronic calendars on their desks, mobile calendars on their PDAs that they didn't synch up with the calendars in their desktop computers, hard copy Franklin Planners, and legal pads with appointments written down on them.

When someone wanted to make an appointment with these people, the situations would become embarrassing as they took out all the different ways of writing down appointments. Their administrative assistants were constantly trying to chase them down to get to meetings and appointments. This wasted triple time: the manager's time, the assistant's time, and the time of the people who were supposed to be with the manager. Stop the insanity. Select one type of calendar and stick with it.

18. Work on Working, Not Reworking

It's true confession time. When I drive, I get lost, a lot. My mind wanders and I miss my exits, I get turned around, and I have to stop and ask for directions over and over. One time I was driving from St. Louis to Indianapolis. That's a four-hour trip for most people. I turned it into an eight-hour ordeal. I drove two hours, stopped to get gas, got back in my car, drove for an hour and 45 minutes, looked up, and read the sign. It said, "15 Miles to St. Louis." I immediately turned around and drove to Indianapolis, again.

Do you ever lose your concentration while you're working, make mistakes, and then have to spend the time to redo your work? That's a time killer. The time you wasted is dead and can't be resurrected. Do one task at a time, concentrate, and don't do it over again.

19. Reward Yourself Every Week

Being a successful manager requires hard work and high levels of concentration. Toss in your responsibilities at home, and now we're talking about a person who is fully engaged in life. If you don't forcefully take some time for yourself, you ain't gonna get any.

Take out a sheet of paper and write down what you like to do. Maybe you like massages, jogging, manicures, pedicures, reading, gardening, biking, or being a couch potato. It doesn't matter, just write it down. Now take out your calendar and schedule at least one to three hours every week that is just for you. This is not for your spouse, kids, neighbors, or anyone else. It's for you. Then stick to that commitment just like you would for your best customer.

20. Review Your Time

Working to take back some of your life is as integral to your ongoing success as exercising, sleeping, and breathing. It's not a one-time deal. Every month, look back and see where your time went. Drucker was right about assessing your time, but don't do it just once. Do it month after month after month. Using your time effectively will differentiate you from many, many people.

RESOURCE RECOMMENDATION

The Effective Executive by Peter Drucker. If you haven't read this masterpiece, do so now.

Acceleration Tips

✓ Money can be lost and regenerated. Equipment can be ruined and replaced. Time goes away and doesn't come back. Acknowledge the importance of priority management. At the beginning of each day, identify the two or three activities you can do that will have the greatest positive impact on achieving sustainable, profitable growth. Start each day with those activities.

Chapter

3

AVOID DISASTROUS COMMUNICATION

"You Said What to Whom?"

A senior executive sits at a dinner table with a group of his direct reports and proceeds to tell stories for two hours without interruption. Everyone laughs and listens closely. When he leaves the table to get a drink, the others lower their heads and say what a bore he has become and how they can't stand working for him. His employees' satisfaction ratings plummet, and he gets demoted despite delivering strong business results.

A newly promoted director walks into his first meeting with his coworkers and says, "I know all of you think the people from the field are idiots, but there's a lot that I can teach you about what really matters." When he describes the incident to me, I replied, "You said what to whom?" He lasts less than six months before being fired.

A senior-level executive stands in front of 300 people and berates the newest product from their top supplier while the supplier is in the room. People's jaws drop open. One person says, "Did he have to say that in front of everyone?"

While speaking to a group of 50 managers, a senior executive continues to refer to herself in the third person about what she's thinking and turns her back on the audience numerous times as she talks to herself. People in the room start to look around, stop listening, and stare off with a glazed look in their eyes.

During his first 30 days as the second-highest-ranking officer in the group, a vice president continually throws his glasses on the table and rolls his eyes in disgust whenever he hears something he disagrees with. His direct reports have no idea what they said wrong, but they become increasingly annoyed with his style.

These are just some of the dozens of examples of poor communication I've seen over the past decade. More than a lack of technical knowledge, developing a bad strategy, or any other factor, poor communication causes managers to lose credibility and damage their careers.

In April 2003, Don Carty, the president of American Airlines, demanded that the pilots and flight attendants support the concept of "shared sacrifice" and take a pay cut in order to save the airline. Shortly after that, it was announced that many key executives would receive a guaranteed bonus regardless of the organization's performance. Carty then reversed that promise and said that the executives would not receive guaranteed bonuses. By the end of that tumultuous month, Carty resigned as president. His demands and secrecy so completely ruined trust in the organization that the only way to move forward effectively was for him to leave the company.

While writing his book, *Work in Progress,* Michael Eisner, then-CEO of the Walt Disney Company, said to his co-author about Jeffrey Katzenberg, the former head of the animation studio at Walt Disney, "I think I hate the little midget." That comment alone cost Disney tens of millions of dollars, and helped to accelerate Eisner into the management abyss. Apparently, he should have called the book, *Work in Need of More Progress.*

In the same way these people damaged their careers in an instant, you can ruin yours through poor communication. Managers don't get fired for poor technical skills; it was their technical skills that got them hired in the first place. Managers generally don't get fired for selecting the wrong strategy. They do get fired for poor execution, and poor execution can usually be traced back to poor communication. For that matter, poor teamwork, poor employee relations, and poor customer relations can usually be traced back to poor communication.

One of the main things I do as an executive coach is sit in meetings and observe how managers communicate with other people. Only then can I point out from my perspective what is and what is not effective in terms of the way they communicate. If we only talk over the phone or behind closed doors, then we're just talking theoretically about how they communicate.

By seeing them actually interact with other people, I can point out when they cut other people off, when they truly listened, when they asked provocative open-ended questions, and when they squelched conversations by talking too much. Another way I gather this information is to ask ten people who know the manger well and frequently see him in action these three questions:

1. What does the person do that makes him effective as an executive?
2. What does the person do that makes him ineffective as an executive?
3. What could the person do that would make him more effective as an executive?

Most of the comments I get back to those three questions relate to the person's communication skills.

TWENTY-TWO STEPS INTO THE COMMUNICATION ABYSS

Following are the main ways I have seen managers ruin relationships and damage their careers through poor communication. By reading about these destructive communication behaviors, you can choose more effective alternatives.

1. Talk and Talk and Talk

Big talkers are small thinkers. They are so busy talking, they aren't listening. They only get away with yapping on and on because they are in charge. Without realizing it, these managers are being ignored and avoided until one day their boss shows up and lets them go.

All the ideas within the group remain trapped in the minds of the employees with no way of getting out and no way of being discussed, improved, and implemented. Big talkers create the classic lose-lose-lose-lose scenario: employees lose, customers lose, the organization loses, and the manager loses his job.

2. Share None of Your Ideas

This is the polar opposite of the big talker. This manager puts her head down and stays busy, but never shares an idea that would improve the performance of anyone. She's smart and hard working, but never shares any of her insights. She views her effectiveness only in terms of the actions she does, and not in terms of the ideas she offers.

When she's replaced by a higher-paid manager, she is absolutely stunned, and wonders how they can pay somebody more than her when she was giving them everything she had. She doesn't realize that the company wanted her brain as well as her brawn.

3. Focus on Faults

The nitpickers are a pain in the butt. Every comment out of their mouths is about what somebody else did wrong. They never say, "Great job on fixing that customer's problems." They say, "Why did you screw up that customer's order in the first place?" They wear people out, and then are stunned when they read the employee surveys. When they get booted, they blame the boss for being too touchy-feely and too worried about how everyone feels.

4. Scream at People

This is the accelerated path to ruining business relationships. The idea of screaming at people is so old fashioned it seems to come from a prehistoric era. And yet it is very much alive today. People only allow themselves to be screamed at if their dignity has already been taken. These people are so desperate to have a job they will put up with a boss who screams in their face.

The screaming manager not only endangers the dignity of other people, but also endangers his own career. One key to management success is to attract and retain talented people. Once a person has developed a reputation as a screamer, the odds of him being able to attract and retain highly talented people goes way down.

5. All Eyes, No Ears

I'll never forget the seminar leader who told the audience members to pair up and listen to each other with soft eyes. He emphasized the importance of listening with empathy and really working to understand the other person's underlying message.

Late in the seminar, the person he had paired up with mentioned how much she appreciated the way he listened to her. He said, "Oh, I wasn't really listening. I was just demonstrating what it looked like." He lost all credibility immediately. Do you really listen to what the other person is saying, or are you all eyes and no ears?

6. Be the Invisible Enemy

A manager becomes an invisible enemy when she talks badly about one employee to another employee when the first one isn't in the room. Eventually word gets back to the first employee, the manager loses her cover, and the trust is gone completely and forever. Guess who's not going to run through the brick wall for that manager the next time?

7. Check Your Watch Frequently

This is the "I'm bored" approach. By checking your watch and sighing a lot, you send a supercharged nonverbal missile at the other person to hurry the hell up and finish talking. Being bored with your employees is not a very effective way to develop talent for long-term success.

8. Give No Specific Positives

Throw around "Good job," "Way to go," and "Boy, do I ever appreciate you!" like feathers after a pillow fight. That fluff feels good for a few minutes, and then it becomes annoying. People will see you as a transparent bag of wind. They will quickly realize you have no substance and no relationship with them. If someone does a good job, let him know exactly what he did well and why you appreciate him.

9. Slam Your Glasses Down

This is the "I'm rude" approach. Throw your glasses down when you don't like an idea, roll your eyes, say, "That's a stupid idea," and throw a fit when the group heads in a different direction from the one you want.

I don't care how brilliant you are in sales, marketing, or operations. This kind of behavior is going to get a stunned look, followed by a chorus of comments behind closed doors about your incompetence as a manager. And don't expect anybody to tell you what an idiot you're being. If you're lucky, you will find out before it's too late.

10. Push Back on Every Idea

If you want people to turn around and walk the other way, then play the devil's advocate on every single issue. This is a very effective way to wear other people out. Eventually they will remain quiet just to get the meeting over with. If no one else talks after any of your interventions, then you can rest assured you have stun-gunned the audience one too many times.

11. Be Arrogant

The arrogant executive is the person who thinks he has nothing left to learn. He ruins relationships, departments, and organizations by acting as though he is the only person with good ideas. I've seen situations when really talented and smart people stopped trying to offer their input because they knew their boss would never listen.

12. Ignore Your Commitments

Tell someone you will get the report done by Monday, and then just don't do it. Promise someone to call them back on Wednesday morning, and then just don't do it. Tell an important customer you will resolve the issues with her bill, and then never get back to her. These are great ways to get a running start before you leap into the abyss from which no manager ever returns.

13. Throw Stuff Out There for the Heck of It

Be polished, prepared, and professional. Be totally organized with every comment you're going to make before an important audience. Then right before you leave the platform, tell an incredibly sexist joke filled with expletives. I know this sounds like a stretch as you're reading it, but trust me, it happens. Managers need to be on guard for their "throwaway comments." Tell me Jimmy Carter wouldn't like to take back the 30 seconds it took to tell the *Playboy* interviewer he lusted after other women.

14. Disempower People

Oh, this is a fun one for the employee. The manager says, "You're in charge of the meeting. Design it any way you want, and I'll just be like everybody else. I'll sit in the audience and jump into the activities just like all the other attendees."

The employee spends a week organizing the meeting and then begins to facilitate the discussion at the actual event. Forty-five minutes into the meeting, the manager steps in and says, "Okay, we're going to head in a different direction. Thanks for getting us together." And then, presto, the manager is up in front and the employee is sitting down. Several months later, the manager can't figure out why he was fired for not developing his employees to take on greater responsibilities.

15. Talk about Politics and Religion

Want to make your employees uncomfortable? Start the next meeting with a statement about why everyone should be an extreme left-wing liberal or an extreme right-wing conservative. Then challenge each employee to talk about where they stand on a current hot issue. Or start every meeting with a prayer. You may not see your employees squirm in their chairs, but you will catch on when the word gets back to your boss.

16. Lie

Make stuff up. Make up the quarterly numbers, make up why you missed a critically important meeting, and make up why your travel expenses are missing important receipts. These are great ways to generate short-term benefits and long-term career disasters.

17. Be Politically Incompetent

Here's a clue: don't say you think the new hire is a "hottie." Clue number two: don't tell a 60-year-old employee "thanks for the memories." Clue number three: don't tell a woman she doesn't have the capacity for certain types of work. I've actually heard all of these and a whole bunch worse.

Believe it or not, there are still people who say disparaging things about African Americans, Hispanics, and Asians, as though "they" are incapable of doing certain things. People, it's the 21st century. Let me set the record straight. Effectiveness is not dependent on gender, race, height, or size. I've met individuals from all possible combinations of gender, race, height, and size. Some of these individuals were incredibly effective and some were incredibly ineffective.

Remember these three steps: think, think again, and then talk. Incorrect statements will cost you many, many career opportunities. However, before you can say proper things, you have to believe those things to be true. If you are racist or sexist underneath the mask, eventually it's going to shine through. Resolve your internal prejudices so you won't have to worry about them slipping out at the wrong time.

18. Be Secretive with Information

Knowledge is power. That old aphorism is generally a ridiculous concept. Keeping important knowledge to yourself does nothing but slow your organization down. Get knowledge in the hands of key people so they can make intelligent decisions and move into action in ways that generate better sustainable results. You may think you're more powerful by holding on to key information, but unless it's truly confidential, the information is only useful if it is moving the organization forward.

19. Start Rumors

Rumors are the byproduct of insecure people who have too much time on their hands. Rather than getting to the facts or confronting people on vague bits of information, rumormongers take the slightest and shallowest pieces of information and start rumors that can destroy careers and ruin teamwork.

Early in my career I spent hours upon hours gossiping about other people. I did it subconsciously because I thought it would make me seem better than others. In the end, it made me feel worse about myself and appear insecure, which I was. People who are focused on adding value simply don't allow themselves to waste time going down the path of starting rumors.

20. Don't Let Anyone Get to Know You

Every business in every industry is a relationship business. You can't build a meaningful relationship by hiding behind your title. Either people get to know you, understand your unique combination of passions and strengths and weaknesses, or they don't.

As I go through a mental Rolodex of the managers I've coached over the years, I would say those individuals who deliberately avoided letting other people get to know them on a personal basis were in almost all cases among the least effective managers. How do you build a relationship with someone if they know nothing about you?

21. Worry about Every Comment

This is the "I'm paranoid" approach. Turn every general comment into a direct attack on you. If the president of the company says, "Personal integrity is critically important to the success of our company," then go to your group and ask, "Why is the president questioning the way I'm running our department?" These comments will send a loud signal to your employees that you are seriously insecure.

22. Brag about Your Wild Days

Self-disclosure can be an ugly thing. No one wants to know about your sexual exploits or drinking binges when you were 20 years old. Keep those "wonderful" memories to yourself. People want a professional to lead them, not a frat boy or party girl.

I've just covered some of the main ways managers ruin relationships. So what is the key to building relationships? In a word, it's "respect." If you respect the people you're communicating with, you will treat them with dignity and honesty. You can still be candid, but you can do so in a way that shows you care. I'll discuss this idea of communicating with respect a great deal more in Chapters 4, 7, and 8.

Acceleration Tips

- ✓ Keep in mind that the fastest way to ruin your career is to have a communication collapse. Consequently, be alert, stay on your toes, and communicate in the manner you truly want to communicate versus the way you communicate when you're worn out and overstressed.

Chapter

4

PROVIDE LEADERSHIP

"My Boss Tells Me I'm a Mood-Ring Leader."

Susan had eight different bosses in three years. You read that correctly. Although she didn't leave her company, the person she reported to changed eight times. One day while I was working with her as an executive coach she said, "Dan, my boss tells me I'm a mood-ring leader."

I asked, "What is a mood-ring leader?"

She said, "Do you remember the mood rings back in the '70s?"

"Vaguely," I replied.

She said, "Mood rings had stones that changed colors every time your mood changed. My boss told me I change my leadership style with every new boss I have. He said I adopt whatever style my boss uses. This is hurting my career and holding me back from being promoted. What should I do?"

I asked, "Can I reach out to people who have known you for the past two to four years and gather their input?"

Susan said yes, and gave me the names of people who worked with her regularly and knew her well. Their feedback was clear and consistent. People said Susan was effective because of her knowledge of the business and her technical skills, but she was ineffective because she acted like she didn't know what she stood for, what her point of view was on a variety of important issues, and what approach she would use at any given moment. They wanted her to take a stand and not fluctuate her opinion based on what her boss felt was the right way to do things.

As she listened to me replay the feedback to her, I saw a transformation begin to happen. She told me she realized she was making herself less effective as a leader by always trying to imitate her current boss. She said she knew she was at her very best when she connected with other people and that if she were ever going to be seen as a top candidate for promotion, she was going to have to go back to her old ways of doing things. In the end, she told me she would have to stop being a "mood-ring leader" and just stick to influencing people the way she believed was the right way.

Susan's focus shifted. She stood up for her staff members even when it wasn't popular with her boss. She consciously carved out what she was, and was not, going to do, and how she was going to do it.

She said, "If I fail, I'm going to go down doing things the way I believe they should be done." She didn't fail. She thrived as a leader. People began to trust her more and their efforts improved. It took time for her new more genuine approach to take hold, but this time she was being true to herself rather than being a copy of her boss of the moment. In the end, she became a highly successful executive.

This pattern of letting go of effective leadership approaches in order to do what "the boss" wants is one I've seen many, many times. In almost every case, the person actually hurt his or her career by trying to do things the way "the boss" wanted things done. To be a great leader, you have to be your own person.

Leadership means influencing how other people think in ways that generate better sustainable results both for the organization and the people in it.

The best leaders I've witnessed determined how they were most effective at influencing other people and then stuck to what worked for them. That said, they were willing to experiment with different approaches. However, in the end, their litmus test for sticking with a certain leadership approach was not what worked for their boss, but rather what worked for them.

Susan found what worked for her. What leadership approach works best for you? Stick with that while continually searching for ways to enhance your ability to influence other people.

In the end, leadership depends on having a relationship with the people you are trying to lead. The foundation of all relationships is trust. Does the other person trust you? As you strengthen your business relationships, you can have a greater impact on how other people think and ultimately have a greater impact on improving the business results. I'll discuss how to build trust in Chapter 7.

For now, Figure 4.1 shows the critical areas for long-term business success: relationships and results.

Managers in Quadrant I have poor relationships and poor results. That's a problem. The temptation is for them to focus on delivering results as fast as possible. That would be a mistake. The way to move forward is to focus on improving both relationships and results. In doing so, you gradually move toward becoming a manager who can deliver sustainable improvement in key business results.

Without a dual focus on both improving relationships and results, you will only land in Quadrants II or III. Neither one of them is sufficient. Great managers operate in Quadrant IV. They consistently strengthen relationships with people throughout the organization as well as with suppliers and customers. They consistently increase their capacity to be effective leaders, while simultaneously guiding the group to deliver better business results.

What follows are a number of leadership approaches you may want to consider. In the end, I encourage you to find the ones that work for you. Of course, you may need to reach beyond this limited list of ideas and find other methods tailored to your personality. The

FIGURE 4.1

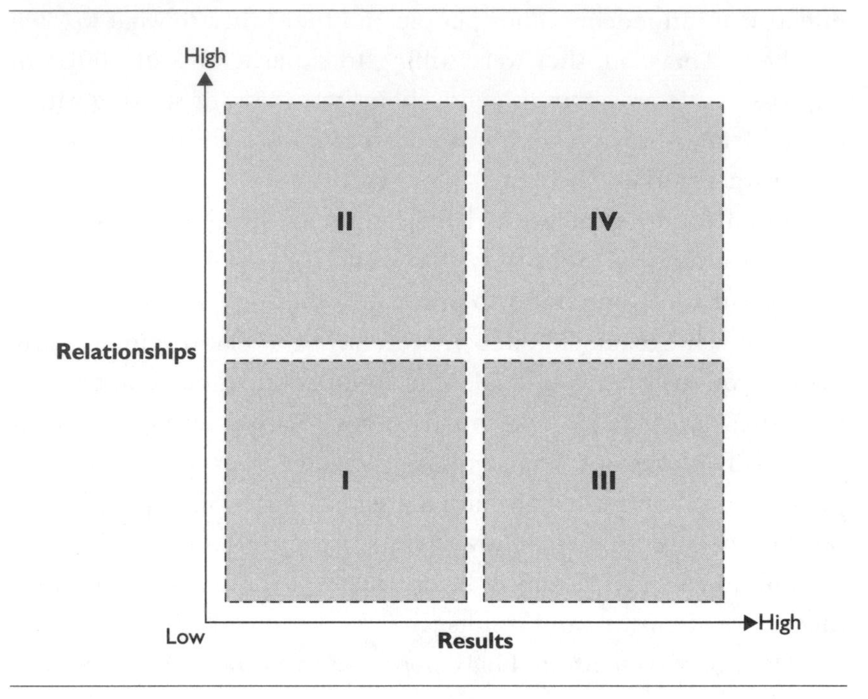

ideas on leadership are placed in five categories—demonstrate, ask, share, challenge, and clarify—and are represented in Figure 4.2.

TWENTY-FIVE WAYS TO INFLUENCE HOW OTHER PEOPLE THINK

Method #1: Demonstrate Effective Leadership Behaviors

1. Act with integrity and be honest. Let me say it again. You can't influence people if they don't trust you. To gain people's trust, you must act with integrity and be honest in every situation. An effective leader is not defined by his charisma, but is someone who acts in a way that makes people feel they can count on him over the long term.

FIGURE 4.2

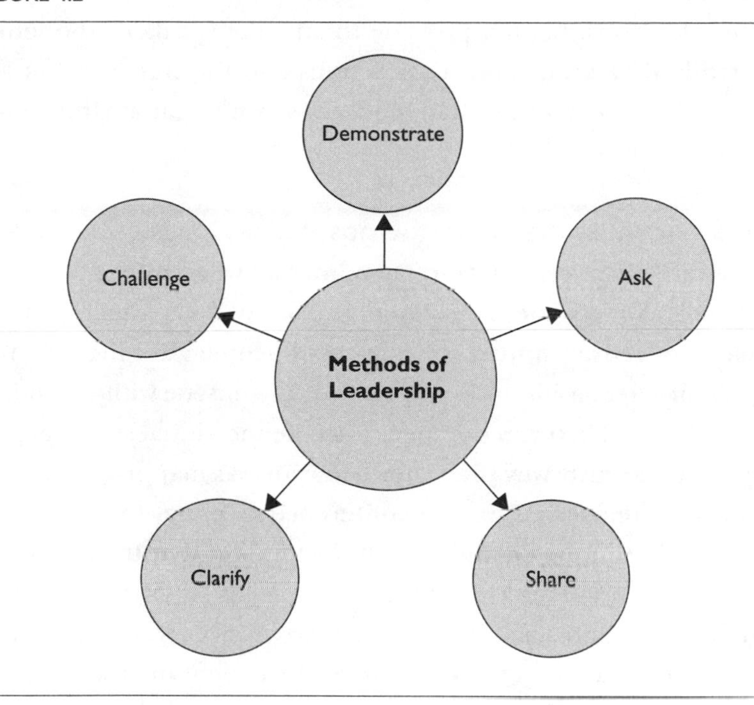

2. Model the desired behavior. I'm always stunned when managers yell at people to be more hospitable. You may want to read that sentence again. One of my clients has a great saying above his desk: "Your actions speak so loudly I can't hear what you are saying." If you want people in your business unit to respond quickly to situations, then you need to model responsiveness and speed.

3. Demonstrate that you believe in their ability to succeed. If you want to send the message that you believe in a certain person, don't tell her you believe in her, show her you believe in her. Tell her she's in charge of the national sales conference coming up in six months. Let her know she's empowered to make whatever decisions are necessary to making it a big success. Give her the budget and get out of her way.

Meet with her every month to hear an update, but don't interfere with her decisions. Let her pick the theme, the speakers, the setup, the agenda flow, and so on. Your actions and the freedom you are truly providing her will speak so loudly she won't hear anything else. That's leadership.

4. Stay calm in the midst of chaos. When things get crazy, and they always do, stay calm. If you stay calm even when one of your staff members is saying something stupid in front of a key client, you will be able to effectively influence a variety of people after the fact. You can pull the client aside and apologize for the miscue without embarrassing anyone. Then you can meet with the individual staff member in private and clarify why his or her behavior was inappropriate.

During a rehearsal for a big conference meeting, I watched as a director became frazzled and started demanding that the A/V technicians rush around and take care of her needs. The vice president calmly watched and waited for his chance to meet with her one on one, then he proceeded to explain in a very patient manner that this was not the way people acted the day before a big meeting.

The director listened, apologized, and everyone moved on with their preparations. The ineffective leader makes mountains out of molehills, and the effective leader defuses situations with his calmness.

5. Step way out of your comfort zone. Demonstrate your willingness to do whatever it takes to help the group succeed. Alarm clocks work well because they jar people from their sleep and cause them to take action. Effective leaders do the same thing. They interrupt people's thinking and cause them to reconsider what they're going to do. If you're always quiet, then raise your voice once in awhile. If you're extremely analytical and numbers oriented, then tell a story about your children or about a touching moment you had early in your career. Create dissonance. Interfere with people's perceptions.

Method #2: Ask Questions to Guide the Other Person's Thought Process

6. Ask a clear, concise, and compelling question. Narrow the other person's focus to simply improving the desired outcome. Leaders do not have to be experts on any one topic. The goal of the leader is not to impress people with what she knows, but rather to cause them to think in a way that will generate better sustainable results.

After sitting through a review of the business results with his staff, one of my clients will often ask, "I know what we achieved, but what did we learn while we were achieving those results? What lessons should we take away from the past year, and how can we use them this year?" These questions really cause the staff members to reflect on what they did, ascertain the sources of their successes and failures, and clarify what they will do going forward.

Another question I heard recently is, "What would it take to double our business in the next five years?" This one question can cause people in every department to reflect on what they're doing now and what they could be doing to generate sustainable, profitable growth.

7. Ask the other person what he sees as his greatest strengths and greatest passions. In Chapter 1, I explained the critical importance of understanding your strengths and passions and deploying them in a manner that will positively impact your organization and your clients.

As a leader, you can ask other people those same questions:

- What are you good at doing?
- What are you passionate about doing?
- Which business results are you working to improve for our company?
- Which client outcomes are you working to improve?
- How can you use your strengths and passions to improve our business results and our client's situation?

Those five questions can generate a person's action plan for business acceleration over the next six months to two years. Your key to success is to ask questions, pause patiently, and then listen for answers. Your feedback and coaching and follow-up can happen later.

8. Ask the other person to recall a success story from her past. A past success story is a gold mine. The trick is to get the other person to stop and recall the story. In other words, go slow to go fast. John Wooden, the great basketball coach at UCLA, said, "Be quick, but don't hurry." The direct route of telling people what to do may seem the most expedient, but it usually builds walls in communication. Instead of rushing into the business at hand, encourage the other person to pause and reflect.

By asking an employee to recall one of her past success stories, you're allowing her to stop and think about the business issues and to find answers from other parts of her life. After she's told her story, ask her to identify what she learned from that experience. Then ask her to identify how she can apply those lessons to her current situation.

Again, all you're really doing is asking questions and patiently listening, but this Socratic approach to improving business results can generate faster and more sustainable results than telling people what to do.

9. Ask the other person to play the role of adviser. People sometimes get blocked when dealing with their own issues, but they usually have no problem giving advice to other people. I think it's human nature. When the pressure is off, we can think clearly. When the deadline or crisis is something we have to deal with, we freeze up.

The next time one of your staff members freezes up in the face of a huge problem, pull him aside and say, "If Mary was faced with that problem, what advice would you give her?" Then stop talking and let the person think. You may need to repeat the question, but I think you'll find that the person you're talking with will start to come up with solutions because it's no longer about him. Write down whatever he says. When he's all done talking, you can say, "That sounds like great advice. I encourage you to put it into action."

10. Facilitate a group discussion. The benefit of facilitating versus lecturing is that you can draw out the best thinking of everyone in the group. By getting people to open up and share their ideas, you can influence the entire group.

Say you want to grow revenues over the next six months. Pull together 50 people and ask, "What can we do to profitably grow revenues over the next six months?" Give everyone the question 72 hours before the meeting, and then again at the meeting.

Then break the large group into ten groups of five people. Have everyone discuss their answers in the small group, and then have each small group present their three best ideas. Then have the large group discuss the ideas and narrow down the choices to the top three ideas. This can all be accomplished in less than 90 minutes. If you do that even once a quarter, you demonstrate that you care about other people's ideas, you probably will gain greater buy-in to the actual business plan, and you might get better ideas than you otherwise were generating.

Method #3: Share Your Insights in Relevant Ways

11. Share a personal story. Make yourself real. A true story about a person who impacted your life can resonate with other people. One of my clients who was the highest-ranking executive in her business unit told a very personal story to a huge audience, and it deeply affected many of them.

She talked about being named a member of the All-State, First Team, Women's Basketball Team her junior year in high school. She went to her coach and asked for advice on how she could get better. She thought he was going to suggest that she watch NBA players, but instead he said, "See that little box above the hoop? I want you to work on your layups." She was stunned and didn't take him very seriously. Then she told us that in her senior year in the state championship game, with five seconds left, the ball landed in her hands about eight feet from the basket. She said she drove to the basket and laid the ball off the backboard, the ball rolled out, and her team lost.

Everyone in the audience froze in their seats as she told this story. Then she said, "For us to succeed, we have to work on the fundamentals. We have to make our layups." That speech generated an extraordinary focus among an enormous group of people to get back to the basics and improve the customer experience. It all happened because she shared a personal story.

12. Provide an analogy that resonates. If the person you're talking to loves sports, then use a sports analogy. If she is into music, use a music analogy. If he is a huge fan of the Marines, then use a military analogy. Don't just assume that talking about winning the Super Bowl is going to mean anything to the other people—they might hate sports. Find the analogy that's going to resonate with them.

13. Suggest a book or a film that causes people to think differently. Rather than making yourself out to be an expert on everything, recommend a few chapters from a good book or recommend a film you saw that might add value to the other person, and then ask him what he got out of it.

Many times I've seen managers purchase a book for all the members of their staff, and then ask them to discuss their perspectives on it at a future meeting. Suddenly the leader is providing influence without saying hardly anything. As the ideas in the book get tossed around, the underlying message gets driven home.

14. Talk about your weaknesses and how you have had to work to overcome them. Again, make yourself seem real. If you're a great public speaker, let the other people know that you were extremely nervous at your first presentation and forgot several key messages. Then explain how you developed your skills over a long period of time.

Or let them know how you struggle with learning technology and you've just conditioned yourself to add one new usage of technology every quarter. If you seem real and human, you may create a place where people can hear your message and be influenced by it.

15. Provide candid feedback. I think Jack Welch was right when he wrote, "The biggest dirty little secret in business is the lack of candor," in his terrific book, *Winning*. Being candid with other people is oftentimes the greatest gift you can give them as a manager.

I encourage you to always do it behind closed doors, one on one. There are times when giving an entire group candid feedback is very effective. However, I'm talking about giving one person candid feedback on his performance. When you give the candid feedback, base it either on actual behaviors that you have seen or on behaviors that you have received input on from multiple people.

I'm convinced one of the main reasons people hire me as an executive coach is that I'm very comfortable being candid with other people about their behaviors, communication styles, decision making, and approaches to the business. I speak candidly because I care about the other person's success and the success of her organization. And, of course, I always do it behind closed doors in one-on-one conversations.

Method #4: Challenge People to Think Differently

16. Challenge your staff member to do even better by asking, "Is this your best effort?" Okay, I'm suggesting one more time that you ask questions. Questions can really force people to think differently. This particular question, "Is this your best effort?" is the question that Admiral Hyman Rickover asked former president Jimmy Carter back in 1955. That question drove Carter throughout his career. Use it with your staff and see what kind of a response it generates. It may cause people to honestly reflect on their efforts and find better ways to generate better results.

17. Help the group define what they will do *and* what they will not do. The easy part of leadership is to get the group excited about what they're going to do to climb the mountain of success. The hard part of leadership is influencing them to give up some of their activities. Challenge people to do less in order to achieve more.

18. Make a bold statement. "Just be right." I don't think I've ever come across a statement by any manager that catches people between the eyes more effectively than this one. After listening to the other person's opinion on what needs to be done to move the business forward, this manager simply says, "Sounds good to me. Just be right."

In other words, he's saying, "I'm trusting you've done your homework and have identified what we should do and what we shouldn't do, and we're going to go ahead with your recommendation. However, I'm going to hold you responsible for the results we achieve." Rather than saying all of that and diluting his point, he simply says, "Just be right."

What bold statement can you make that would immediately influence how other people think in ways that will generate better sustainable results both for your organization and the people in it?

19. Establish an extraordinary goal. I'm sure you know about "stretch goals." They either inspire people or turn them off. If your company has generated 2 percent growth in revenues each year for the past four years, then stating that the company is going to double its size in ten years is a real turnoff. However, if your company has doubled in size in the past five years, then saying the goal is to double in size again over the next five years is inspiring and realistic. Extraordinary goals do galvanize people as long as they are realistic stretch goals.

20. Compete with your best competitor. I think you have to put a face on the enemy. Assuming you're not the runaway best performer in your industry, I encourage you to set your sights on your top competitor. Make it clear to everyone what is being measured and how you stack up against the other company. Don't copy their every move, but instead look for innovative ways to move past them.

When PepsiCo found it to be impossible to win the cola wars against Coca-Cola, they moved into noncarbonated beverages and energy drinks and snacks. They took the indirect approach to grab market share from a redefined revenue pie.

If you are the best in your industry, set your sights on being the best company in any industry or the best company in a newly defined category or on making history. Whatever objective you decide upon, just make sure that it gets the competitive juices flowing in your organization.

Method #5: Clarify to Reduce Confusion and Increase Understanding

21. Clarify the desired business outcome and why it's so important. I think you should be able to clearly communicate your desired business outcome in one sentence. Clarity creates effective teamwork, brainstorming, and combining of operational efforts.

One of the most important things you can do as a manager is to clarify the desired outcome and why it is so important. If everyone understands the end game and the value of achieving it, you may very well influence them to think differently and behave differently in ways that will accelerate the achievement of that desired outcome.

22. Clarify the risks and the rewards of taking action. Don't leave people hanging out to dry with their concerns. Get their issues on the table right away. Take out a flipchart and draw a vertical line down the middle. Write "risks" on the left side of the line and "rewards" on the right side.

Ask them to identify all the risks involved in implementing the new approach. Then ask them to identify all the possible rewards for implementing the approach. Work with them to clarify any changes that need to be made to the new initiative so that the potential rewards are greater than the potential risks.

23. Clarify the potential impact of being successful. This is similar to the previous suggestion. The difference is rather than focusing on the rewards the group might gain if they are successful, this approach focuses on the improved results other people might gain if the group is successful. In other words, the focus shifts from "what we will gain" to "what impact we will make beyond our group."

24. Clarify the expected behaviors and results. Essentially, I'm talking about culture and business performance. The more you clarify the expected behaviors, the more you increase your chances of building a sustainable culture. The more you focus on the importance of delivering real results, the more you generate sustainable, profitable growth.

This is really an everyday responsibility for leaders, and your title doesn't matter. One business unit I worked with was focused on enhancing hospitality at their retail units. The lead administrative assistant organized all the other administrative assistants around a theme called, "We serve the people who serve our customers." Each month they found one additional way to add more value to the department heads and staff members in the office. It was a beautiful example that leadership is not dependent on titles.

25. Follow up to clarify priorities. Follow-up is the grunt work of leadership. It's fun and sexy to give the inspiring speech, but it's also pointless if it's not followed up with by the person giving it.

I've seen senior executives invest an enormous amount of time and money in gathering input from across the country on what would make their company better, and then not get back to anyone on what was going to happen with their input. That's not effective.

If you ask for input or you gather ideas, then you need to follow up with folks to see what is working, what's not working, what they are learning, what they are doing with what they are learning, and what adjustments they've decided to make. If you don't follow up with them, then you will actually influence them to not take you seriously.

RESOURCE RECOMMENDATION

I encourage you to read Marcus Buckingham's book *The One Thing You Need to Know,* particularly the section on leadership. He makes a powerful point about the importance of providing clarity as a leader.

Acceleration Tips

✓ I've given you 25 ways to influence how other people think. Now come up with 25 more of your own. Constantly search for ways to be more effective in influencing how other people think that will generate better sustainable results both for your organization and the people in it. You need to be the final filter on which approaches you use. Decide how you are most effective in influencing other people, and then put those approaches into action.

Chapter

5

KICK START CREATIVITY

"People Don't Pay Me to Sit Around and Think"

Tom was an enormously successful and highly respected executive. Over a period of 20 years, he had worked his way up the ladder to be the vice president of operations for a $500 million business unit. Everyone respected Tom because he got things done. Whatever he said he would do, he did it, and he made sure his teams did the same thing.

His efficiency levels and customer satisfaction scores were extraordinary. After six months of working with him as an executive coach, Tom said to me, "Dan, I have some bad news. My boss says I need to change. He wants me to become more strategic. He wants me to think bigger."

I said, "Tom, that's not a problem. I've heard this many, many times before. By thinking bigger and being more strategic, you can leverage yourself and have a greater impact on the business. Rather than you doing so much, you can help guide your team to even greater successes."

Tom looked at me and became even more intense. He said, "Dan, you don't understand. People don't pay me to sit around and think.

They pay me to get stuff done. I'm a doer, not a thinker. If I just sit around the office, I'm going to lose all my credibility."

I have had virtually this exact conversation dozens and dozens of times in my executive coaching career. Hard-working people have gained increasing levels of responsibilities until one day their main job is not to execute the tactics but to develop the concepts that other people will execute. Many managers stall at this point in their careers. The declining manager never buys into the value of setting aside time just to think, and he never sees practical ways to develop breakthrough ideas.

When this happens, I have two objectives:

1. Get the manager to understand why creative thinking is critically important to moving the business forward.
2. Help the manager see how they can find and develop ideas in a practical manner.

WHY CREATIVITY IS A CRITICALLY IMPORTANT MANAGEMENT SKILL

When I asked managers what the benefits would be of taking time to get away from their work and think about the business, these were some of the answers they came up with:

- "I might see things I might otherwise not notice within our company."
- "I might get an idea from a competitor that would add value to what we're doing."
- "If I stopped working so hard doing everything, I might have more energy to put into the few things that really matter."
- "I might find an idea from outside my industry that could help us."
- "I might get an idea from another part of our company."

- "I might see some connections between ideas that I just don't have time to explore right now."
- "I might realize that we're barking up the wrong tree, and that we're spending a ton of time, money, and energy on things that don't matter to customers."
- "I might find that I'm spinning my wheels on things that really don't matter."
- "I might be seen differently inside the company if I came up with some big ideas rather than always being the one who executed other people's ideas. Maybe I'd get a promotion."
- "Perhaps I could leverage my experience in the field in a way that would make things easier for a lot of people and deliver better results."

Once the person starts to buy into the value of thinking creatively about the business, I work with them to develop processes for thinking differently. Before I go into those processes, here's a simple but powerful quote from the Disney Imagineers' book, *The Imagineering Way: Ideas to Ignite Your Creativity:*

> We pondered for six months just what comprised the process of imagination. Was there a basic process in common that held true for both a scientific breakthrough and a beautifully decorated birthday cake? Indeed, we discovered, there is. Everyone goes through a process of gathering information, storing it, and recombining it with other thoughts to produce something new.

Imagineers are the people at the Walt Disney Company who come up with the ideas for all the rides and attractions at the Disney theme parks. Then they convert those ideas into realities. The term "imagineer" was originated by Walt Disney and refers to the combination of imagination and engineering. Imagineers come up with ideas and determine how to deliver those ideas.

The first time I read the aforementioned quote from *The Imagineering Way,* I was extremely unimpressed to say the least. I thought, "That's it? That's not very useful." Then I read it several more times, and I began to see the genius in the simplicity of that statement. That basic process of gathering inputs, storing them, and then combining them with other ideas is where creative breakthroughs occur. Here are some suggestions on how to make that simple process real and practical in the midst of your busy days.

TEN WAYS TO INCREASE CREATIVITY

1. Use Your Scheduled Thinking Time to Be Creative

As I mentioned in Chapter 2, when I interact with people like Tom, the first thing I suggest is for them to put one hour a week of thinking time on their calendar, and to make that hour as sacrosanct as an important meeting with a great customer. These people are used to doing things, so the first thing I want them to do is schedule an activity. Now it feels like they are doing something.

Then I say to the person, "Take one important objective you are working toward achieving and turn it into an open-ended question. Go into that hour of thinking time and devote the first 45 minutes to answering that question from as many different perspectives as you can. Generate as many different ideas as you can. Then take the last 15 minutes to identify your best ideas and develop an action plan."

Over the years, I've found that people rarely do this simple exercise the first time I recommend it. Like water on a rock, I stay on the person just to try it. Then after about seven weeks, the person starts to try this process. And then almost magically she starts to uncover ideas that will help to move the business forward effectively.

Every person has the capacity to develop new ideas for positively impacting the business. What keeps most people from doing it is either they don't value taking the time to think creatively, or they don't think they are in a position to develop breakthrough ideas.

Consequently, they just stay focused on doing things, which are inputs, versus generating ideas that could dramatically improve the outcomes, which are outputs. Creativity begins with the discipline to stop doing things and just focus on thinking for one hour a week.

2. Be Naïve and Ask Lots of Questions

As you interact with people from different departments, ask open-ended questions like:

- What are the key factors for your department to improve the corporation's desired outcomes successfully?
- What are the biggest strengths of your department?
- What do you see as the biggest obstacles our business has to overcome in order to move into the upper echelon?

By asking questions and listening to the answers, you will begin to accumulate a variety of insights. At some later point, you may very well be inspired and see those insights in a way that can be applied to improving key results.

3. Walk in the Other Person's Shoes

To really understand another person, you need to spend time with him or her. If you work in operations, then spend some time with the people in marketing or finance to better understand their role. Spend a day just shadowing the other person in meetings and client visits.

Don't do it to evaluate someone. Do it so you see what the people performing various functions really deal with on a regular basis. I have a client right now who is a regional vice president of operations. She meets once a month with the head of finance and the head of marketing. In doing so, she broadens her pool of knowledge and then looks at the business from a different, enhanced perspective.

4. Put Yourself into New Nonwork Situations and Observe What Is Happening

Walt Disney developed the idea for Disneyland by visiting amusement parks with his daughters. Toyota engineers in the 1950s developed the idea for just-in-time inventory by visiting U.S. grocery stores. They noticed how the shelves never went bare; every time someone took a loaf of bread, another loaf appeared just in time for the next customer to take it out.

If you are working 70 hours a week and never allow yourself to be immersed in a new setting, you will not get very many new connections for driving your business forward.

5. Read, Read, Read

Books are fuel for ideas that can be connected to drive great business results. Feed your mind insights on a wide variety of industries and corporations and not-for-profit organizations of all sizes and from all parts of the world. Books provide us with the working material to make connections we otherwise could not make.

6. Listen to a Variety of Talk Shows

Interviews with highly successful people can provide unusual insights into the hidden rules of success. Oprah Winfrey and Larry King can extract powerful insights from people that can have application in many different scenarios. Just one good idea from a superstar can ignite the ideas you already have within you. Suddenly you may generate a breakthrough approach for growing your business that you never saw before.

7. Talk to Different Types of People

Make a list of everyone you've talked to in the last month. Look at your list and analyze how diverse the members of the group really are. Do they all work in the same organization or industry? Do they all do the same type of work? If you're up to two yeses, then you're not going to get very many new insights that will cause your pool of stored information to spark and flourish into a full-fledged breakthrough idea.

8. Be the Customer

Whenever I work with a new client, I step into his world to understand his business from his perspective, which is infinitely more important than understanding the business from my perspective.

If you work as a manager in a public accounting firm, then spend two days "working" at your most important client's organization. Stand shoulder-to-shoulder with people throughout the organization and see their world from their eyes. It may help you understand opportunities for the business to grow that you had never seen before. With this additional understanding of your client, you may come up with ideas that can add value to your client and possibly increase your revenue streams.

9. Optimize Your Breadth of Knowledge

In terms of making connections, breadth of knowledge trumps depth of knowledge. Rather than being the world expert on one topic, expand your experiences, reading, and conversations to grow your breadth of knowledge. By doing this, you will have a broader pool of ideas to draw from when necessary.

10. Connect Seemingly Unrelated Ideas

Go back to the process of imagination as described by the Imagineers. They said it's a three-step process: gathering information, storing it, and recombining it with other thoughts to create something new. It's the third part, the recombining part, where the magic happens for you.

Asking the question, "What if?" is a powerful way to make connections.

What if our service department had the speed of service of a 911 emergency department? What if we conducted talent management the same way Harvard University creates its student body? What if we used iPods to distribute our monthly updates by recording our message on an MP3 and then e-mailing it to all our employees who could listen to it while they are sitting in traffic?

Another question to create useful combination of ideas is a "How" question.

How can we deliver twice as many products in half the time? How can we double the size of our business in five years? These questions force us to rethink every part of our business and what needs to be done differently.

Acceleration Tips

✓ As a manager, your job is to generate better sustainable results than have been achieved before. Your job is not doing as many activities as you can possibly fit in. In order to increase your own creativity, you need to see the value of being creative, and then you need to have a repeatable process that can produce meaningful and relevant ideas on a regular basis.

Part Two

ACCELERATE YOUR STAFF'S RESULTS

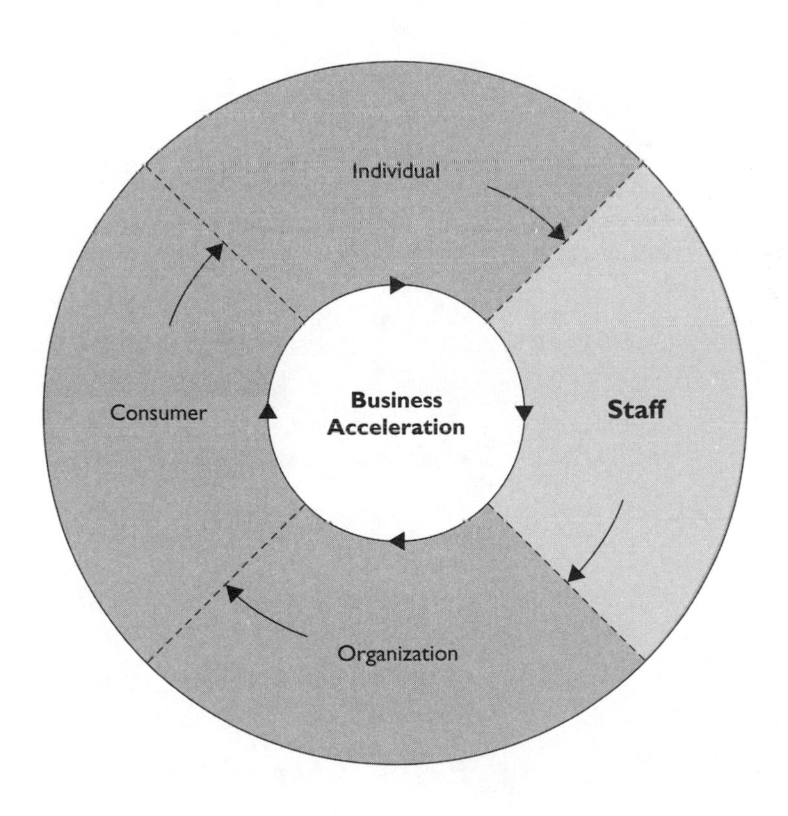

Chapter

6

IDENTIFY REASONS FOR LACK OF UNITY

"You Call That a Team?"

I once asked a receptionist, "What time does the management team meeting start?" She said, "You call that a team? The meeting starts at 10 AM, but I certainly wouldn't call it a team." Her words were prophetic. The meeting consisted of department updates, finger pointing, and a far greater emphasis on individual goals than on fulfilling the group's purpose in a tangible manner.

The harsh reality of business teamwork is that it almost never happens.

Most business groups called "teams" are the opposite of a true team. All too often individuals talk about the performance of their department, the issues their department is facing, the resources their department needs, and the bonuses their department wants. The only problem is customers don't care about departmental performance. They only care about the net result of all the departments' efforts.

Since no one department completely serves the customer, departments are dependent upon one another to add value to the customer. Consequently, there's a dangerous dichotomy in motion:

many individuals focus solely on the performance of their own department while it is only the work done between departments that matters to customers.

When I ask people to describe their work environment, one word I hear a lot is "silos." As in, "It's like we all work in silos. The operations people think the marketing people ruin any chance of improving operations, and the marketing people think the operations people are afraid to try any new idea that might throw them off. The finance people just crunch the numbers and have no real idea what is going on with the customers." While I'm convinced people want to be part of a vital team, there are forces at work that greatly diminish the chances for any true teamwork to occur.

TEN PRIMARY REASONS WHY TEAMWORK FIZZLES AND SILOS MULTIPLY

1. The Best Intentions of Family and Friends

The people I've worked with and observed over the years do not come across as greedy, self-centered, money-grubbing individuals. They seem like caring, kind, considerate, hard-working folks. So why don't they create great teamwork more often?

The first reason is they go home at the end of the day. When they get home and start interacting with their spouse, parents, friends, and neighbors, the questions shift from, "How can we add more value to our customers?" to "How's your year going?" Neighbors don't want to hear about the level of teamwork in your organization or how departments support one another toward generating breakthrough ideas. They want to hear about the new deck you're building or the vacation you're going on or the new car you're buying or what colleges you're sending your kids to.

The same holds true for your spouse, parents, and friends. They want to hear that *you* are doing a great job at work, and that *you* are being rewarded handsomely for it. While the focus from people at work is on how the organization can deliver better value and generate sustainable and profitable growth, the focus you will get at home is on how you are performing and how you are being rewarded.

This focus on personal rewards frequently takes over the focus on the team's efforts, and teamwork breaks down. This dual set of expectations is true for every employee in every organization. When I coach a person, I always say that she has to keep in mind both what's good for the organization and what's good for herself and her family.

Sometimes she will have to take the long view on both of those perspectives. Taking time to go watch her daughter's dance practice may not help her company in that two-hour time period she's gone from work, but her enhanced energy may help her team succeed over the next 90 days. Moving to a new city may not seem like a thrill ride for her family, but over the long term it may open up opportunities her family could never have experienced.

Being a team player at work doesn't mean you have to forget your needs and wants as an individual. You do have to know what is important to your organization, your work group, your customers, your family, and yourself. Keeping those desired outcomes in mind increases the chances you will make decisions that can meet a variety of objectives.

Saying that you won't go to a happy hour with your work group doesn't mean you're not a team player. It just means you want to be with your family or with your friends away from work. Traveling on a Sunday night doesn't mean you don't love your family. It means you're trying to be rested for an important meeting on Monday.

2. The Manager's Lack of Vision

There's a fine line between creating a competitive work environment that brings out the best in people, and creating a hostile work environment that brings out their fangs. When managers play favorites, they bring out the worst in everyone. When managers pit employees against one another and one has to "lose" and another has to "win," he builds a culture in which employees focus more on how they're being seen than on the value they deliver to customers.

Here's a simple example. If in an automobile dealership the manager praises the sales force for moving new cars off the lot and blames the finance department for having to repossess cars due to customers missing their payments, she creates a silo mentality. From now on, the finance manager will protect himself by turning down car sales to prospects with even small finance problems, and the sales manager will keep making promises to customers he knows should never get financing. Shazam. The manager has magically destroyed any hope for teamwork.

Acceleration Case Study

I'll never forget the time I spoke to a company that had been created by merging two competitors. This was the first day they were operating under the new name, and the company was set up to have representatives from the two product lines call on the same customers. You read that right. Two salespeople from the same company would call on the same prospective client and try to sell him two competing products.

Each salesperson would leave behind a business card with the name of the new company and the name of the product line he or she was selling. The idea was to capture as much market share as possible.

At the meeting where I was the keynote speaker, the tables were divided by the competing product lines. So the employees from one former company filled half the tables, and the employees from the other former company were seated at the other half. The topic was, "How to Build World-Class Teamwork." I tried to keep a straight face as I had the audience members do an interactive exercise and they literally walked right by their new "teammates" and turned their backs on each other. I can only imagine what it was like for the customers.

3. The Bad Apples Require a Doctor Every Day

Imagine this scenario: the purpose of the group is very clear and most of the members of the group support one another toward fulfilling that purpose. However, a few members of the group insist on returning to their sophomore year in high school. They talk out loud during meetings, show up late to high priority and low priority appointments alike, and laugh when other people put ideas on the table. As long as the manager and the other members of the group allow this behavior to go unimpeded, the group has no hope of ever building effective teamwork.

Over the years, many executives have asked me whether or not a troublesome employee should be let go. Oftentimes, they ask if I will work with the employee as a coach to see if I can help the person turn his or her behavior around. I always say no to coaching people like that because I think it's a poor investment of their money and my time.

I encourage them to ask themselves several times why they should bother keeping the employee. I encourage them to make the difficult decision and let the employee go. Without exception, shortly after the manager has fired the employee, he or she said to me, "I wish I had done it much sooner." The worst employee is the one who can't do the job, doesn't want to do the job, and robs other people of huge amounts of time and energy. Let those people go so the others can move from surviving to thriving.

4. The Individual's Ego

Essentially I'm talking about the times when you are the problem. You're human, you can get tired and overstressed, and you can make sniping remarks about other people just as easily as can anyone else. Consequently, you need to be on guard against yourself.

Over the years and in a variety of organizations that I belonged to, I know I ruined the group's efforts when I let my ego get involved. I would raise my hand and push back on every point that was made.

Subconsciously I wanted the group to acknowledge my presence, but essentially I acted like a selfish child.

The underlying question you, and I, can always ask is, "Am I saying, asking, or doing this to help the group achieve its overall purpose, or am I saying, asking, or doing this to gain more attention to myself?" If it's the former, then your passion is really about the good of the team. If it's the latter, then your emotional responses are really about your ego.

5. Lack of a Crisis

For a few years I was a member of the St. Louis Regional Commerce and Growth Association's Leadership Circle. Each year a group of business, civic, and community leaders would travel to another city to study their best practices. One year we traveled to Denver, and everyone was very impressed with all of the great things that Denver had accomplished in the 1990s. Throughout the presentations, we consistently heard that the key to Denver's turnaround was the series of crises they faced as a community.

In the 1980s, Denver's economy had gone through a shock of epic proportions. It was heavily dependent on the energy business. When oil prices plummeted, Exxon shut down a major project, and almost immediately 28,000 energy-related jobs evaporated. Then more than a dozen industrial banks and three large savings and loan institutions left. The downtown became so empty that people joked about how many mountain views one could see through the empty buildings. It became so bad that at one time someone posted a billboard that said, "Will the last person out of Denver please turn out the lights?"

Near the end of the second day, I raised my hand and asked, "Do you have to have a crisis in order to turn things around?" The panelist from Denver said, "No, but it certainly helps." Instantly from the back of the room one of my fellow St. Louisans yelled out, "Well then let's hurry up and have a real crisis," to which everyone laughed.

Every group needs either a compelling purpose or a compelling crisis to pull the members of the group together. For some reason,

Acceleration Case Study

Here's one more story from my hometown. In the summer of 1993, St. Louis experienced its worst flood in over 100 years. Whole neighborhoods were washed away and many streets were deemed unusable due to the floodwaters.

Through it all, white collar workers, blue collar workers, rich people, poor people, and everyone in between stood shoulder-to-shoulder to support one another in fending off the natural disaster. The problem with teamwork-by-crisis is that eventually the crisis goes away, and then the old prejudices and silos reappear. It wasn't long after the flood had subsided that the old factions and issues reemerged.

I saw the same phenomenon from afar when Hurricane Katrina overwhelmed New Orleans and the entire Gulf Coast. Acts of heroism occurred every day for months, but then the efforts began to flag in the midst of political and personal aspirations.

people seem to be more motivated by a crisis than by an overarching purpose. After the attacks of September 11, 2001, Americans supported one another at an incredible level. Without a crisis, even the smallest and most unintentional snipes tear apart the fabric of the team. There are ways to get past this reliance on crises, and I'll explain those in the next chapter.

6. "Are We Winning or Losing?"

Motivational speeches have a short shelf life. No matter how inspiring the quarterly sales rally was, the group will lose a sense of cohesion if they don't know what kind of progress they're making. Without some sense of how they are performing, people will feel like they're driving through a tunnel with their eyes closed. They know they're moving, but they don't know if they're heading in the right direction, about to hit the wall, or about to collide head on with a truck. This lack of awareness can create fear and anxiety for top performers and poor performers alike.

7. No Truth or Consequences

When managers avoid establishing positive and negative consequences because they don't want to reward some people over others and want to avoid conflicts at all costs, they create a massive state of confusion. A stated purpose and objective loses its credibility if people can behave any way they want and achieve whatever they want with no consequences.

I once sat in a midyear performance review and all but one of the 42 employees in a region were awarded an above satisfactory rating. However, that region's operational performance was in the bottom 50 percent of all the regions in the country. As politely as I could, I asked how this could be possible.

The group of managers doing the ratings immediately became very defensive. They told me the only reason they rated the employees the way they did was because they weren't allowed to give them higher ratings. Huh? I was thinking they should give out lower ratings.

This lack of connection between individual evaluations and the group's performance caused many members to feel they were being unjustifiably held back in their careers. When they didn't get a promotion, they would point to their performance ratings and say they should be paid more and promoted more often. The inability to provide negative consequences to poor performance increased the lack of teamwork.

8. Removal of the Domineering Executive

Having a domineering executive at the top of a work group does have its upside. When the organizational chart becomes "the CEO and then everyone else," it's a lot easier to keep the decision making streamlined and efficient. The problem is that the "teamwork" is illusionary. Department heads aren't really working together. They are all simply walking in step with what the domineering executive wants. When that person resigns, gets fired, or dies, the department heads quickly realize they have no common cause and they don't really know how to support each other. The only thing they had in common before was to please their boss, but now that boss is gone. It can quickly become a culture of every department for itself.

9. No Collaboration, No Teamwork

And now it's time for the world's fastest teamwork test. Write down what you did to support other members of your organization toward achieving the organization's desired business outcomes. Notice I didn't say, "Write down what you did to achieve better results." Now write down what other people did to support you toward achieving the desired organizational outcomes. Take a look at your lists. If you have nothing written down, then you have no teamwork.

10. No Money, No Mission

In all the literature I've read on teamwork, I've never seen anything on the importance of maintaining cash flow in order to maintain teamwork. When paychecks don't go out, when there's no money to hold a meeting, and when your organization can't afford to provide any resources for recognizing strong performances, then the members of the group will start to wonder what kind of a mess they've gotten themselves into.

Teamwork is a business driver. When people support one another toward achieving a high priority business outcome, they will move the organization forward. Just as there is a human price to pay to build great teamwork in the forms of sacrifice and energy invested in listening and responding intelligently, there is also a financial price to pay in terms of giving employees time away from their day-to-day tasks and finding appropriate space for meetings and providing food for the attendees.

In this chapter I've explained how work groups can spiral downward into individual silos. In the next few chapters, I will explain how groups can reverse those negative trends and accomplish extraordinary results through teamwork and collaboration.

Acceleration Tips

✓ Don't ever assume that a group is a team. Without serious intention and significant work, it is far more likely that a group of individuals will splinter off into self-centered silos than into a synergistic approach toward achieving a common objective.

Chapter

7

STRENGTHEN TEAMWORK

"We Just Sit Wherever We Want."

One time I asked a flight attendant what it was like to work at Southwest Airlines. She said she loved it. I said, "C'mon, you love it? What do you love about it?" She said, "I used to work for another airline. When we would have meetings at that company, they would put the pilots in one area, the mechanics in another area, and the flight attendants in another area. At Southwest Airlines, we just sit wherever we want. We all know what the purpose is and so we just sit anywhere because we're all in it together."

Now that's a powerful testimony to the teamwork at Southwest Airlines. Amazingly, as I was writing this chapter, I was sitting in Houston's Hobby Airport. Herb Kelleher, the chairman of Southwest Airlines, went through the check-in area, slipped off his shoes like everyone else, and went through security. He had no fancy airs. It was the first time I ever saw him, but his actions backed up what I had heard a few years earlier from the flight attendant. At Southwest Airlines, everyone knows the purpose and so nobody needs to worry about who sits where at a meeting.

No manager is an island.

I've never worked with a manager who provided value to a customer all by himself. All the value that is created and delivered from an organization to a customer is created and delivered through groups of people. In running a business unit, it is critically important to remember that point. Even though we operate in a business environment in which some CEOs are ridiculously overpaid, the truth is that groups working throughout the organization generate the business results. True teamwork is a driver of improved business outcomes. Practical managers understand that and work toward making teamwork a reality.

Teamwork happens when individuals support one another toward achieving a meaningful purpose.

That was so easy to explain, and it's so difficult to make happen. In the last chapter, I explained ten forces that cause teamwork to fray apart into department silos and individual agendas. Before we go any further, please keep in mind that creating teamwork is real work and requires time. This is not like making popcorn in a microwave.

Okay, here goes. There are four types of groups as represented in Figure 7.1.

Quadrant I is the tragic zone. The members of the groups in Quadrant I have no common purpose, and no one supports each other. What a horrible way to spend a career. Clearly these people go to work for one reason: the paycheck. In many cases it's doubly sad because those individuals could seek out employment in a place where they would feel they are doing meaningful work and be supported by others. Often, they don't seek other groups because they think this is the way work is supposed to be.

Quadrant II is la-la land. The people in this group all talk about a meaningful purpose, but no one supports anyone else. In my opinion, this is what happened at many of the dot-com companies in the last part of the 20th century. Few people have ever exuded as much

FIGURE 7.1

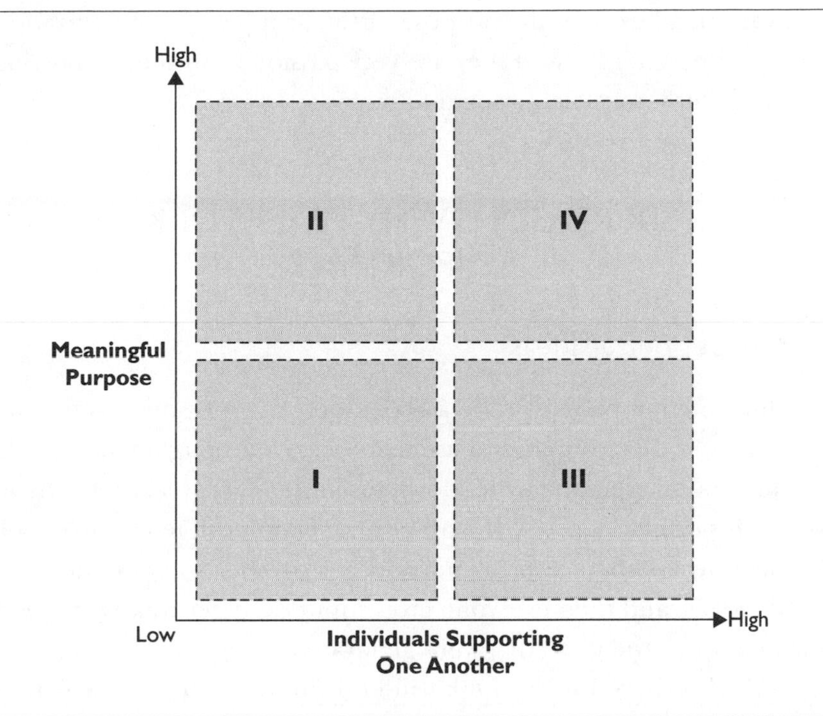

passion as the members of dot-com nation. Unfortunately, in many cases the focus wasn't so much on supporting one another as it was on selling their companies to the highest bidder and cashing out. When the stock prices fell, the imaginary teamwork collapsed as well.

Quadrant III is party central. People in the group support one another, but the group has no overarching purpose. As in, "Let's all go to a happy hour and talk about what a crazy organization we work for." That may be fun for a while, but eventually people realize there's not much depth to their conversations. I operated in this quadrant for more years than I care to recall. It finally dawned on me what a waste I was making of the time I was given.

Quadrant IV is where true teamwork happens. This is the place where people fall in love with their work, primarily because it doesn't feel like work. These instances might be rare, but they are the ones people look back on with the fondest memories. Members of these groups can all explain the purpose of the group or the organization in very simple terms, and they are very passionate about supporting one another toward achieving that purpose.

SIX REASONS WHY TEAMWORK IS IMPORTANT

1. You Get Better Ideas

Imagine ten people are in a room, only one person gets to state an idea, and the group has to use that idea. Now imagine ten people are in a room, everyone writes down his or her best idea, each person shares his or her idea with the other nine people, all ten people look for ways to combine two or more ideas together to generate even better ideas, and then everyone gives input on determining the best idea out of all the ideas that were generated.

Which group do you think will end up with a better idea? In a nutshell, this is the difference between a group with a dictator and a group that has teamwork.

2. You Attract and Retain More Talented Employees

If a talented and hard-working person wants to be part of an organization, then she is going to want to be part of a great organization. Great organizations attract great people. When you create a great group, you have individuals who support one another toward achieving better results, and they will attract more good people who can achieve even better results and the cycle goes on and on.

3. You Attract and Retain Better Customers

Notice the difference between a great team in Quadrant IV and the la-la land group in Quadrant II and the party group in Quadrant III. Great teams support their members in ways that add more value to customers and generate better long-term business results for the organization. In doing so, the customers they delight tell other potential customers, which causes the base of happy customers to grow and grow.

4. More Money Flows to the Bottom Line

I sometimes laugh aloud when I hear people say teamwork is the touchy-feely part of a business. Have they lost their minds? Great teams attract and retain great talent inside an organization, add more value to customers, attract and retain more good customers, and spend less time and money on having to hire and train people to replace those good employees who have left.

Do you notice how all these things contribute not only to an increase in top-line sales, but also to an increase in bottom-line profit? Great teamwork is a business driver, not fluffy stuff.

5. Teamwork Is the Golden Goose That Keeps on Giving

When creating effective teams becomes engrained in your organization's culture, you have something very special. When people throughout your organization are supporting one another toward fulfilling a clear purpose, you become far less reliant on having one superstar executive. Instead, the team emerges as the driving force behind generating sustainable, profitable growth.

6. Great Teams Give Birth to Great Leaders

I don't disagree very often with Jack Welch, but one thing he and I differ on is what constitutes a leader. He says that when a person gets promoted to the head of a group, she needs to realize that now she is the leader of the group. I disagree. I think people need to realize they can be leaders of a group from day one.

Leadership is the ability to influence how other people think. Great teams create an environment in which people listen to one another, regardless of whether that person is a ten-year veteran or a rookie. In this kind of culture, people can hone their ability to influence others without being shot down for opening their mouths. When there are lousy group dynamics, people reject other people's ideas all the time until no one ever attempts to challenge any one else's ideas. Lousy cultures do not develop great leaders.

THREE THEMES OF GREAT TEAMS

As I've watched practical managers strengthen their staffs into great teams, I've seen three major themes emerge consistently regardless of the industry.

Teamwork Theme #1: Keep the Spotlight on Desired Results

Clarify one meaningful purpose. The only way to avoid "teamwork by crisis" is to constantly communicate a clear and compelling purpose for your group. Sometimes it's obvious. The American Cancer Society has a pretty clear purpose: they save lives. Pleasant Rowland, the founder of the American Girl company, used to say, "We're in the little girl business." That's compelling. People get that.

If you're in charge of a group of department heads from eight different business functions, the purpose of the group may not be so clear. In that case, your first and most important job is to clarify why the group exists. One way to do that is to ask the group, "What's the purpose of our group?"

Give everyone the question a few days before the meeting, and then at the meeting give everyone a few minutes to write down their ideas. Then break the large group into small groups of five people, give them time to discuss their answers, and then hear responses from each small group. By giving everyone a chance to weigh in on the purpose of the group, you may very well increase the buy-in to the final statement of purpose.

Then have everyone stand, pair up with another person in the room, and practice explaining the purpose of the group in a conversational manner without a cheat sheet. Keep practicing until everyone in the group can explain the purpose of the group with the same meaning and in a down-to-earth way that other people who didn't attend the meeting can understand.

Once the group hones the purpose to something clear, compelling, and conversational, then your responsibility as the manager is to make sure that purpose is communicated clearly and consistently from that point forward.

Remember that teamwork happens when a group of individuals support one another toward achieving a meaningful purpose. Without a clear and meaningful purpose that stays at the forefront of activities and decisions, you won't create a true team.

Maintain urgency in the absence of emergency. When your organization or business unit is getting great business results, you are in danger of destroying teamwork. As the good times roll in, people can very easily lose focus on the purpose of the group. However, the long-term successful managers don't let this happen. They make the purpose real and tangible all the time and create a sense of urgency when there is no real emergency.

One company I studied was fanatical about their purpose of customer service, and they maintained an extraordinary sense of urgency around creating and maintaining a call center that could answer each of the over 50,000 incoming calls a week in less than one second. They achieved a 95 percent success rate at answering their phones on less than one ring and were constantly working to achieve an even higher percentage. Customers were not complaining that their service was slow, but they still maintained a high level of urgency.

Anticipate the next adventure. During the past ten years, I've worked with clients at AT&T, Toyota, Coca-Cola, McDonald's, Marriott,

St. Louis Cardinals, and GSD&M. What do the people at these extraordinary companies have in common? I think one thing is they eagerly anticipate the next adventure. All companies have goals, strategies, and tactics. These people go after adventures. I encourage you to read *The Toyota Way* by Jeffrey Liker; *Grinding It Out* by Ray Kroc, the founder of the McDonald's Corporation; and *The Spirit to Serve* by Bill Marriott Jr. All these books explain in depth different stages in each company's history, and they explain some of the many adventures those companies have gone after.

Whether these companies are coming out with a new car, a new sandwich, a new type of hotel, a new way to attract fans, or a new way to create an effective advertising campaign, the people inside the companies talk and act like pioneers heading off to discover a new country. Their passion and common focus are exhilarating to be around. I find myself caught up in their enthusiasm to achieve the unimaginable and deliver what no one has done before.

Build in championship objectives regularly. I think there's a reason why the NCAA Division I men's and women's basketball tournaments are among the most exciting athletic events in the country. Their seasons start around Thanksgiving, build momentum in January and February, and climax with March Madness and the road to the Final Four. If those seasons were 12 months long and they just ran from one to another, I think people would lose interest. When the tournaments are over, the sports fans are ready to move on to another sport and another championship.

I feel the same way about year-long business objectives. They may be too long to hold the interest, passion, and commitment of your team members. I encourage you to establish clear and challenging objectives that last for six months. That's enough time to achieve something without getting caught up in the quarterly mindset, but not so much time that people lose sight of what they're going after.

People want to experience the thrill of victory and the agony of defeat. It puts juice in their days. As a manager, establish clear objectives and clear rewards for achieving specific objectives, bring them up frequently to the group, and encourage people to support one another toward achieving those objectives.

Then after six months, get the group focused on a different set of objectives or focused on the same type of objectives but start the clock over again. That way each year can have different seasons and different championships to go after. Having these objectives in front of the group can help the members pull together rather than be drawn apart by the reasons I described in the last chapter.

Keep the good of the organization at the forefront of decision making. The manager's position is a tad tricky. You need to create an environment in which people support one another toward achieving a meaningful purpose, but you also need to make some very difficult and unpopular decisions when it comes to strategy, tactics, hiring people, and, particularly, firing people.

I believe the overarching screen for all management decisions should be "What is the best decision for the good of the organization?" If the best thing to do to generate better sustainable results is to move into a new area of technology that is going to affect a number of people's careers, then you need to do it.

Over the short term it will hurt teamwork, but over the long term people will know that doing what is best for the organization is overriding a manager's likes or dislikes of the various members of the team. Jack Welch took a lot of criticism for buying up companies, increasing efficiencies, and letting go of employees in the 1980s and 1990s at GE. His successor, Jeff Immelt, took a lot of criticism for not buying up as many companies and instead focusing on organic growth. The key here is they both did what they thought was the best thing for the organization.

Many times professional football and baseball teams will overhaul the lineups of moderately successful teams in order to do what is best for the team itself. In this way, the good of the team ranks higher than the good of any individual member.

Acceleration Case Study: Teamwork Hollywood Style

As the television show *Friends* reached the end of its ten-year run, the six stars on the show were constantly interviewed. One of my favorite comments came from David Schwimmer, who played the character Ross. He said the key to the show's success was the ensemble approach, which he described as the way in which the actors worked together to make sure that each of the different characters created hilarious scenes on different shows.

Teamwork Theme # 2: Relationships Provide the Fuel That Drives Results

Use the ensemble approach. The practical manager sells his employees on the value of the Ensemble Approach. The Ensemble Approach says that the best ideas always come from the group, no one person always has the best ideas in any group, and no one knows who is going to have the insightful idea or which combination of ideas will ultimately be used.

Just like the members of a great jazz band playing a piece of music, the members of a true business team are all willing to step up or step back depending on the flow of the conversation. When this happens, ideas can develop, gain momentum and buy-in from the group, and move toward effective implementation.

How can you create that environment? The four keys to creating a successful Ensemble Approach are:

1. Use open-ended questions
2. Draw input from a wide variety of people
3. Steadily guide the group toward a desired end state
4. Frequently recognize and reward people for contributing, listening, and collaborating

Learn from the past. Have the members of your group recall a situation in their lives when they were members of a true team. Then have them answer these questions:

- What was the group?
- What was the purpose of the group?
- How did people in the group support one another?
- How did that experience affect me?
- What lessons did I learn from that experience?
- How could I apply those lessons to our current group?

Then have them recall a group they were a part of that fell apart due to lack of teamwork and answer the exact same set of questions. You can help your staff members learn from their past group experiences and apply those lessons to improve the current group, but only if you take the time to help them clarify what they learned.

Members seek to add more value. Have the members of your group pair up with another member and ask, "What am I doing that's adding value to you, and what can I do to add more value to you?" Be sure that each person in the pair gets the opportunity to ask the other person this question. Asking this question doesn't mean that the person has to do everything he or she is told. It just increases awareness around what is of value to the other person and what would be of more value.

The best bosses I've observed regularly ask their employees these two questions. They are simple, but very powerful because they create opportunities to strengthen relationships, clarify what really matters to the other person, and identify ways to move the business forward.

Teamwork Theme #3: Each Member Has Responsibilities and Deserves Consequences for His or Her Actions

Use a team impact reality check. Continually examine how you impact the teamwork in your office, and have the members of your staff do the same thing, by asking everyone to answer these two questions: "What am I doing that strengthens the teamwork within our group" and "What am I doing that hurts the teamwork within my group?"

Those two questions cause a great deal of personal reflection, and can lead you to some powerful insights into your own behavior. They help you see what you need to keep doing and what you need to stop doing. I encourage you to answer those two questions a minimum of every six months, and have the members of your group do the same thing.

Keep things in perspective. One of my favorite quotes is from Lou Holtz, the former college football coach, who said, "Things are never quite as good as they seem, nor as bad as they seem, but somewhere in between reality lies."

It's very easy to lose perspective and see your issues as vastly more important than anyone else's issues. This is what creates individual and department silos. Suddenly the marketing people think the operations people have hurt the desired outcomes, and the operations people think the marketing people act as if they're from another planet. Boom. Walls go up and teamwork goes away.

I encourage you to ask yourself this question: "What, if anything, do I need to keep in perspective right now?" Take the time to answer this question. By understanding how your perspective can enhance or destroy teamwork, you can make the necessary adjustments to resolve your individual concerns while still focusing on how to support the other members of your team. Again, this requires stepping off the train of constant activity and taking the time to reflect. It also means carving out time for all the members of your group to answer the same question.

Release toxic habits. Just as chemical toxins ruin the environment, individual toxic habits are the words or actions that ruin teamwork. You can release these toxic habits by following three steps. You can help the members of your staff release their toxic habits by walking them through each of these steps.

Step one: increase awareness. By raising your level of self-awareness, you begin the process of releasing your toxic habits. When you do something often enough, you turn it into a comfort zone. You begin to break the negative, toxic comfort zones by becoming aware of them. You won't be able to go comfortably back to your old behaviors with this new level of self-awareness. To gain this awareness, ask yourself, "What do I do or say that ruins teamwork?"

Step two: accept that this habit is yours. You can further release a toxic habit by accepting it as part of who you are. If you deny having the habit, it will continue to control you. If you gossip about other people, you can begin to let go of that negative habit by accepting that you actually do it. Until you accept that you do it, you can't let go of that particular toxic habit.

Step three: take action to remove the toxic habit. There are varieties of actions you can do to release your toxic habits. Here are some of them.

- Experience and express your negative emotions. Take out a sheet of paper and write a letter to the person who is bothering you. Get all of your negative emotions onto the sheet of paper. Then you can burn the paper, rewrite it without the negative energy and send it to the person, or keep the letter and reread it from time to time. But get that toxic stuff out of your system. It's not healthy to carry it around.
- Mentally detach yourself from the end result. It does no good to use up your time and energy worrying about achieving a desired business outcome. Pour your efforts into the process of achieving the desired results and into the process of being an effective manager. The results will take care of themselves.
- Forgive yourself for the mistakes you have made and other people for the mistakes they have made. For a group of people to truly support one another toward achieving a meaningful purpose, they have to be willing to forgive each other and

themselves for the mistakes they've made. If you don't forgive yourself and other people, then you carry all that baggage around for years and years. And that baggage gets in the way of improving relationships and results.

- Reduce the complexities of your life. Complexity creates stress and frustration. That stress and frustration can easily cause you to focus more on your personal issues than on the success of the business team. It can cause you to stop listening and shut down. Wham. There goes the Ensemble Approach. Eliminating some of the complexity in your personal life can help you bring a better energy to work. Maybe it means you won't be on 15 boards simultaneously or maybe you won't be able to volunteer for four different fundraising efforts this year. Be reasonable so that you can bring your best energy at work and at home.
- Replace a toxic habit with a more life-enhancing habit. No matter what toxic habit you want to release, the key is that you consciously replace it with a more life-enhancing habit. If you want to stop gossiping, then perhaps you can fill up your time writing handwritten notes to people throughout your organization and congratulating them on their efforts on a variety of projects. If you don't replace the toxic habit, eventually it will return to fill the void that has been left empty.

Build trust. Trust is never built in a workshop or a retreat. There are three requirements to building trust and they must be delivered over an extended period. These steps can be useful for you and the members of your team to experience together.

1. Work to understand the other person. What do they want to achieve? What do they need to achieve? What is important to them? What could you do to add even more value to them?
2. Clarify what they can expect from you. Consider what you've learned about the other person in terms of what they want and need, and decide what you will do and what you will not do

and the rationale behind your decision. Communicate to the other person what you will and will not do and why it will be that way. Be clear as to what he or she can expect from you.

3. Deliver at a minimum what is expected of you. Do what you said you would do. Before adding any new ideas to your plate, follow through on what you said you would do. If anything causes you to be unable to do what you said you would do, communicate immediately with the other person and let him or her know what expectations you are not going to meet.

These three simple steps can be applied over and over with people in your group, with your suppliers, and with your customers. When those three steps are repeated, the other person will trust you more. When you fail to deliver step three, trust begins to break down.

With trust, people will consider your input. Without trust, people will ignore your input and work toward making you unsuccessful. This dynamic is described in Figure 7.2. When people trust you, they will accept your constructive criticisms as you attempt to help them be more successful. When they don't trust you, they will be personally offended by your nerve in telling them what to do. Teamwork, the ability to support one another toward fulfilling a meaningful purpose, is completely dependent on the members of the group trusting one another.

The next obvious question is "What can I do if I've broken my trust with other people?" That requires five steps. First, be patient and know that it's going to take a long time. Second, apologize and

FIGURE 7.2

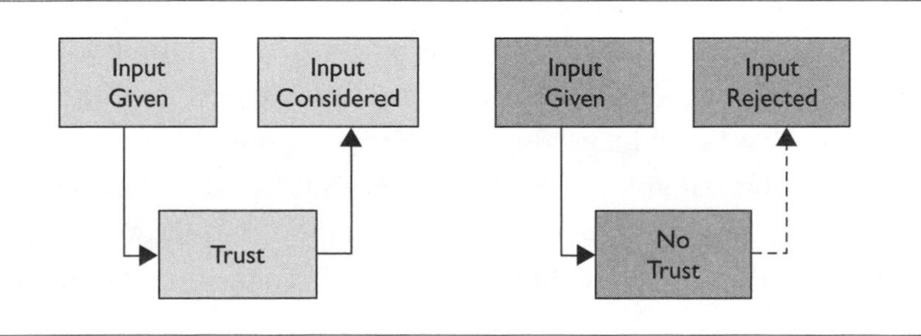

ask for forgiveness. I know that sounds like it belongs in a different book, but apologizing and asking for forgiveness is a big part of building effective business relationships. Then repeat the three steps for building trust I previously outlined: listen for understanding, clarify what you can and cannot do, and do what you said you would do.

Recognize and reward the supporters. Members of great teams support one another. However, far too often recognition and rewards only go to the individual who achieved extraordinary results. If an employee offered an idea that played a critically important role for the high achiever, then that person should be recognized as well. If an employee is only out for himself, then it's important that you provide some form of a negative consequence.

The organizations with the best teamwork make sure that everyone who played a role is rewarded. I knew of one company that as it grew from $100 million to $1 billion in annual sales gave every employee the same bonus in direct correlation to that year's annual sales.

Make sure individuals experience success as well. No group ever becomes a great team if the individual members suffer while they are a part of that group. On great teams, the individuals feel they are significant, they are doing purposeful work, they are being heard, they have important responsibilities, and their careers will be better off because of being a member of that group.

Recently I attended a department head meeting with more than 30 people in the room. One person stood up and shared with the others that at her latest performance review her boss told her what she did well and what she didn't do well that year. Then she told the group, "At that point, he looked at me and said, 'Now I think you have a responsibility to tell me what I did well this year, what I didn't do well, and what I could have done better. So tell me what you think.'"

She said it was an extraordinary growth experience because she felt her thoughts were significant, her responsibilities were meaningful, and that her contribution mattered. That's how you build a great team.

ACCELERATION ADVICE

From an Interview with Ashley Andy, Director of New Business Development, GSD&M (National Advertising Agency)

In 2005 and 2006, I served as an executive coach for Ashley Andy. During that time, Ashley was responsible for guiding the five-month, three-phase pitch process for the $100 million BMW account. GSD&M won the BMW account. It was one of the best examples of business teamwork I've ever seen. Here's her story:

Coughlin: *How many people both from within GSD&M and partner groups that you brought in were involved in the five-month, three-phase BMW pitch?*

Andy: Two hundred people within GSD&M touched the BMW pitch at some point. In addition, we had eight outside marketing partners/experts brought in to add value and different perspectives as we tackled the challenge of reinvigorating the BMW brand.

Coughlin: *What made the group effective as a team?*

Andy: To take on such a challenge of capturing the business, it was critical for the team to embody an unrelenting passion and a desire for the BMW business. When you have a committed and passionate team focused on one goal, the results can be phenomenal. We had a clear sense of what the real challenge was for BMW, and the team worked from the same page attacking the same issue. Our core new business team provided leadership and direction by facilitating and guiding the unruly and chaotic nature of the process.

Other key success factors were the group's ability to take risks, collaborate together, swing for the fences to try new ideas, and push beyond our functional roles and overlap with one another to build comprehensive and innovative solutions. Essentially, we landed on the idea that "BMW is a company of ideas. This concept emphasizes BMW's independence and innovation." Sounds simple, but it was a tough place to get to. Making something complex simple is the ultimate challenge.

Coughlin: *What were some of the obstacles the team faced and how did it overcome them?*

Andy: The key obstacle with that many people involved was keeping the level of communication consistent and clear so that no one individual or group within GSD&M would spiral off on its own and head down a different direction. Time was of the essence and every step we took needed to be consistent and purposeful in meeting the challenge of solving BMW's desired objectives.

Another obstacle was not succumbing to the pressure. We had pitched several car accounts over the past couple of years and had declined other opportunities in anticipation of the jewel of all car accounts. When BMW came knocking at our door, we knew this was the chance of a lifetime to add one of the most prestigious car accounts to our client roster. The stakes were really high and we had to rise to the occasion.

We overcame the pressure by trusting our gut and staying focused on what we were trying to achieve, which was to solve the issue of making the BMW appealing to a broader market.

As far as communications goes, the goal was to overcome miscommunications. We installed a weekly update meeting, and created an online destination (microsite) to capture everyone's ideas and provide continuity in thinking and direction.

Coughlin: *How was such a large group able to stay focused and motivated over such a long period of time?*

Andy: In addition to some of the things I mentioned earlier, every once in a while, it was important to introduce some fun. We had all the BMW cars from the dealership at GSD&M so people could drive and truly experience the Ultimate Driving Machine™.

We also gave people the ownership to do what they really do well, and then brought their thinking to light and plussed it. Ultimately, that's my job. Utilizing everyone's expertise and ideas and packaging it in an innovative way for the prospective client. When people started to see their ideas come to life, it reenergized everyone and motivated us to push harder. It also helps to have a team that thrives on the thrill of competition and winning.

Of course, feeding our people always is a good idea. With all the hours invested in working on this pitch, we had to keep them happy and full. We had ice cream trucks stop by and brought in catered food and occasionally hosted Friday happy hours to blow off some steam.

Coughlin: *How were you able to customize your approach and your pitch to BMW?*

Andy: We started from a place of strength. We identified what BMW stands for and what we stand for, and then we looked for places where we were aligned. As I initially studied BMW, I thought, "Wow, there is a lot of similarity between their beliefs, culture, and language, and GSD&M's beliefs, core values, and experience with tackling their issues."

We knew the only way we could win was to stay true to ourselves. There was a lot of overlap in our corporate cultures. For example, we knew there was a real belief at both BMW and GSD&M to let the best ideas win.

It was critical to have interaction with the clients prior to showing up for the final presentation. We treated these as mini-pitches. You'd be surprised how you can win or lose before you ever get to that final presentation. We had touch points with BMW early on to hear what they liked and didn't like, what sparked and what didn't, and how we could take that learning back to our teams and redirect it appropriately. It showed the clients we listened to them and this provided an indication of what it'd be like to work with us in the future.

Hint: Clients love to be listened to. We collaborated early on with them instead of working in a vacuum. This created a sense of ownership on the client side before we came in with our final recommendation. When we did, they could see their affect on the end product.

Coughlin: *How do you build breakthrough relationships with a prospective client?*

Andy: You have to live and breathe the product. We drove their cars, we went to their performance center, we talked to dealers, and we canvassed every opportunity we could to develop a comprehensive, in-depth understanding of the company, the clients, and the products. It's the only way to build the right solution. And clients love it when you love who they are and their products.

Acceleration Tips

- ✓ Your most important job as a manager is to create a culture in which people understand the overall purpose of their group and support one another toward fulfilling that purpose. This is more important than incorporating the newest technology or finding the hot new product for the marketplace or starting up a pet project that you're dying to dig into. Focus your time and energy on continually clarifying the compelling purpose for why the group exists and rewarding people for supporting each other toward the fulfillment of that purpose.
- ✓ Be certain to focus on how your behaviors positively and negatively affect teamwork.
- ✓ And finally, keep in mind that teamwork is completely dependent on building trust with your team members and between your team members. That doesn't happen at a two-day retreat.

Chapter

8

EMBRACE COLLABORATION

"What Do You Mean It's Not Enough to Be Right?"

Colleen sought me out.

She had discovered a new technology that she felt would definitely make her company more successful. Colleen was an expert on this new value-added technology, and she knew it.

When we sat down, she said, "They just don't get it. My boss told me many times to find technology that would make our company more successful. I worked a long time to find this new piece of technology. Our company could earn a ton more money from current and new customers if they would just listen to me. I've written explanation after explanation on what they need to do to implement the new technology, and they won't listen. I know that I know what I'm talking about, they know I know what I'm talking about, and they still won't listen to me. What am I supposed to do?"

I said, "There's a lot you need to do. You haven't done enough yet."

She exploded by saying, "What do you mean it's not enough to be right?"

I looked at her and said, "If you continue to do what you've been doing, you have zero percent chance of success. You've said 'I' and 'they' in every sentence. My guess is nobody likes you, nobody trusts you, and absolutely nobody wants to see you succeed."

She stared at me and then she wiped her eyes. She put her head down for a long time, and then she looked up. She looked me right in the eye and said, "I made a mistake. I wanted so badly to help the organization succeed and prove that I deserve to be promoted that I made a huge mistake. I trampled over anybody who stood in my way. I wanted to shove this new technology down everybody's throats to show how much I knew. And now nobody wants to be around me. What should I do?"

This was one of the many examples in my work with executives when rugged individualism got in the way of a person's career. Colleen seemed to think that if she knew enough, she could make other people do whatever she wanted.

I looked Colleen straight in the eye, and I said, "Go in there and apologize. Tell people you wanted to add value so badly that you tried too hard. Let them know how sorry you are and that the situation was your fault, not theirs. And then be patient. You're not going to gain their trust for a long time. Don't push your agenda. Go to your boss and explain that this new technology is going to have to be put on the back burner until you provide support to other people, gain their trust, and are able to move forward as a true team member."

Colleen listened carefully, and then she walked back into the building. It took several months for people to set aside her rude behavior of the past and trust her. Then together they implemented the new technology and it did generate a ton of revenue and a lot of value for customers. Colleen simply did one thing differently. Instead of telling people how right she was, she worked to support other people so they would all end up being right.

COLLABORATE TO ACCELERATE

Competition happens when two people try to beat each other. Competition is fun. One month you're winning, and the next month the other person is winning. Competition brings out the best in both of you.

In terms of moving the business forward, one step above competition is cooperation. Cooperation happens when two people look at all the work that needs to be done, agree on what each person will do, and then each of them goes and does his or her part. By dividing the workload, they get more done than they did when they were competing.

The highest form of acceleration is collaboration. Collaboration happens when each person offers his or her ideas on how to achieve the desired outcome, they both listen to each other, and then they work together to combine ideas to come up with even better ideas.

Is it time consuming to collaborate? Yes, it takes a lot of time. Is it hard work to collaborate? Yes, it is very hard work. Is it painful to the ego to collaborate? Yes, it's very painful to the ego to come up with the very best ideas you can, put them on the table, and have someone else look at them and immediately come up with an improvement. Will you achieve better sustainable business results through collaboration? Yes, and that's why it's so important to collaborate with other people.

If you want to be a successful manager over the long term, you have to develop your capacity to collaborate effectively with other people. Business dynamics are so complicated today that no one person delivers all the value to any customer. So-called self-made men are really the net result of huge collaborative efforts. Even if you're the CEO, and probably even more so if you're the CEO, you need to be able to collaborate with other people.

SIX WAYS TO CREATE COLLABORATION

1. Ask for the Other Person's Priorities

Don't start the conversation off with how smart and successful you are. Enter the conversation with a question like, "What business outcomes for the organization are you hoping to improve with this project?" Discuss these outcomes until you both agree on the objectives that you're both trying to improve together.

Then work to add value to the other person to help him or her succeed. This is a dramatic shift from focusing on your priority outcomes to focusing on the other person's priorities. Now you're working to be the guide on the side rather than the sage on the stage.

2. Listen to Their Ideas First

As the conversation moves toward ways to improve the desired results, listen to the other person's ideas first. If he insists that you go first, offer a couple of ideas and then say, "Now I'm really interested in hearing your ideas. What do you think we can do to achieve the desired outcomes?" It doesn't matter what your title is or what the other person's title is. You can still ask for his ideas before you jump in with yours.

3. Use "And" Instead of "But"

When the other person has finished offering some ideas, say, "And another thing we might want to consider is _______." Don't say, "But the reason we can't do that is ______." Collaboration is about building on ideas, not aborting them. You can always discuss later what the final actions will be, but for now just focus on springing off the other person's ideas.

4. Offer Suggestions, Not Solutions

Regardless of the brilliance of your ideas or how "right" you are, avoid telling the other person that you have the solution. Instead, offer suggestions. Say, "Here's a suggestion we might want to consider as we move this project forward . . . What do you think about that idea?" This allows the other person to build off of what you just said rather than putting them on the offensive to attack your idea.

5. Don't Just Talk the Talk, Support with Your Actions

Collaboration doesn't end with the brainstorming sessions. As the execution phase evolves, continue to maintain the conversation so that you build on each other's ideas and efforts. Executing a plan requires a lot of hard work and long hours. Rather than getting stressed and pointing your finger at the other person for all of his mistakes, keep exchanging perspectives and potential approaches to each step along the way.

6. Keep Exchanging Ideas Even When the Project Is Over

Jack Welch used to say his main job was creating a boundaryless organization so ideas moved throughout GE regardless of departments or business units. Collaboration is a business driver. Yes, it's an intangible activity. You can't measure the exact impact of collaboration on the bottom line, but the impact on the quality of ideas, execution, relationships, employee retention, and customer retention will most definitely impact your organization's most important business outcomes.

Acceleration Tips

✓ Great managers are great collaborators. They know nothing occurs just through the efforts of their individual groups. Effective marketing managers work to exchange ideas with operations managers and human resource managers and business research managers and sales managers. They understand they don't deliver any value to customers by themselves. The same is true about effective managers in every part of the business. And the best corporate presidents are those people who work to learn from others and create an environment in which ideas piggyback on top of other ideas. Collaborate to accelerate.

Chapter

9

EXPEDITE EXECUTION

"We Could Get More Done If We Had More Time."

John was putting in extraordinarily long hours. He was driven to get as much accomplished as was humanly possible. Yet he felt frustrated a great deal of the time. He never seemed to get as much done as he wanted to, no matter how many hours he worked. One day he looked at me and said, "We could get more done if we had more time." I thought about that for a moment, and then I said, "I think you could get more done if you put less time into your work."

That comment didn't sit well with John. It was counterintuitive for him, and he let me know he didn't appreciate my sarcastic comment. I moved to defend my position by saying, "John, if you had 20 fewer hours a week for work, what would you do?"

He thought about that question for several minutes and then said, "I would just pick out a couple of things to concentrate on and try to do them well."

"Bingo," I said. "That's the ticket to getting more done. Just concentrate on moving the needle forward on a few items at a time. You're working on so many projects simultaneously that you're wearing yourself out, and you're not making the kind of impact you want on anything. Think about a professional basketball player in the NBA. He gets 48 minutes to accomplish something. That's it. If he had more time, eventually he would wear out. Having more time doesn't make a person more productive. Making a more concentrated effort does increase productivity."

John didn't buy in to my idea totally, but he did start to go home at a reasonable hour and he stopped working so much on the weekends. As he worked less, he actually accomplished more.

When it comes to management, know that there are two things you can't manage: time and people.

You still have 24 hours a day, 7 days a week no matter how much you would like to reconfigure that, and every person in your business unit can still do what you don't want them to do. Okay, now that we have that cleared up, let's move on to what you can manage: execution.

HOW TO MANAGE EXECUTION

In Chapters 12 and 13, I'm going to provide thoughts on how to establish for your organization or business unit the strategy, tactics, and planned activities that constitute your business plan. Those are organizational issues either for your entire organization or for your part of the organization.

For now, I want to focus on how you can guide your group toward converting those organizational decisions into well-executed activities that generate better sustainable business results. Specifically, I'm going to focus on two areas: before planned activities occur and after planned activities start to occur. It doesn't matter whether your planned activities include the launching of a new product, the opening of a new retail space, or the implementation of a new software program. These steps will still apply in all those situations.

These 11 steps were developed over two years as I was working with the top executive team of a billion-dollar business unit. While much of our approach consisted of trial and error in finding out what did and did not work, we also found value from Ram Charan and Larry Bossidy's book, *Execution,* which is powerful.

BEFORE THE PLANNED ACTIVITIES HAPPEN

1. Clarify Expected Behaviors and Results

Before you ask any employee to take action, clarify what you expect from him in terms of his behaviors and the results he should produce. In terms of expected behaviors, I'm really talking about clarifying the desired values for your organization or business unit. Values are beliefs that determine behaviors. Values are the underlying beliefs that ignite behaviors in any situation.

If a person truly values honesty, then she will be honest in any situation. If she values teamwork, she will always look to support other people toward achieving the common purpose. This is why great organizations like the Walt Disney Company send their employees to extensive orientation programs before they ever interact with customers. Without really clarifying the expected behaviors and results, you won't be able to hold people accountable effectively.

Providing a positive or negative consequence for an action or a result will only confuse your employees if they don't realize that's what you did or didn't want all along. What I'm really talking about here is building a culture, a set of consistently displayed behaviors in your organization. Posting mission statements and core values on the wall does not constitute a culture. It is consistently displayed behaviors—not slogans—that create a culture. By continually talking about expected behaviors and results and holding people accountable for those behaviors and results, you will instill the desired culture in everyone in the business unit.

2. Sequence the Planned Activities

It's not enough to know the list of activities that need to be accomplished over the course of the next 12 months. The activities need to be sequenced in the proper order to optimize the impact on results.

If you manage multiple departments, then it's best for each department head to bring in a list of all the activities they are planning to implement. I suggest they write down each activity onto a single index card. Then everyone can see all the potential activities from all of the departments at the same time, and you can easily move the index cards around until the activities are sequenced in the most logical order.

Here's a very simple example. If the marketing department is going to promote a big spring sale and the operations department is looking to revitalize the look of the retail stores, then it is better for the operations department to do their activity before the marketing department.

While that's a simple and obvious example, the same thought process can go into sequencing all the activities in the business unit. The question to be answered is "What is the best sequence for all the activities in terms of accelerating the achievement of our highest priority business outcomes?"

3. Sacrifice Some Planned Activities

Even during the most disciplined planning sessions, managers still tend to pile on too many tactics and planned activities. Just because the planned activities are on your business plan doesn't mean you have to execute every one of them. Be willing to sacrifice some planned activities in order to improve the execution of the most important activities.

Many times during the planning stage, my clients think their employees are superhero action figures and can do way, way more than people in any other organization could ever do. I remind them their employees are not superheroes, but real people with real lives to live. It is far better to do less and achieve more than to do more and achieve less.

4. Establish a Critical Path for Each Planned Activity

The critical path consists of the answers to the *who, what, when, where,* and *how* questions. Say you want to provide training courses on customer service. The critical path will answer the questions: Who will put on the training courses and who will take them? Who will train the trainers? What information will be covered? When will that training take place? When will the courses be taught? Where will the courses be taught? How will the information be gathered and assembled for the course to be taught? Why will this approach fit within the tactic of implementing training courses across the business on the fundamentals of great customer service?

Your answers to these questions constitute your group's to-do list, the roles and responsibilities for each piece of the planned activities, and the validation that you are doing things that fit within your strategy and one of your tactics.

5. Schedule the Activities and Stick to the Schedule

At the end of a strategic planning process, you will have a set of planned activities that need to be executed over the course of the next year. Focus on these planned activities in six-month increments. At the end of six months, you may decide to alter some of your planned activities for the remainder of the year. Now that you have sequenced the activities for optimal impact and you have sacrificed some of those activities, you are in a position to put those activities on the calendar.

Write down the actual dates when each step in every activity will be executed. Don't estimate and say it will happen in the May-June timeframe. Put every piece of every activity on a specific date on the calendar. If you need a train-the-trainer session before the actual training course on customer service takes place for your employees, then put a date on the calendar for this session along with the names of who will be affected by that event.

By putting everything on the calendar, you will now see very clearly when scheduling conflicts will occur. You can then make adjustments to avoid those conflicts. This is crucially important for achieving success.

Another crucial factor is to have the self-discipline not to change the calendar once it's set. It's been my experience that way, way, way too many managers are their own worst enemies when it comes to disrupting effective execution. They change the calendar for an "emergency meeting," which affects 30 other people's calendars and throws the timing of the critical path off dramatically. After you put the calendar together, have the discipline not to mess it up.

AFTER THE PLANNED ACTIVITIES HAPPEN

6. Follow Up with Your Team Members, Evaluate Their Performance, and Provide Guidance and Feedback

Keep in mind everything that has already been done up to this point. The strategic planning work is finished. It's been decided what the approach will be to the marketplace, the tactics have been selected, and all the activities supporting each tactic have been selected, sequenced, and scheduled. It is clear who is responsible for doing each task.

At this point, your job as the manager is to stay out of the way, let the people on your team do their job, and then follow up with them. In this follow-up phase, check up on their progress and give candid feedback both on their behaviors and their results so far. In addition, provide guidance by asking open-ended questions, offering suggestions, giving additional insights, and discussing any issues or opportunities they are facing.

Do not micromanage. Micromanagement happens when you either tell your employees exactly what to do or you step in and do it yourself. When you micromanage, you hurt your company in two ways. First, your employees never learn to think for themselves, which keeps you from ever developing a prepared workforce, and you dramatically decrease productivity by spending your time doing activities rather than managing the overall process of execution.

7. Give Top Performers Rewards and Greater Responsibilities

When a person has executed her work at a very high level, then give her both public and private recognition. Raise her up as an exemplar in the organization, and let her know on a one-to-one basis what a terrific job she has done. Reward her both in terms of recognition and financially. And give her even more important responsibilities to take on.

However, do not burn out your best employees. You can shift the person's specific responsibilities so she is doing more important work, but avoid the temptation to keep overfilling her plate.

8. Work to Improve the Average Performers

Business acceleration occurs as you work with your average performers to improve their capacity to execute effectively. As you can see in Figure 9.1, a person's capacity to perform well is based on whether he can do the job and whether he will do the job.

Your best performers are in Quadrant IV. These people can do the job and will do the job. Consequently, give them more important responsibilities that will help the organization achieve sustainable, profitable growth.

Your average performers are in Quadrants II and III. Either they can do the job but don't want to do it, or they want to do the job but can't do it. In the former case, they need to find a reason to do the work, and in the latter case, they need more training in order to increase their chances for success.

If it's a case of the person needing to understand the purpose of the work so that he will want to do it, then you as the manager need to explain why the work is so tremendously important. If it's a case of the person needing to understand better how to do it, then you as the manager can either provide more explanation on how to do the job or you can send the person to further training. Of course, you have to determine whether you think the investment in additional training is worth it for this individual.

FIGURE 9.1

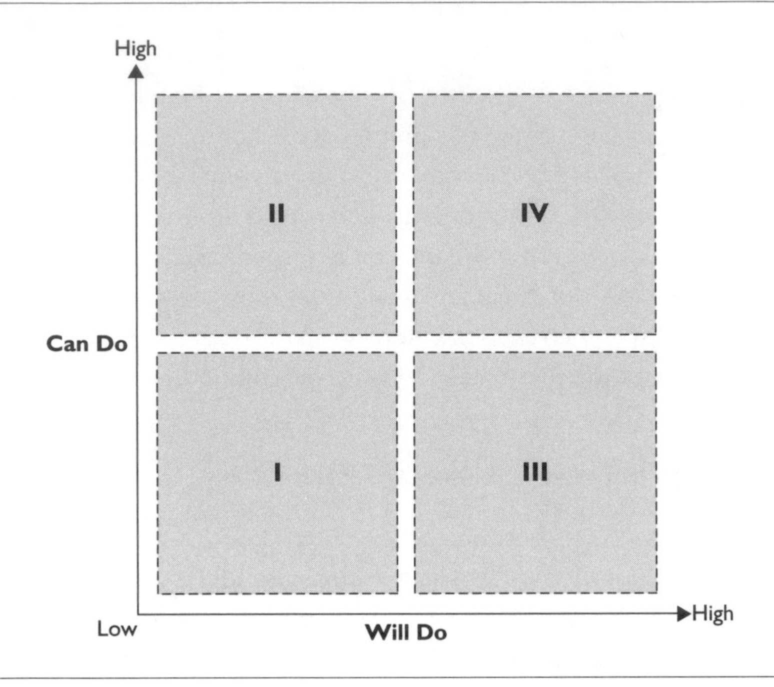

Basically, in working with an average performer, you are either trying to answer a "why" question (Why is this work so tremendously important for the organization and the customers?), or you are trying to answer a "how" question (How should this work be done most effectively and efficiently?). With average performers, you need to provide both positive and negative consequences in order to hold them accountable. They need to be rewarded for their efforts or performance, but they also need some negative consequences in order to realize they have room to grow and improve.

9. Remove Poor Performers

Your poor performers are in Quadrant I. Poor performers are people who can't do the job and don't want to do the job. They've gotta go. Many, many times managers have complained to me about specific employees and have questioned whether they should keep the employee. My first suggestion every time is to let the person go.

That sounds very cold, but I really want to push them to identify why the person should be given another chance. Occasionally the truth will come out that the person needs more training because his desire to succeed and willingness to work are in place. In those situations, I recommend that the manager provide that training and give the person another chance.

Unfortunately, many times the manager cannot come up with a good reason why the person should stay, but he will give the employee another six months to improve. In virtually every one of those situations, the manager will end up firing the employee and then tell me that he should have done it six months earlier.

Truly poor performers disintegrate a culture of execution. For your sake, the sake of your group, and the sake of your organization, remove poor performers as quickly as you can.

10. Continually Evaluate the Efficiency and Effectiveness of Each Planned Activity

Assuming that your team members executed the details of a planned activity at a high level, the next step is to analyze whether or not the activity itself was both an efficient use of your group's time and an effective way to move the desired business results forward in a sustainable manner. If the activity took up an enormous amount of time, money, and effort relative to the impact it had, then it either needs to be tossed aside in favor of a different activity or it needs to be redesigned.

If the activity had a negligible impact in terms of moving the desired result forward, then it may need to be dropped or redesigned. Just because a planned activity appears on the original business plan doesn't mean that it was the right activity for the long term. Continually analyze what is being done and whether or not it should stay on the to-do list.

11. Be Aware of Opportunities and Dangers and Make Adjustments

Finally, the world around you is dynamic, not static. Be willing to let go of a set of planned activities if the changes in the marketplace create new opportunities for you to pursue or new dangers that need to be avoided.

If the product you're selling suddenly becomes the hottest item on the market or if you find a faulty part in one of your products and need to conduct a major recall, you will need to adjust your planned activities. Notice that this is different from changing the schedule of your planned activities because you want to insert a meeting that is not on the calendar.

When an opportunity or danger arises, you may need to actually alter your plan. This means proactively changing what your group will do in terms of activities. You're not changing the schedule and then trying to go back to the planned activities and execute them well. You are actually changing the planned activities that your group will execute. In doing so, select the strategy, tactics, and planned activities that will best leverage the opportunity or avoid the impending danger, and then execute those new planned activities to the best of your ability.

Acceleration Tips

- ✓ Execution is boring. It's boring to write all the potential activities on index cards and then keep moving them around until you have the best sequence. It's boring to go through the entire calendar and put down who is going to do what part of each activity. It's boring to follow up with people to see how their activity is moving along. It's boring unless you see how incredibly important execution is to accelerating the achievement of your most important business outcomes. Essentially, effective execution is the difference between greatness and mediocrity. Know the steps, do the steps, and constantly get better at completing the steps.

Chapter

10

MANAGE CHANGE

"When Are All These Changes Going to Stop?"

October 2001 was the perfect storm for change.

I was coaching about ten people at two national organizations: one in the retail industry and one in the hospitality industry. For the previous four months, the retail organization had been working on a plan to reduce their number of regional offices by 50 percent and their corporate workforce by 600 people. The announcement of this reduction came just 30 days after the terrorist attack of September 11.

The hospitality organization, which had been experiencing unprecedented growth just 18 months earlier, had been depressed by the collapse of the dot-com bubble in March 2000 and was decimated by September 11. Suddenly no one was traveling. In addition, the widespread use of the Internet allowed consumers to find transportation and lodging at unheard of low prices. Shortly after these massive changes happened, corporate scandals at Enron, Arthur Andersen, and WorldCom became public knowledge and further damaged consumer and investor confidence.

I saw how people dealt with every imaginable change. Some of these changes were selected by the individuals I knew, some were implemented by people higher up in their organizations, and some were delivered by forces completely outside of their control.

Some of the people I knew were promoted while others were fired. Some were given the opportunity to stay as long as they took a demotion. Of those, some took the demotion and others left. Some people ended up with the same title, but had their geographic responsibilities double in size. Some people left their industry to find new jobs while others went to work in new departments within their same organization. I watched the heartbreak some people went through as their friends were fired, and I saw how people reacted when new "teams" were instantly created in which individual members had never even met each other before.

During one memorable coaching session, one of my clients looked at me, paused, and then said, "When are all these changes going to stop?" I looked down for a moment, and then I looked her in the eye and said, "They're not going to stop. The rate of change is only going to increase going forward. We need to focus on how you can leverage change to achieve what you want both for your organization and for yourself." And with that, she and I got busy shifting our focus from being worn down by change to converting change into opportunities.

In this chapter I will take each of these types of scenarios and offer some perspective on how to effectively create change and deal with change.

FIVE TYPES OF CHANGE

1. Creating and Clearly Communicating Changes

Alan Weiss, a highly successful international consultant and author of *Million Dollar Consulting,* taught me three powerful questions to help manage the process of implementing change in an organization:

- What are we changing from and why?
- What are we changing to and why?
- How are we going to make that change?

He pointed out very effectively that people have the biggest problem with changes they don't understand. This vagueness creates confusion and increases anxiety. As Marcus Buckingham wrote in his book, *The One Thing You Need to Know,* the most important job of a leader is to provide clarity.

Before you implement a change, write your answers to those three questions. If you are not clear in your own mind about what is being changed and why it is being changed, what the new reality is going to be and why that is being created, and how this change is going to occur, then don't make the change. If you are clear about those three items, then communicate your answers to the people in your organization or business unit. Your employees don't have to agree with you, but they do need to understand you in order to move forward effectively with the changed reality.

Be honest and candid. It does no good at all to try to avoid communicating the changes that are being made. Actually, it's extremely counterproductive to put your head down and push forward with the attempt to change when no one understands what is being changed or what the actual change is going to look like. You won't have a perfect answer most of the time, but do the best you can with what you know to communicate your answers to those questions.

2. Responding to a Societal Change

You have no control over societal changes. Whether it's a horrific event like a natural disaster or a terrorist attack or a shift in trends in fashion or technology, you can only respond to these changes as they arrive. The key is to be honest about the new reality. Ask yourself, "What is the new situation we are dealing with?"

By accepting the fact that you're operating in a new reality, you can decide how to respond to the circumstances. If you deny that the reality has changed, then you are making decisions in a world that no longer exists.

To deny the proliferation of digital communication and entertainment or to say that all manufacturing jobs need to stay in the United States and deny the explosive growth of China is simply a failure to confront reality. To stay in a business that cannot remotely compete on price with companies in India and not make any adjustments in terms of your approach to the marketplace is a failure to respond to a societal change.

Be honest about the world you're living in at this moment. Write down what has changed. Then develop a plan for achieving your desired outcomes that takes into account the true reality you are working within.

In terms of leading your business unit, be sure to clearly communicate to everyone the new reality that the business is facing. The more you get your employees to understand that the old reality has changed and what the specifics of the new reality are, the more they can accept their new surroundings and begin to accelerate within that new framework.

Again, the key to effective leadership is to influence how other people think in ways that generate better sustainable results both for the organization and the people in it. This influence begins with honest and clear communication.

3. Dealing with Change from Above

If your boss has determined that changes need to take place in your organization, then you are in a situation similar to a natural disaster. Essentially, you are working in a new environment. Just as you would deal with the societal changes discussed in the second type of change, responding to this type of change requires a two-step process. First, be honest with yourself. Second, be honest with the members of your group and the other people who are affected by this change.

When the members of your group have come to grips with the new direction from above, they can then shift back into the basics of great teamwork: identifying their purpose as a group and how it supports the overall organizational goals, and working to support one another toward fulfilling that purpose.

4. Changing from Two Competing Teams to One United Team

When top executives decide to merge two companies or two regions within the same company, a common mistake managers make is trying to do some things the way one company or region used to do them and some things the way the other company or region used to do them. A far more effective approach is to admit that things have changed and the new group, which consists of people from both former companies, is dealing with a new reality. This new group has to clarify for itself its purpose within the organization and how the members will support one another.

You have to look upon this consolidated group as a completely new group. Otherwise people tend to live in the past, and they keep bringing up old gripes that no longer apply in the new situation. For example, if you were the southern region and you just merged with the old western region, then call your new group something other than the southern or western region. Gain a new identity, clarify a new purpose, and establish how the members of the group are going to work together.

5. Accelerating Through a Career Transition

Even though this section of the book is on group performance, I want to step aside for a moment to take on an important personal issue: career transitions. In a nutshell, a career transition occurs when your career changes. This could mean you received a promotion, gained significantly greater responsibilities, changed departments, or went to another organization. In one sense, all these situations are really the same. You are faced with new circumstances, but you still have the same strengths, passions, and desires as before.

The first step to accelerate during a career transition is to identify the desired outcomes of the organization you are working for and the desired outcomes that your new role should deliver. The second step is to ask yourself how you can leverage your strengths and passions in this new situation to accelerate the achievement of those desired business outcomes. Essentially, this takes us back to the beginning of this book. And that's my whole point: a career transition is merely a new version of an old situation. You're still in a position in which you're expected to deliver value and increase the chances that other people will achieve what they want to achieve.

While you may need to develop some new technical skills, the human dynamics and business dynamics that were important in your previous role will be as important in your new role. No matter what industry you end up in or what business function you work in you will still need to be effective as an individual, influence how other people think, communicate effectively, build true business teams, establish an effective strategy, and execute properly.

Of course, being fired is one of the hardest changes to deal with. Following are a couple of suggestions on how to deal with that harsh reality.

First, don't become paranoid and think that the world is out to get you and no one likes you. Accept the reality that your boss simply chose to go forward without you. The sooner you can accept that, the sooner you can move forward with your career.

Second, ask yourself what organizations you could add value to that would truly leverage your strengths and your passions. Then identify what those organizations are trying to achieve. As you prepare for an interview, clarify what you can do to add value to the organization that will help them achieve what they want to achicvc.

Third, make a list of actual experiences from your past jobs that demonstrate your strengths and your ability to add value in a way that is relevant to the organization you are interviewing with. Then go after it!

Acceleration Tips

- ✓ The old saying that change is constant is constantly true. Accept it and deal with it effectively.
- ✓ If you generate the change, then clarify what the group is changing from and why, what it is changing to and why, and how that change is going to occur. Then clearly communicate those three things in multiple ways to people throughout your business unit.
- ✓ If change is being thrown at you by a force outside of your organization or by higher-level executives in your organization, then accept the new reality as quickly as you can. Operate within that reality by identifying the desired outcomes, the role your group can fulfill toward improving those outcomes, and how the members of your group can support one another toward the fulfillment of those objectives.
- ✓ If your job transitions to a new set of circumstances, then accept those as the new reality and work to add value effectively by leveraging your strengths and passions within that new framework.
- ✓ If you lose your job, keep your dignity by realizing that you are still in control of your decisions and your destiny.

Part Three

ACCELERATE YOUR ORGANIZATION'S RESULTS

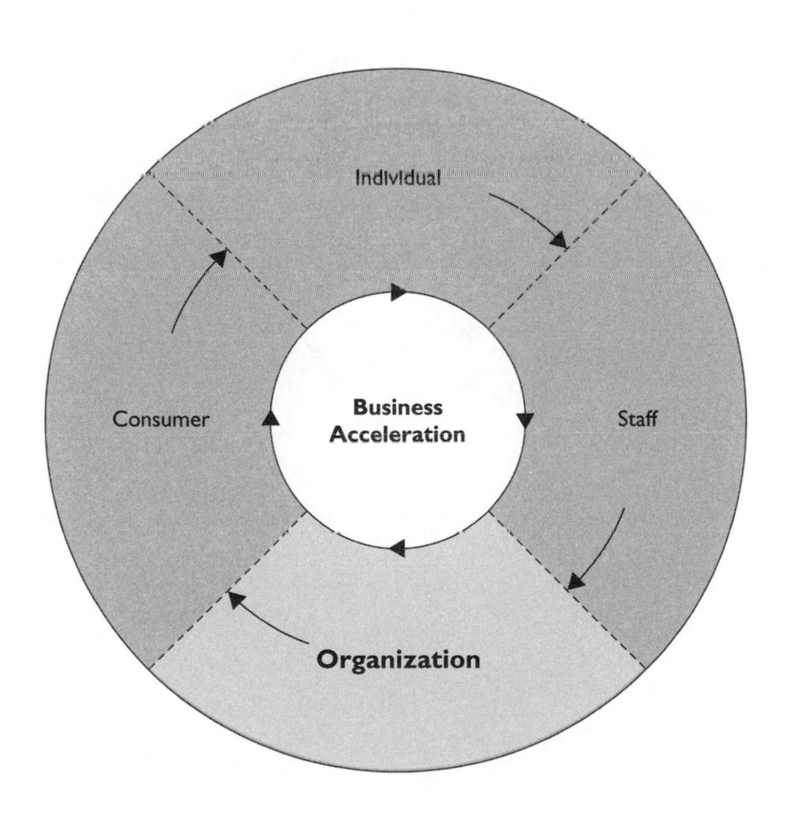

Chapter

11

ESTABLISH YOUR LEADERSHIP COUNCIL

"How Do I Get My Leadership Council to, You Know, Lead?"

I was coaching an executive who had just come back from his first Leadership Council meeting. He said, "Dan, how do I get my Leadership Council to, you know, lead? Right now they're blaming the company for all of their problems. One guy even said, 'We need leadership to step up and fix these issues.' I looked around the room and said, 'I think you're referring to me, but the leadership of this business is this group, not one individual.'"

After I thought about his question, I said, "I don't know the answer. I'm not even sure what a 'Leadership Council' is. However, I believe we'll work together and figure this out." Little did either of us realize how exciting the journey over the next several years would be. In a nutshell, we discovered that an effective Leadership Council is the golden goose that generates sustainable, profitable growth.

An effective Leadership Council represents a wide array of constituents, defines the strategic direction of the organization, serves as a liaison between individual parts of the organization and the senior corporate decision makers, resolves issues effectively as they come up in any part of the organization, seizes opportunities for business growth, and makes sure the organization doesn't go off on meaningless tangents. In addition, I came to realize that any organization in any industry can set up an effective Leadership Council that drives sustainable, profitable growth.

KEYS TO ASSEMBLING AN EFFECTIVE LEADERSHIP COUNCIL

There are two keys to establishing an effective Leadership Council: passion and diversity.

First, you need people who want to be there, who want to represent the opinions of other people, who are willing to speak up, who care about the big picture, and who are willing to put in the time and effort necessary to generate success in terms of the overall purpose of the extended organization.

The worst type of Leadership Council is made up of people who really don't want to be there, and are only involved because no one else was willing. In these situations, you get half-hearted efforts and half-completed projects, which make a complete mess of the Leadership Council.

You want a position on the Leadership Council to be seen as an honor and a privilege. You want people to have to work hard to get on the Leadership Council, and for others to talk about membership on the Leadership Council with a certain amount of reverence. The members should be looked upon as the true leaders of the overall organization, and not as the suckers who drew the short straw.

The second key in assembling an effective Leadership Council is to value diversity. You want each of your organization's constituencies to be fairly represented. If your company is a franchise organization, you will clearly want franchisees in a variety of key positions, including chairman of the Leadership Council. If independent business owners play a key role in your extended organization, then make sure they make up at least part of the key officers of the Leadership Council.

Reach out to your suppliers and gain a strong, diverse group of people who will represent this critically important aspect of everyone's long-term success. Make sure that key departments within your company including sales, marketing, operations, finance, human resources, and so on are represented. Be certain at every meeting to have a strong business research person who will give a solid overview of how the organization is doing in key measurement areas. This will help ground the conversation in facts and not just subjective opinions.

Look for diversity in terms of talent and skills as well. Some people may be strong at giving honest pushback or thinking big picture or understanding the trends in the marketplace, while others may be strong at getting things done behind the scenes or reaching out to get new people involved or seeing the obstacles that will be created on the front lines by certain strategic decisions. As you encourage people to run for election, try to create as wide an array of talent as you can assemble.

Also, work to diversify the group in terms of race, gender, and ethnicity. The more diverse Leadership Councils that I have seen are the ones who maintain the broadest perspective on developing ideas and making decisions. They tend to do a better job of understanding how a wider group of people will be affected by the projects they put into motion.

To increase diversity of perspective, bring outsiders in to specific meetings. You might bring in an expert on a particular topic and have the person give a lecture or a seminar.

You could bring in a panel of your associates who are working on the front line with customers to hear their thoughts on the plan for next year. I've seen this work very effectively. Have a facilitator up front who takes questions from the members of the Leadership Council for any member of this panel. That way the Leadership Council can see right away the reactions from people who actually implement the strategic plan, grapple with the issues, and see the opportunities on a daily basis.

KEYS TO OPERATING AN EFFECTIVE LEADERSHIP COUNCIL

It does no good to assemble a wonderful Leadership Council of 25 diverse people representing all aspects of the extended organization if no one is allowed to speak up. The worst Leadership Council meetings are ones in which eight people each give 30-minute updates, and then the group goes off to dinner. Don't need to do that. The whole point of a Leadership Council is to have meaningful dialogue on important issues that affect the customers, the success of the various groups represented, and the long-term success of the business.

Members of Leadership Councils usually volunteer their time to attend meetings. Make sure these meetings value openness and honesty. Publicly reward comments that challenge the thinking in the group. Put open-ended questions on the meeting agendas. Have short reports followed by meaty and open discussions. Break the large group into a series of small groups to increase the level of dialogue, and rotate the groups so each person sits with different people on a regular basis.

As in making any strong team, work to clarify the purpose of the group and how each person can support other people toward fulfilling that purpose. This doesn't happen by sitting and listening to updates for five hours and then going off to party together.

If possible, create three-year terms for membership so one-third of the group is being replaced each year. At the beginning of each year, go on some type of Leadership Council retreat so members get to know each other on an individual basis, and the overall group gets to further clarify its purpose, specific objectives, and mode of operating together.

Work to ensure that this is not run as a top-down group in which the officers simply tell others what to do. The point of a Leadership Council is to collectively provide influence for the extended organization that generates sustainable improvement in high priority results. Council members should be seen as equals and not as part of the group reporting to another part of the group.

Clarify Roles and Responsibilities

People generally get on Leadership Councils because they are highly successful in their day jobs. They get asked to be part of a lot of groups both in terms of the business and in the community. In a nutshell, they are very, very busy people. They have no time to waste and no patience for long meetings that accomplish nothing. They want the group to be purposeful and successful, and they want to play a useful part within the group. My point is, you have to provide clear roles and responsibilities or people will get bored and leave.

Here is one way to delineate responsibilities: set up subcommittees that are responsible for conducting research on different aspects of the business. Each member of the subcommittee plays a role in gathering information about that aspect of the business and bringing the insights back to the other members. Then the subcommittee crafts a recommendation on how the organization could approach that area of the business while staying within the overall strategic direction that the Leadership Council has determined.

In this example, each person knows whether he or she is a member of the Executive Committee for the Leadership Council, which I'll explain in a moment, the head of a subcommittee, or a member of a subcommittee. They know specifically what role they need to fulfill in order to move the business forward.

They also know what information they need to gather, organize, and present on which dates to which groups. In this manner, each person understands how he is helping to make the organization more successful. The more purposeful members feel as individuals, the better the chances will be for the success of the Leadership Council.

The members of the Leadership Council also need to have a clear understanding of their general responsibilities as members. Do they speak for the organization in public venues? Do they share what has been discussed at the Leadership Council meetings with their staff members? Do they cast a vote on the strategy and tactics for the organization? Be sure to clarify both the general responsibilities of being part of the group and the responsibilities of each role within the group.

Review Business Research

I've seen Leadership Councils that actively use business research and those that don't. The former tend to beat the latter by a long shot. When a group of successful people come together, they bring a lot of strong emotions and forceful opinions into the room. The role of business research is to provide a perspective based on actual data that outlines general market trends, areas where the business is succeeding and where it is failing, and an understanding of what is happening with the competition.

Based on this business research, the members of the Leadership Council now have a common base to return to that is fact-based. Their individual perspectives can now be delivered in light of actual customer behaviors. Without this factual basis in place, the loudest or highest ranking person may dominate the group toward doing something based entirely on his or her gut feeling. At the end of the day, someone will have to go with his gut and make a decision, but why not base that gut feeling on well-researched evidence?

Determine Strategy and Tactics Together

This is the first of the two main areas where the Leadership Council, you know, leads. The members examine the research, collaborate on what they've learned, and establish a clear and focused strategy for the organization. Then they take the components of that strategy and establish subcommittees to do further research and develop meaningful tactics around each component of the strategy. In this manner, the Leadership Council will collectively impact decisions and behaviors throughout the business.

The next two chapters focus on strategy and planning. Chapter 9 concentrated on how to execute a plan successfully. The point here is that the Leadership Council plays the critical role in defining the strategies and tactics for the business. Once this framework is put in place, the entire organization can now move forward with alignment and focus toward executing the tactics and planned activities.

Craft and Implement an Issue/Opportunity Resolution Process

This is the second area where a Leadership Council can provide true leadership. As we discussed earlier, leadership means influencing how other people think in ways that generate better sustainable results for both the organization and the people in it. A critically important aspect of leadership is listening to other people.

For a Leadership Council to be effective it must have a mechanism in place for people throughout the extended organization to voice their concerns, share their ideas for the growth of the business, feel like they are really being heard, and believe their ideas are being considered. Imagine a funnel of issues and opportunities flowing downward from customers, employees, suppliers, and business partners or franchisees. There are two ways to deal with these issues and opportunities.

The first way is to put the funnel over the head of the highest ranking executive in the organization and let all the issues and opportunities pour over him or her, and then put the onus of responsibility on this person to resolve all these issues and opportunities.

The other way is to set up subgroups within the Leadership Council who are responsible for different aspects of the business plan. When an issue or opportunity presents itself to the Leadership Council, the first question to answer is, "Which group is going to take the first crack at resolving this issue or optimizing this opportunity?" Once that has been decided, then the small group leader reaches out to the person who presented the issue or opportunity for more information and clarification.

Then the small group researches the relevant background information needed to form an opinion on the issue/opportunity. The members of the small group collaborate to determine their best recommendation for that situation, and present their decision to the larger Leadership Council. The Leadership Council discusses the recommendation, and if there is some disagreement about what to do, they vote on what action to take, if any.

Once the decision has been made, it is communicated back to the individual who brought the issue or opportunity to the Leadership Council. Even if the decision is to do nothing, that decision is communicated back to both the individual and other people across the extended organization. In this manner, trust is built up between the Leadership Council and the larger body of people across the members of the corporation, suppliers, business owners/franchisees, and other relevant constituents.

Empower the LCEC (Leadership Council Executive Committee)

Even in the most effective and collaborative groups, you still need a small number of decision makers to put the finishing touches on what the larger Leadership Council has discussed. This small decision-making group is known as the LCEC (Leadership Council Executive Committee). It usually consists of about six to eight people including a chairman, vice chairman, secretary, and treasurer. It also includes a few ad hoc members, who are usually the leaders of the strategic component teams.

The LCEC makes the decisions on what the final draft of the business plan looks like, what the final say is on particular issues and opportunities, and on which outsiders are invited to attend the Leadership Council meetings. Generally the LCEC members are the ones who speak at public events and share with the extended organization what has been decided, why these decisions were selected, and what actions will happen as a result of those decisions.

One subtle but important job of the LCEC, and particularly the chairman of the Leadership Council, is to decide when to shut down the conversation on one topic and move on to another. Without a clear understanding of who plays this role, meetings could go on ad infinitum. Everyone cares about improving results, and no one wants to admit when it's time to leave the great discussion and move on to the next item.

ACCELERATION ADVICE

From an Interview with the Senior Executive of a Billion-Dollar Business Unit

This interview was with an executive I coached who was responsible for managing a billion-dollar business unit in the retail industry. This executive wanted me to focus on the ideas we discussed rather than on his name or the company name. I think you will find some powerful insights from this person's responses that you can use in your business.

Coughlin: *What is the process your business unit used to develop and implement an innovation?*

Executive: We always start by focusing on consumers of today and what consumers of tomorrow might look like. When we considered a new initiative, regardless of whether it already existed in our industry or not, we looked at seven bullet points.

1. Industry Leader. Would we be the first to market or would we dominate the market if we did it?
2. Ownership. Is it something we would want to own versus implement? When people own an initiative, they won't let it fail.
3. Sequencing. Will it come in waves that will contribute to our ongoing momentum, or is it a one-time fix, a one-time big idea?
4. Headwind or Tailwind? In other words, if we do this initiative, will we have to fight resistance within our company and from consumers or will it have support from within our company and from our customers?
5. Business Plan. Does it fit within our business plan? If it doesn't, should it or could it be on our business plan? What's the sales impact? Is this an idea that will generate revenue that is left of the decimal point (i.e., 1 percent growth? 3 percent growth? 5 percent growth?)? Is the ROI

worth the investment? Is the idea operationally friendly? Does it fit our operational plan?

6. Promotion or Base Builder? Will this idea help strengthen our ongoing base of sales, or is it just a promotion that will generate one-time sales?

Once we go through those screens, we then decide whether or not we want to move forward with the idea.

Coughlin: *What do you think it takes for a Leadership Council to be effective? How do your Leadership Councils develop business strategies and tactics, resolve business issues, and capture opportunities in the marketplace?*

Executive: It starts with getting the right people. These are people with proven track records, good business results, solutions to real business issues, and ideas that are not the industry norm.

The group has to be focused on consumer insights and trends. We should be asking questions like, "How does the consumer look at my business as opposed to the way I look at my business?"

Together the Leadership Council needs to decide what the vision is. What are we trying to achieve? What are the roles and responsibilities of each team within the Leadership Council? Who does what? How will tomorrow's leaders describe what we were trying to achieve today? What will they say was important to us? How will they describe our values and the way we treated each other? How will they describe the way we worked together?

The Leadership Council needs to develop a business plan, a focus. Then we need flawless execution with timely follow-up. There needs to be two levels of measures. Level One is a roadmap. You use a roadmap to see where you are and to identify where you want to go. The roadmap is used to identify the last three years' progress and project the next three years. Level Two is a scorecard. Where are you on any given day compared to the desired results on the scorecard?

As business opportunities and issues present themselves, we apply our processes to solve them. We look at consumer insights, we put the opportunities through our business model, we identify which team within the Leadership Council should look deeper into the opportunity or issue, they bring their recommendations to the Leadership Council, and we make a decision.

Coughlin: *What have you learned about how to effectively deal with change or make changes?*

Executive: When I think about change, I ask three questions: Is it good for my customers? Is it good for my business? Can my organization execute it?

When it comes to dealing with changes, understand the reasons for the change. Work to find those reasons. Know the "why" behind the "what." Evaluate the risks versus the opportunity. Evaluate yourself and what changes you will have to make to implement the change. If you get three yeses to my three questions, and you can't change, then find someone who can.

Coughlin: *When you're looking to add a new person to your organization, what do you look for?*

Executive: Look for competent people who have experience that resulted in success. I look for relationship builders and not policy enforcers. I want people capable of planning and managing their own time. I want people who understand the need for balance between their work life and their personal life. I don't necessarily look for people who fit in. We should look for people who bring new or different ways of approaching the business.

Coughlin: *How do you apply talent management in your organization?*

Executive: Focus on the consumer and then you can judge whether or not an employee or a prospective employee focuses on that consumer. If they just focus on company hierarchy, I would question whether they are in it to build the business.

Once you get the team together, get the leadership aligned, develop the plan, provide resources, break down barriers, and then get out of the way and let people do their jobs. Along the way, ask open-ended questions when progress is disrupted to gain other's insights.

Acceleration Tips

✓ An effective Leadership Council is the engine inside an organization that studies relevant information, drives strategy and tactics, resolves what to do with issues and business opportunities, and provides clarity and focus for the extended organization.

✓ Finding diverse and passionate members, creating a culture of open and honest dialogue, and truly listening to and responding to every concern and every opportunity are critically important elements of a highly effective Leadership Council.

Chapter

12

ACKNOWLEDGE THE MISTAKES OF STRATEGIC PLANNING

"Are We Doing Enough?"

It was mid-November and everyone on the planning team felt good about the strategic plan that had been assembled. Beginning in August, a group of 30 business leaders representing every aspect of the business studied the analysis from business research, looked at the trends in the marketplace, identified what the competition had done, and crafted a clear and concise strategic plan for the upcoming year. The overarching strategy was to focus on improving service and the overall customer experience.

However, a small group of key leaders continued to ask, "Are we doing enough to reach a billion dollars in sales?" I served as the facilitator of this small group discussion. Our goal was to become a billion-dollar business unit. Clearly it was only a matter of time before it was going to happen, but we wanted it to happen as soon as possible.

We had settled on a three-year goal. This business unit had experienced significant sales growth over the previous five years, and so we thought three years seemed like a reasonable stretch goal. In order to accelerate the achievement of that goal, we started to add additional initiatives to the original plan. It seemed reasonable to us that in order to get to the desired goal faster, we had to do more than what we had initially set out to do.

We thought wrong.

By the following May, our service scores ranked in the bottom third across the United States. How could this be? Our main strategic focus was to improve the customer experience, and we were actually getting worse in this area. What had gone wrong? One of the officers picked up a marker and said, "All right, let's list everything that's impacting our front-line work force." We identified 41 new items that affected these people in addition to what was already on their plate. Simultaneously, we realized the mistake we had made.

We failed to improve service, which was our main strategic focus, because we tried too hard to succeed. We added too much to an already full plate. Immediately the group began to develop a maniacal focus on execution. We had the right strategy, but we weren't being disciplined enough in terms of implementing a reasonable number of activities, sequencing and scheduling those activities, and staying on top of the details of those projects.

We turned it around and went on to achieve our goal of becoming a billion-dollar business unit a full year ahead of schedule because we dove into the details of why the strategy wasn't working.

Strategies fail.

Despite the best strategic planning efforts of very intelligent people all over the world, strategies still fail to deliver the desired outcomes. It's important to keep this in mind because of the euphoric state that often accompanies the completion of a strategic planning process. There is work involved in selecting an appropriate strategy, and even more work involved in operating within that strategy long enough to generate sustainable improvement in results.

In my opinion, just as true teamwork is the exception rather than the rule in group dynamics, selecting an effective strategy, establishing the proper tactics, and executing a reasonable number of planned activities in a way that generates sustainable, profitable growth is the exception rather than the rule in organizations.

Following are the main reasons I have seen that explain why strategies fail.

EIGHTEEN REASONS WHY CORPORATE STRATEGIES FAIL

1. Obsessed with the Sizzle, Bored with the Steak

This is by far the biggest reason why strategies fail. The strategic decision-making group, and specifically the senior executive within the group, gets extremely excited about a strategic concept for the organization. He talks about it as a cutting-edge approach to creating value for customers in the industry. Everyone in the group is jazzed about the idea.

Almost without noticing it, a day goes by with nothing actually happening that supports the strategy. Another day slips by and no one says a thing. Suddenly two months go by and people within the organization start to talk behind closed doors. They ask, "What's going on with our new strategic direction?" Curiously, they hear nothing. What has happened is that the senior-level executive has lost his enthusiasm for actually doing the things that need to be done within this new strategy. And the great idea peters out before it ever got started.

2. Right Strategy, Wrong Culture

A strategy is only effective if the people inside the organization can execute it. That seems so obvious, but far too often strategies that sound great in the boardroom fall flat at the execution level.

Say, for example, an automobile manufacturer has a culture in which employees focus on quickly producing low-cost cars with no frills. These employees take pride in not being fancy and see expensive automobiles as a waste of money. If the senior executives suddenly decide to grow market share by designing more stylish, higher cost cars, their corporate culture won't support it. It would be like telling Southwest Airlines flight attendants to sell caviar and cappuccino to customers standing in line.

3. Right Strategy, Wrong Customers

Many years ago, the Coca-Cola Company made an extraordinary strategic error by introducing New Coke. They thought since Coca-Cola had been a smash hit for years, they could introduce a new and improved Coke and grow market share even further.

However, customers didn't want to be told they needed a new and improved product. They felt refreshed by Coca-Cola, the drink was a reward for working hard, they felt they were taking a break when they drank a Coke, and they most definitely did not want some big corporation taking that away from them. Coca-Cola wisely and quickly shifted back to their original magic formula.

4. The Microwave Popcorn Mindset

If after three and a half minutes your bag of microwave popcorn has not started popping, you get concerned. That's approximately how long many people think a corporate strategy should take to start producing results. Not just activities, but actual results. And they better be substantial results. This obsession with the microwave mentality causes corporations to change their strategies so often none of them ever produce sustainable results. To produce sustainable results, you actually have to have a sustained strategy.

5. Bored with Success

Handling success is often more difficult than handling failure. When things aren't going well, the "hope in better things to come" can sustain your efforts. However, when success arrives, you might become bored quickly with how you became successful and want to dash off to another approach. This happens when an executive comes back after attending a new seminar or reading a new book and instantly wants to change the direction of the company. One of the keys to long-term corporate success is remaining comfortable with staying the course.

6. Scared to Confront the Industry

Industry norms are not nearly as sacrosanct as some people think. Not all dentists need to run their own small business, not every grocer needs to know the name of every customer, and not every airline needs to provide assigned seating. When a company willingly pushes back on industry norms, good things can happen.

Heartland Dental Care now owns more than 100 dentist offices, which provide extraordinary service to their customers and great benefits to their employees. Wal-Mart decided to focus on low prices when the industry was focused on small stores and personal attention. Southwest Airlines focused on fun and low fares and didn't worry about assigning seats.

7. "Me Too" Strategies

Imitation may be the sincerest form of flattery, but it usually makes for a lousy business strategy. If your company is following a strategy just because another organization used it and achieved great results, you're almost certainly destined to fail.

The underpinnings of a successful strategy include a company's culture, resources, passion, and so on. The odds that your company has the same infrastructure assets as another corporation are infinitesimally small. You're much better off crafting your own strategy based on your situation than on trying to copy someone else's.

8. Addicted to Change

I've sat in meetings at which the executive in charge will say, "We're going to try this approach to the business for this year, but it won't be around next year because we try something different every year." The problem was the individual saying it didn't see that as a problem. The employees were so resigned to constant change for the sake of constant change they didn't even bother putting up a fight.

The results didn't just go up and down every year, they basically just went down. Strategies are like skateboards. The rider needs some momentum before he can jump off a ramp and fly through the air. Annually changing strategies is like making the skateboarder jump onto a different skateboard every three feet.

9. The Arrogant Executive

Some day I'm going to write a whole book on the problems associated with arrogant executives. Suffice it to say that an arrogant executive thinks he knows it all. He thinks he knows what the customers want and need, he thinks he knows how best to deliver that value, and he thinks he knows what his employees should be able to do.

When the strategy fails, the arrogant executive blames everyone except himself. Arrogant executives usually get into their role by achieving some spectacular short-term results on lower rungs of the corporate ladder.

These short-term results fuel the problem in two ways: first, the individual starts to believe even more that he knows more than anyone else, and, second, he has been rewarded even though he has never achieved sustainable results. This causes arrogant CEOs to shut out other input and focus on the short-term. Thus, the corporate strategy fails in terms of generating significant, sustainable, and profitable growth.

10. Desire to Leave Your Fingerprints

I've seen consultants convince executives to develop a ten-year corporate vision by replacing the word "Wall" in "Wall Street Journal" with the executive's name. For example, if the executive's name is Tom Brown, then it becomes the Brown Street Journal. All his top reports then work to write articles for this fictitious paper describing what their area of the business will look like in ten years.

The intent of thinking long term is a good idea, but the net result of this approach is an organization that focuses on serving the boss and not on adding more value to clients.

11. Obsession with Complexity

Some senior executives are in love with simplicity and others are in love with complexity. Based on my informal research, I would say the former beat the latter in terms of generating sustainable, profitable growth by a long shot. Effective top decision makers talk about their company's strategy in a few sentences and they do it with pride. They say things like:

"Look, we keep things pretty simple around here. We give the customer what they're looking for and we do it faster than anybody else."

"Our job is pretty clear: we manufacture planes and we take care of those planes so our clients can focus on their customers."

"Our customers want a break. They want to feel refreshed. So we give them not only a great dessert, but also a comfortable place where they can eat and talk with their friends."

However, some senior executives get embarrassed when they talk about their business in simple terms, and to make up for it they give long dissertations describing their organization and how it adds value to customers. Usually the people in these organizations are running all over the place trying to do too many things and not delivering any extraordinary value to their customers.

12. Passion Outage

If you burn out your employees, pretty much any strategy will fail. If your organization reaches a point at which people simply put in their time to get a paycheck, you have virtually no chance for success. How do these passion outages occur? Here are three ways to suck the life right out of your employees:

1. Use layoffs as the answer to every problem. When your revenues don't reach the desired number, fire a bunch of people. When your profit doesn't satisfy the analysts, get rid of 15 percent of your workforce. When your productivity per employee hour doesn't improve the way you want, force every manager to lay off the bottom 10 percent of their employees.
2. Hire every key person in your organization from the outside, and your employees will believe no matter how hard they work or how much they achieve, they will never be promoted. They become like the dog that hits the electronic fence over and over and eventually stops trying to go into the street. These employees will eventually stop trying to support any strategy.
3. Change your strategy every year regardless of how the company performs, and employees will not support any strategy with passion. They'll say, "Why get excited about this approach? It's going to change in a year anyway."

13. No Money

There's a great old quote that says it's okay to build castles in the sky as long as you build a foundation underneath them. Having a glorious corporate vision and an approach to converting it into reality loses all momentum when the reality hits home that you don't have enough money to do what the strategy calls for. Every strategy has parameters within which it has to operate. One of those parameters is your organization's financial strength.

14. Lack of Skill

All the money in the world won't matter if your employees don't know how to deliver the value your strategy calls for. What competencies or skills are necessary for your strategy to be effectively implemented? Do your employees have those skills? If they don't, do you have the resources to develop those skills in your employees or to get employees with those skills? If not, you need to pursue a different strategy.

15. Better Competitor Strategy

The toy industry has gone through a massive upheaval in the past few years. While some stores focused on providing extraordinary toys at relatively high prices that provided great learning experiences, other stores focused on selling toys in mass quantities at very low prices.

By and large, cheaper toys won out over expensive toys and some companies that focused on high-end toys went out of business. If your strategy doesn't provide differentiating value that matters more to your customers than what your competition is doing, you're doomed to working hard and getting terrible results.

16. Lack of Leadership

I believe people at all levels in an organization can be effective leaders. As I explained earlier, leadership means influencing how people think in ways that generate better, sustainable results both for the organization and the people in it. Leadership is not based on a label, an income, or a position of authority. It's based solely on the ability to influence how other people think.

If you have an absence of effective influencers in your organization, your strategy will never gain buy-in from the people who need to execute it at the point of customer interaction. If your desire is to be the fastest deliverer of service in your industry and you have a lack of leadership in your organization, the concept of speed will remain a dream.

17. The Charismatic Consultant

If you hire a consultant to help you in the strategic planning process, be careful not to be seduced by the charm with which he or she presents a potential strategy. Sometimes consultants jump to an idea for a strategy on pure intuition, and then spend their time selling the members of the group on why that strategy is the best one for the organization. That's a bad move. Consultants can effectively facilitate the strategic planning and implementation process, but they should never be the one to determine an organization's strategy.

18. Can't Execute

This final reason is really a summary of a number of other reasons. No strategy can deliver results if you have not developed an execution culture in your organization. An execution culture happens when employees focus on identifying what needs to be done, why it needs to be done, how it will be done, who will do it, when it will happen, and where it will happen.

In an execution culture, employees get busy using the proper tactics and stay on top of the details that need to happen in order to get the job done. In the absence of this culture, strategies remain meaningless statements in the corporate boardroom.

STRATEGIC QUESTIONS

Is your organization or business unit achieving the type of sustainable business results you want? If not, why do you think the strategy is not generating those results? Use the reasons presented in this chapter as your first set of screens and then look at other possible reasons.

Acceleration Tips

✓ Don't let your group get too excited about having a strategic plan. Clarifying an approach to the marketplace and mapping out your tactics and planned activities for the upcoming year merely constitutes a starting point. Just like a marathon runner doesn't celebrate getting to the start line, don't have a celebration for putting a strategic plan on paper.

Chapter

13

GAIN STRATEGIC FOCUS

"Let's Just Pick One Thing and Do It Really Well."

After two hours of what was becoming an excruciatingly painful strategic planning meeting, a soft-spoken man in the back of the room yelled out, "Let's just pick one thing and do it really well." Suddenly all the eyes stopped rolling and the shoulders stopped shrugging.

Another person stood up and one said, "Tom's right. Let's stop pretending that we can do 50 things well. Let's just select one thing to improve in each area of our business and stop worrying about everything else." More people chimed in with support for the idea. I was sitting off to the side and observing the drama as it unfolded. It was one of the most effective moments I've ever witnessed in a strategic planning session.

The usual arguments over whether something was a strategy or a tactic went away. The piling on of ideas went away. Each subgroup had to sacrifice a lot of ideas in order to present the one thing they felt would have the greatest positive impact on generating sustainable, profitable growth.

In the end, the group emerged with a strategy known as the "Main Six." The group broke its business down into six areas:

speed, friendliness, facilities, marketing, profitability, and product launches. The people responsible clarified one thing to improve for their specific area that would matter to customers and could generate sustainable, profitable growth.

And away we went. The six items appeared on one side of a laminated index card, and six questions related to those six items appeared on the other side. The questions helped bring discussion happening throughout the business unit into an immediate and common focus. This business unit had more than 25,000 employees. Within six months of the launch of this strategic plan, virtually all the employees knew the Main Six and were prepared to answer the six questions on the back of the card.

The Main Six remained the central strategic focus for the next three years while the business unit achieved the best three-year stretch in its history. The Main Six wasn't just a theme. It was a way of thinking that impacted behaviors that resonated with customers in a way that drove sustainable, profitable growth.

This story represents the central theme of this chapter. An effective strategy emerges when a group of people really understand their assets as an organization, the market conditions including the actions of their competitors, their desired business outcomes, and their current approach to the market. The successful business units then discipline themselves to do less by operating within the clear strategy in order to achieve more.

KEYS POINTS TO REMEMBER ABOUT STRATEGIES

Know the true end game. A strategy is only effective if it helps you to achieve your desired end game.

A strategy is not something you do. A strategy is a guideline for making decisions. A strategy helps you to decide what to do *and* what not to do.

A strategy defines your business, or a part of your business, and the way in which it adds value in the marketplace.

In the absence of a clear strategy, you can do anything, which can lead to customer confusion. For example, how much does a purse cost? The answer is it depends. If you put a $20 purse from Wal-Mart, a $300 purse from Nordstrom's, and a $1,000 purse from Louis Vuitton side by side in one store, customers will get confused. They may question the logic of the pricing and possibly walk away.

The point of having a clear strategy in place is that it causes you to make decisions that are consistent with one another.

Acceleration is the art of sacrifice. You define your business by the opportunities you turn down. When you say no to a potential strategy, tactic, or customer, you are defining the work you will go after and the work you won't go after. That's very powerful.

You need a strategy that slices through all the possible actions you could take like a knife slicing through butter. The butter on one side of the knife goes on the piece of bread, and the vast majority of the butter on the other side of the knife stays on the plate. If you put the whole stick of butter on the piece of bread, you have a mess. If you do all the activities you're capable of doing, you have a mess. An effective strategy clarifies the few actions you can consider doing and the vast majority of actions you should not consider doing.

Give your group a very limited amount of time to develop a vision statement for your organization or business unit. I know that runs counter to what you might expect from a consultant, but my reasoning is based on real life business circumstances. Organizations only have a certain amount of time they can dedicate to developing their strategic plan.

When subgroups develop a vision statement, they invariably spend an inordinate amount of time philosophizing about what they want the future to look like. There's nothing wrong with doing those exercises, but in reality, I find that groups end up using a disproportionate amount of their time doing the "fun" stuff, which is perfecting a vision statement. They then run out of time to do the "grunt work" of establishing a strategy, tactics, planned activities, milestones, roles, responsibilities, and timelines, and then actually executing those items effectively.

Rather than conducting a full-blown strategic planning process each year, I encourage you to do it every three years. By taking a three-year slice of time, you'll force yourself and your group to look at a longer view of the business and to be more disciplined in the strategy you select.

One of my clients who was suffering through a period of unusually poor results dramatically turned around her performance by gathering input from a wide body of constituents and then putting in place a three-year plan to succeed. That strategic plan became the foundation of unprecedented sustained profitable growth for the organization.

Great strategies emerge from great awareness. In order to find a simple, clear, and effective strategy, you need to do the hard work of increasing your awareness of your organization and its surroundings. The people in my story at the beginning of this chapter all had ten or more years of experience in the business. They had studied business research consistently quarter after quarter. Their simple, powerful strategy emerged in an instant, but only because they had done their homework in terms of being aware of what was going on.

Some people think Sam Walton was an unsophisticated businessman who would never spend time in some fancy strategic planning session. And they're probably right. However, Walton was in his stores every day, counted the cars in his parking lot, and kept close tabs on which items sold well and which ones didn't. He knew what his competition was up to at all times. Ultimately he developed one of the most powerful retail strategies in history: we sell for less. Those four words affected every decision within Wal-Mart from their inventory management to their office space to executives rooming together when they traveled.

THE FIVE PREPARATION STEPS BEFORE SELECTING YOUR STRATEGY

If you put one child on one end of a seesaw and another child on the other end, the larger child will lift the smaller child up in the air. However, if the fulcrum is moved toward the larger child, the smaller child can gain the leverage he needs to lift the larger child in the air. This relationship is shown in Figure 13.1.

Because the weight of the children and the length of the board are fixed, the only changeable variable is where you place the fulcrum. If the smaller child moves the fulcrum too close to the larger child, he loses his leverage and can't lift him. If the smaller child places the fulcrum too close to his end, he can't lift the larger child either. Finding the optimal fulcrum point allows the smaller child to lift the larger one off the ground.

This analogy represents the four components involved in establishing an effective strategy:

- Your organization's strengths—represented by the smaller child.
- The market conditions—represented by the board.

FIGURE 13.1

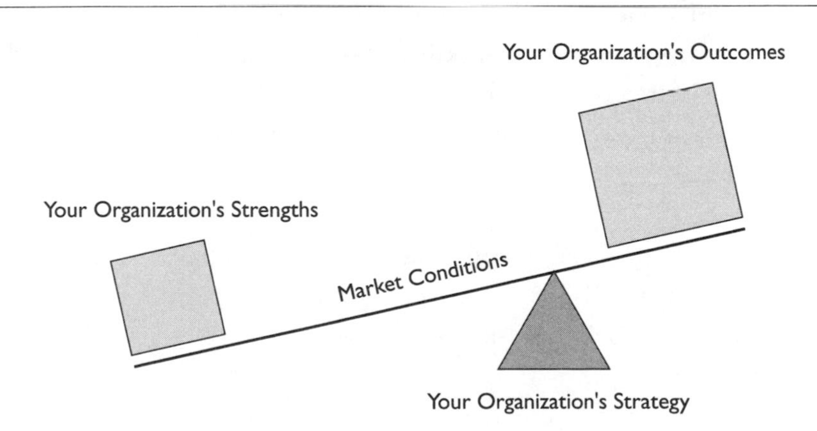

- Your organization's outcomes—represented by the larger child.
- Your corporate strategy—represented by where you place the fulcrum.

The goal is to determine what strategy, if executed properly, will best help your organization or business unit achieve your desired objectives. An effective strategy leverages your organization's assets in a way that adds meaningful and differentiating value to your desired customers, operates within the conditions of the market, and generates significant, sustainable, and profitable growth.

Choosing the wrong strategy means your company either has no leverage or does not impact the marketplace in any meaningful manner. In order to establish an effective strategy, you first need to really understand your current organization, the market conditions, your desired business outcomes, and your current business strategy. Then you can decide if you want to keep your current strategy or change to a new one.

Step One: Conduct an Organizational Asset Audit

No strategy is effective unless it can be executed. In order to understand what an organization can effectively do, you need to understand what makes up the organization. Every organization has five components: values, skills, passions, resources, and knowledge. The better you understand each component, the better you will understand what strategies will and will not work for your organization.

Values. Values are beliefs that determine behaviors. An organization's culture is its set of consistently displayed behaviors. What values are being demonstrated on a consistent basis in your organization?

Walk around and observe the employees in a variety of situations. Notice how the executives behave. Notice how people talk about each other. Observe how they refer to the stated corporate values. Do they consider them to be a joke or do they use them as the basis for making decisions? Observe people at different levels in the organization and see if there are consistent behaviors displayed by people in different groups.

Skills. What do your employees have the ability to do well? That's no small question when you consider the vast array of talent in your organization. These skills don't necessarily need to be in action at the moment. The more you can understand the variety of skills in your organization, the more you will understand what strategies can be implemented.

Apple Inc. has a vast array of talent in its workforce, but most people in the company thought their skills could only be applied to personal computers. Little did the world know that those same skills could change the music industry through the creation of the iPod. What skills do your employees have that could add value to customers in ways you never dreamed possible?

Passions. Ask your employees why they work. What motivates them to take purposeful and effective action? What trips their trigger and gets them to perform at their highest levels?

By understanding the real passions in your organization, you can clarify which strategic approaches will be enthusiastically supported and which ones won't. To understand the passions among your employees, you can survey them and interview them, but I think the best way is to observe them. Watch them in action and see what turns them on.

Resources. What physical and financial assets does your organization have to leverage that could add value to some customers? Does your organization own facilities or land that could be used for other purposes? What capital assets do you have inside your facilities?

Make a list of your organization's reserve funds, short-term and long-term debt, available lines of credit, and any long-term financial

Organizational Audit Exercise: Skill Identification

Respond to the following questions, each of which begins with the same part. Your answers could describe just a few of your employees. The skills present in your organization do not have to be shared by all employees.

How would you describe your employees' capacity to . . .

- Respond to customer questions in a rapid fashion?
- Manage financial resources?
- Learn new technologies and apply those technologies in ways that add value to customers?
- Develop long-term relationships with customers that lead to repeat business and referrals?
- Manage multiple projects simultaneously and move each of them forward in a steady and productive manner?
- Take on a new, extremely large, risky, and multiple-year project and convert it into a financial success?
- Incorporate multiple cultures both within your organization and in your client base?
- Open new successful operations in a variety of cities around the world?
- Manage the flow of mass volumes of inventory?
- Implement a variety of nuances that continually enhance the customer's experience?
- Teach new ideas and processes in ways that add value to customers?
- Create a fun and exciting environment for customers?

You just answered a dozen questions, some of which may not directly apply to your operation. Create a dozen more that will cause you to really examine the range of skills specific to your organization.

commitments on your books, for example pensions, retirement plans, insurance, and so on. Know what resources you have available to deploy against any strategy.

Knowledge. What do your employees know well? Again, this doesn't have to apply to all your employees. Clarify what industry knowledge is strong in your organization. What knowledge do employees have of different cultures, demographics, and buying patterns? Identify the technical knowledge that your employees have. The better you know what your employees know, the better chance you have of finding the best strategy for your corporation.

Step Two: Understand Market Conditions

Market conditions exist outside of and are independent of your organization. There are two kinds of market conditions: temporary and long term. The dot-com era was a short-term market condition. The Internet is a market condition that will affect corporations for many years to come. The economic downturn at the beginning of the 21st century was cyclical. The economic expansion that occurred in China at the same time will have a lasting effect on the world's economy, although it's hard to predict what that impact will be. Population trends can generally be predicted for a period of 20 to 30 years. These affect a vast array of organizations.

Make a list of the current market conditions. Make your list as comprehensive as possible. For example, what are the current market conditions in regards to technology, digitization, gasoline prices, personal and organizational security, buying habits by different demographics, makeup of the workforce, starting salaries, disposable income, consumer confidence, economic expansion, and population trends?

Divide your list of items into two categories: short-term conditions and long-term conditions. Understanding the conditions of the markets in which you want to operate will give you a strong feel for which strategies can be successfully implemented and which ones won't generate sustainable success.

Desired Customer Audit Exercise: 25 Customer Defining Questions

1. Which three of your desired customers' highest priority outcomes can your organization help them to improve?
2. How would your desired customers prioritize the following items for the product or service you sell: quality, cost, reliability, personal attention, speed, user friendliness, customer service, ease of purchase, and convenience of delivery?
3. Do your desired customers want to pay a premium in order to be a member of an elite group?
4. Do your desired customers want to pay the lowest price on the market for products and services?
5. What are the age demographics of your desired customers?
6. What are the geographic demographics of your desired customers?
7. How often would your desired customers make a purchase from your organization? Once every three years? Once a year? Once a month? Once a week? Once a day? Once an hour?
8. Do your desired customers want to build a long-term relationship with your organization?
9. Do your desired customers want to buy from you in bulk?
10. Do your desired customers expect your organization to be a one-stop shop that can solve all of their problems in a given area?
11. Do your desired customers expect you to work in collaboration with other suppliers to meet their needs?
12. In general, how long will the sales cycle take with your desired customers?
13. Do your desired customers make buying decisions in the form of a committee or by a single individual?
14. Is providing your desired customers with ongoing guidance an important aspect for them?

Continued

15. Are your desired customers coming to you for an enriching experience? If so, what type of experience would this ideally be?
16. Are your desired customers only interested in buying the best product or service on the market?
17. Are your desired customers focused on maintaining certain buying traditions?
18. Do your desired customers want to work with suppliers they know personally?
19. Is the ability to leverage the Internet with suppliers an important consideration for your desired customers?
20. Are your desired customers looking to demonstrate their current level of success through their purchases?
21. Are your desired customers more focused on the functionality of a product or service than on its name recognition?
22. Is price the differentiating factor for your desired customers?
23. Is brand name recognition the differentiating factor for your desired customers?
24. Are your desired customers obsessed with buying cutting-edge products and services?
25. Are your desired customers willing to take a risk in making a purchase?

By answering these questions and providing a written rationale for each of your answers, you will sketch a very clear picture of your desired customers. Add any additional questions you feel are important to better understand your desired customers.

A subset of the general market conditions is your desired customers. Define your desired customers as clearly as you can. See the Desired Customer Audit exercise for some questions that may help you better understand your desired customers. The better you understand them, the better your chances of establishing an appropriate corporate strategy.

Step Three: Understand Your Desired Outcomes

A strategy can only be effective in helping an organization achieve its desired outcomes if the people in the organization know those desired outcomes. Seems obvious, but it's most definitely not always done.

If you think this is obvious, ask everyone in your work group to write down the three most important business outcomes your group or organization is working to achieve this year. Then compare the answers. Many times I've seen a group generate a huge number of important outcomes. This means the members don't agree on what is most important. It's impossible to implement an effective strategy without knowing the most important measures of success because the point of a strategy is to generate specific results.

Step Four: Understand Your Current Corporate Strategy

The final component to clarify before you select your strategy is the corporate strategy your organization currently uses. Remember, a corporate strategy defines an organization and the way in which it adds value to the desired customers. It is the statement that guides all decision-making in an organization.

In order to understand whether your corporate strategy is effective, you need to know what it is. I'm not talking necessarily about the corporate strategy hanging on the wall or written in your business brochures or posted on your Web site or placed in your annual report. I'm talking about what actually guides decision making in your organization today. You can accomplish this by completing the following statement: We are a _______ organization that provides _______ to _______ through _______.

The Walt Disney Company could complete that sentence by saying, "We are an entertainment organization that provides quality entertainment to all members of the family through television shows, theme parks, films, cruises, ice skating shows, videos, Web sites, and licensed products."

Results Clarification Exercise: Defining Desired Outcomes

When you define your desired outcomes, you can determine if you have selected the right strategy, and whether or not you are implementing it well. These business outcomes could fall into, but are not limited to, the following areas:

Financial

- What revenue do we want to generate?
- What do we want our operating income/cash flow to be this year?
- What do we want our operating costs to be this year?

Market Share

- What do we want our client mix to look like this year?
- What percentage of our business do we want each client to represent next year?
- What percentage of our business do we want our current clients to represent next year?
- What percentage of our business do we want each revenue-producing activity to generate next year?

Long-Term Growth Potential

- What products/services do we want to develop to generate sustainable, profitable growth in the future?
- What percentage of next year's operating budget will we commit to developing these potential products/services?

Your answers don't need to be perfect down to the minutest details. You just want to emphasize the types of business outcomes that are the most important for your organization to achieve in the next year. For example, if it is decided that diversifying your client base is a critically important business outcome, then you might set a goal that no client, or type of client, will represent more than 20 percent of your revenue.

Continued

Continue to build your list of questions for clarifying desired business outcomes. Just make sure you're focused on business outcomes and not on internal activities. For example, hiring 50 new employees is a goal, but it's not a business outcome. If someone said that was his goal, I would ask, "What business outcome are you hoping to generate as a result of hiring 50 new employees?"

Starbucks might complete the sentence by saying, "We are a retail organization that provides high-quality coffee and music to a wide range of adults through our relaxing, comfortable, and conveniently located restaurants."

If you ask 20 employees and 20 customers to complete this statement for your organization, you will get a much clearer idea of your actual business strategy. Look at the commonalities between their answers and craft the best statement you can to reflect the reality of what they say. In Step Five, you will use that statement as a point of comparison to other possible strategies in deciding what would be the best strategy for your organization or business unit as you go forward.

Step Five: Make a Strategic Decision

The question now becomes "Is this the most effective strategy for leveraging our organizational strengths, addressing the needs of the marketplace, and generating our desired business outcomes? If not, what strategy should we select?" In other words, has your organization selected the best fulcrum point? The other key question to ask is "If this is the best strategy, what other people do we need in our organization, if any, to execute it, and what desired outcomes, if any, do we need to adjust?" I'll talk more about talent management in the next chapter.

THE SIX STRATEGIC OPTIONS

There are four components to consider in terms of developing an appropriate strategy: your organization's assets, your desired business outcomes, the market conditions, and your current strategy. While you can't change the market conditions, you can change your organization, the outcomes you decide to pursue, and your corporate strategy. Consequently, you have a variety of options to choose from when you are developing a strategy for your organization.

Option #1: Change nothing
Option #2: Change your corporate strategy
Option #3: Change your desired business outcomes
Option #4: Change your organization
Option #5: Change two out of the three
Option #6: Change all three

Option #1: Change Nothing

If you want to accelerate your organization's most important business outcomes, a valid decision may be to change nothing. Deciding to keep your organization the same, to keep pursuing the same types of customers, and to keep using the same approach with your customers may very well be the smartest approach. Of course, you can still work to improve your organization, your understanding of your customers' changing needs, and the execution of your strategy.

Option #2: Change Your Corporate Strategy

You might decide you have the right organization for your desired customers, but the way in which your organization adds value to them needs to be changed. In that case, the question becomes "What corporate strategy should we use instead?" Remember, an effective strategy optimally leverages your organization's assets, adds differentiating value to your desired customers, and generates significant and sustainable improvements in your desired outcomes.

Option #3: Change Your Desired Business Outcomes

This really is not as easy as it sounds. Regardless of your success with your current customers, you have built up a certain amount of "client equity" in the marketplace. People associate your organization with serving certain types of people. These associations generate referrals, testimonials, and recommendations that lead these people to you.

If you suddenly change your focus in terms of the business outcomes you're pursuing, you may create some confusion in the marketplace. You may receive calls from prospects that no longer fit your screens. And you're going to have to work to build relationships with new types of customers.

Having said all that, sometimes this is the decision that makes all the difference in the world for a corporation. Deciding to diversify your customer base, optimize short-term cash flow, increase long-term ROI, or any number of other desired outcomes can enhance the relationship between your organization's strengths, its approach to the market, and the results it generates. Even though it's painful, going after a different type of outcome may be the best strategic decision you can make.

Option #4: Change Your Organization

Regardless of the size of your company, this is no small trick. We're talking about changing the values, passions, skills, resources, and/or knowledge in your organization. However, in many situations, this needs to be done in order to fully execute the strategic direction for your organization. If you choose this option, where do you begin? I suggest you take each of the five variables within your organization (values, passions, skills, resources, and knowledge) and decide which ones you can keep the same and which ones need to be changed.

If you decide you need to change the values and passions in the organization, you're really talking about changing your corporate culture. This is doable, but not an easy thing to accomplish. In order to change organizational values, you need to change the behaviors you recognize and reward, you need to have role models at high levels demonstrating those new behaviors, and you need to provide negative consequences when people use old behaviors. This is very hard for some people to accept and many people will leave.

In order to change passions, which are the things that get people really excited, it may mean you have to hire different people. Employees can't fake their passions. If you've built an organization of people who are passionate about improving manufacturing processes and you now want an organization where people are passionate about customer service, you may not be able to flip a switch and get these same people to change their focus with enthusiasm.

If you want to modify the skills and knowledge in your organization, you can provide training and development for your current employees, hire new people who bring the desired skills and knowledge, or do both. In any case, it's a costly proposition, but it may be the step you need to really gain leverage out of your current strategy.

If you want to change your resources, you will need to alter your patterns of investment. This takes time and effort to do effectively.

Option #5: Change Two Out of the Three

This option really provides you with three choices:

- Change your organization and your corporate strategy, and go after the same desired outcomes.
- Change your corporate strategy and the outcomes you pursue, and leave your organization the same.
- Change your organization and the outcomes you pursue and stick with your corporate strategy.

All three choices are viable. Keep in mind a strategy can only be executed if the organization in place has the capacity to execute it. No strategy can be executed by a "hoped for organization." First, the organization has to be in place, and then the strategy can be implemented. Many times, executives establish a really exciting strategy and then blame its failure on the organization's inability to execute. Clearly, those executives missed the point. First, the necessary organization has to be created before a strategy can be effectively executed.

Option #6: Change All Three

Essentially, this means you're starting from scratch. You're changing your organization, your approach to the marketplace, and the outcomes you're pursuing. There really are two reasons to do this:

- Your current situation has completely failed.
- Even though your current situation has been moderately successful, you believe your organization will only decline if it continues on its current path.

In the first scenario, you will want to change everything as quickly as possible. Cut your losses, apply the lessons you've learned, and start over. If you and the other key decision makers have made mistakes on all three fronts, then admit the error of your ways and start over. You'll never achieve greatness sticking with a completely flawed business approach.

In the second scenario, you can reasonably buy yourself some time as you transition your business. Begin with your organization. Start to hire and develop the type of employees you want to execute a new strategy. Once the necessary employees, incentive programs, and management approaches are in place, then you can begin to implement the new strategy and direct it toward your new desired outcomes.

In time, you can shift a higher and higher percentage of your employees toward these new desired values, passions, skills, and knowledge either through replacing your current workforce or retraining your current employees. By steadily shifting your organization, your strategy and your desired outcomes, you will steadily create a completely new business scenario. Your organization will develop a different brand, a different reputation in the marketplace.

This really takes double effort because not only do you need to shift your organization, strategy, and desired outcomes, but you also have to be patient enough to allow this shift to take place in the minds of your customers and prospects. And before I make this sound too easy, keep in mind the strain this type of shift places on current and new employees.

Current employees will likely want to hold on to some of the old ways of doing things while new employees will likely push for new methods. This culture clash can be agonizing and can create an enormous amount of wasted time, effort, and money. Stay focused as you transition from one phase to the next, and keep the train moving forward.

Choosing an Option

The key question to answer in selecting one of these six options is "Why did you select that option?" No one option is better than another, but you need to determine why you've decided to do what you're about to do. All three variables (your organization, your desired outcomes, and your corporate strategy) are dependent on one another for success.

Ignoring any one of them will likely result in failure to generate significant, sustainable, and profitable growth. However, when all the pieces connect properly, you create an organization with extraordinary leverage in adding value to targeted customers that continually delivers profitable growth.

FOUR WAYS TO DEVELOP A STRATEGY

If you decide to develop a new strategy, here are four ways to actually do it. Strategy development processes are the poetry of business. Some people like Robert Frost, some like Maya Angelou, and some like Led Zeppelin. Every company seems to develop their business strategies in different ways.

Before I explain these four strategy development processes, I do want to recommend several books that I have found useful in understanding how to develop a business strategy and a tactical plan for operating within that strategy: *Blue Ocean Strategy* by W. Chan Kim and Renée Mauborgne, *The Discipline of Market Leaders* by Michael Treacy and Fred Wiersema, *Profit from the Core* by Chris Zook with James Allen, *Beyond the Core* by Chris Zook, *Managing for Results* by Peter Drucker, and *Execution and Confronting Reality* by Larry Bossidy and Ram Charan. I think each of them brings some useful insights on the topic. In the end, I encourage you to establish an approach to developing a business strategy that works for you.

Define Your Approach to the Marketplace

One way to develop a business strategy is to define how your company positions itself. In their excellent book, *The Discipline of Market Leaders,* Michael Treacy and Fred Wiersema explain three ways to move into the position of a market leader. They call the three approaches *product excellence, operational excellence,* and *customer intimacy.*

They define product excellent companies as having the best product on the market and always improving their product at a faster rate than the competition. The goal of product excellent companies is to make their own products obsolete before the competition can do it. They provide very high quality products at a relatively high price to the customer. Apple Inc. is a great example of a product excellent company.

Treacy and Wiersema define operationally excellent companies as those companies that produce massive volumes of products or services in a very efficient manner at relatively low prices to customers. McDonald's and Wal-Mart are examples of operationally excellent companies.

Finally, they define customer intimate companies as companies that gain extraordinary insights into their customers and provide their customers with the best total solution for what they are trying to achieve, and they provide those solutions at a relatively high price to the customer. Home Depot was listed in the book as an example of being customer intimate.

The goal is to be good in two out of the three areas and to be outstanding in one of them. If you try to be great in two areas, you end up diluting your efforts. For your company or business unit, which of these three approaches do you want to concentrate on? Making that decision and sticking to it can have a significant impact on many aspects of your organization, but it can also greatly clarify for your customers the value they receive from your organization.

Differentiate Your Approach

The second way you can develop your business strategy is find a way to distinguish yourself from your competition. If you have virtually the same strategy as your competition, then you will always battle it out on the ability to execute within that strategy. If the execution of the two companies is very similar, then you will put your organization into an elongated price war. That's not a fun place to be.

In their book *Blue Ocean Strategy*, W. Chan Kim and Renée Mauborgne do a beautiful job of explaining how to find a strategy that differentiates you from the competition so you are not competing on price. Their concept of a blue ocean strategy is an analogy about sharks. Imagine two sharks fighting. One dies but the other one gets cut very badly and loses a lot of blood. That's a red ocean. Now imagine that one of the sharks finds a space all to itself out in the middle of the ocean. Because there's no fighting, the water remains clear. That's a blue ocean.

In the marketplace, you create a red ocean when you use the exact same strategy as your competitor. Both companies get bloodied. You use a blue ocean strategy when you find a unique approach to the marketplace that allows you not to fight directly with other companies. When deploying a blue ocean strategy, you have the market space to yourself.

Here are two key questions I learned from Kim and Mauborgne's book. First, what are the factors organizations similar to yours compete on from the customers' perspectives? Choose up to five key factors that people consider when choosing between your organization and your competition.

Second, what is the offering level that customers currently receive on each of these factors from your organization and from your top two competitors? Grade each factor for you and your top two competitors on a scale of one to five, with five being excellent and one being terrible. Compare your organization to your competition.

The goal now is to find an approach to the market that differentiates you from your competition. In order to do that, choose one factor that you would emphasize in your organization for improvement and one factor that you would deemphasize in your organization. Of course, make certain that the factor you're emphasizing adds meaningful value to your customer and the area that you're deemphasizing is not going to ruin your relationship with customers. Also make certain that in choosing the area to emphasize and the one to deemphasize, you are truly differentiating yourself from your competitors.

When Dell Inc. first entered the computer market, they deemphasized selling through retail stores and product excellence, which were the two areas where the competition performed at their best. However, Dell did emphasize selling direct to customers at dramatically lower prices.

Dell created massive savings by reducing inventory and avoiding the middle person. In turn, they passed those savings on to the customers. For many years, this served as a blue ocean strategy in which

Dell had no competition and grew exponentially. Today Dell may very well have to recreate their strategy for the next decade.

Louis Vuitton used the opposite strategy. It separated itself from other luggage companies by making incredibly high quality bags at incredibly high prices. No one strategy is a cure-all. You decide on the strategy—the approach to the marketplace—that will be most effective for your organization.

After you decide which factor to emphasize and which one to deemphasize, then describe the value your company would bring to customers in ten words or less. This will help you determine whether or not you have a clear and concise strategy that will effectively affect behaviors and decisions in your organization in a way that will generate sustainable and profitable growth.

Stay True to Your Core Business *and* Move Strategically Beyond Your Core

The third way to develop your strategy is to look at the core of your business and consider if you should move beyond your core. Apple's core business is personal computers, and they extended that core profitably by creating the iPod and iTunes. PepsiCo's core business is beverages, and they extended that core by getting into the snack category and selling Fritos, Doritos, Tostitos, and Sunchips.

One of the hardest questions in all business is "When do we stick with our core business, and when do we move beyond our core?" There are no cookie cutter answers to that question. I do encourage you to answer these two questions:

- How would you describe your core business?
- What else can your organization profitably do that connects to your core business and would add value to your desired customer base?

For more insight on this topic read Chris Zook's books *Profit from the Core* and *Beyond the Core.*

Compare and Contrast with the Best of the Best

The final way to develop your strategy is to look at the strategies pursued by model companies. The purpose of this section is to give you a breadth of different business strategies. My hope is this will help you to see whether or not a company already exists that you can use as a model for your strategic approach to the market. Here are twelve approaches companies use:

1. The democratization strategy. eBay democratized the auctioneering business and IKEA democratized buying quality, stylish furniture. This approach is not about offering the lowest prices. It is about expanding the horizons of millions of people who otherwise could not operate in the given arena.

2. Depth and breadth. The Walt Disney Company so dominates family entertainment, both in terms of the breadth of ways they provide entertainment and the depth with which they deliver each method, that "Disney" is synonymous with some forms of entertainment.

3. The friendliness factor. It is possible for a company to use "friendliness" as an economic advantage over competitors who simply aren't as friendly? Corporations using this approach understand that few people can deliver friendly service day in and day out. Nordstrom's and Marriott stand out in their respective industries because of the extraordinarily friendly service they provide on an ongoing basis.

4. Price matters. Budget Rent A Car and Wal-Mart are examples of corporations that use low price as a competitive advantage. This corporate strategy continues to attract customers and generate profitable growth through small margins and massive volume.

5. The value of elitism. Louis Vuitton and Mercedes-Benz demonstrate the capacity for profitable growth founded on some consumers' need to feel part of an elite group. The status derived from an "elite purchase" is critically important for these consumers. Organizations that successfully overcome the vast challenges of remaining an elite brand can enjoy extraordinary customer loyalty and highly emotionally charged purchases.

6. Iconic status. Rarely do organizations fall in this category, but when they do, they enjoy a rare blessing. The blessing is the extraordinary demand for their products or services that remains constant for years and years. Coca-Cola and Microsoft represent the rewards of having reached iconic status.

Of course, it is hard work to remain an icon forever, and you have to be open to adjusting your strategy. Otherwise you leave yourself open to a strategic attack such as what PepsiCo has done to Coca-Cola and Google has done to Microsoft.

7. The neighborhood brands. This corporate strategy is as old as Tupperware and Mary Kay Cosmetics and as new as Pampered Chef, Southern Living, and Creative Memories. The idea quite literally is to get potential customers to open their doors and invite your organization into their homes. This creates a unique advantage over traditional retail stores, but it also provides challenges in the area of marketing and distribution.

8. "I feel a need for speed." These organizations understand that, all things being equal, they separate themselves from their competitors by delivering the product or service faster than any other organization. Dell and QuikTrip gas stations provide maniacal emphasis on speed and delight their customers all the way to the bank.

9. Aspirational qualities. Ralph Lauren, Starbucks, and L'Oreal provide products that embrace consumers' desire to inhabit a loftier position or a more relaxing lifestyle. This age-old focus on providing hope for millions of consumers brings with it a variety of challenges in terms of maintaining staying power in the minds of the target audience.

10. The family traditions. John Deere and General Motors sell products that are promoted from one generation to the next. Organizations using this strategy focus on items that have been ingrained in the minds of family members. They emphasize how these items are part of a family's legacy and have historic value. This strategy requires both a great deal of time to develop such a reputation and a great deal of care in maintaining the integrity of the brand.

11. The best and always getting better. Organizations in this category separate themselves from their competitors by developing a reputation for always improving their current work at a rate faster than any competitor can maintain.

Intel and Nokia have successfully used this approach to differentiate their products and generate sustainable, profitable growth. The challenge is not to get stuck in a niche that sucks the life out of an organization like quicksand. Another challenge is not to remain in an industry that has become obsolete. This concept of fanatical continuous improvement has to be applied to a general concept and not to a single product.

12. Combined strategies. The secret to McDonald's success over the past 50 plus years has been its ability to deliver quality products with fast, friendly, and accurate service in clean and inviting environments. These strategies simply cannot be unbundled and delivered sporadically. As you might imagine, that level of expectation put on 30,000 business units is pretty tough to live up to every day with every customer, but that's how you become one of the best brands in the world.

Organizations deploying a "combined strategy" approach are very different from organizations that change their strategy on an annual basis. Their combination of strategies actually becomes a single strategy in and of itself because this unique combination remains constant for the organization.

At this point, it's decision time. Given the conditions of the marketplace, what strategy do you believe would best leverage your organization's or business unit's assets in a way that will generate your desired outcomes? You can choose the one you currently have, or another one. However, you must clarify a strategy or set of strategies for the different areas of your business before any effective planning or execution can take place.

THOUGHTS ON THE PLANNING PROCESS

Once the business objectives and strategy have been determined, you can begin to put in place the remaining components of your business plan, which are the tactics and planned activities.

Sometimes groups I've observed in establishing a strategic plan have wasted a huge amount of time and energy debating over what a strategy, a tactic, and a planned action are. This semantics death spiral ends up driving people over the edge, and then they just want to get the whole darn process over with as fast as possible.

Keep it simple. A strategy is about what to do; a tactic is about how to do it. Planned actions are the actual steps that will be carried out for a given tactic. If the strategy is to diversify your client base, the tactics might include defining and pursuing new market segments, creating a referral bonus program with existing customers, and redesigning your Web site in order to appeal to a broader audience. The planned activities would clarify what steps need to be carried out for each of these tactics.

Two important filters need to be kept in mind for tactics and planned activities.

First, do each of the chosen tactics truly fit within and support the strategy?

It does no good to establish a strategy if the tactics you select don't fit within that strategy. As you consider a tactic, ask yourself if it supports the strategy. If your goal is to increase short-term cash flow and your strategy is to focus on the basics of providing great customer service, then the tactic of buying your largest competitor would not make sense right now.

Second, have you established planned activities that support each tactic?

A tactic is a broad statement. Your tactic might be to implement training courses across the business on the fundamentals of great customer service. However, nothing gets accomplished until that tactic is converted into planned activities.

If you get a "no" or a "maybe" as the answer to either of these two questions, then go back and discuss the tactics and planned activities again with the members of the Leadership Council until you can answer "yes" to both questions.

Once you have finalized your strategies, tactics, and planned activities, you are in a position to focus on managing the process of execution, which was explained in Chapter 9.

ACCELERATION ADVICE

From an Interview with Karen Wells, McDonald's Corporation, Vice President of U.S. Strategy

I coached Karen over a four-year period as she moved from regional vice president of operations to regional vice president/general manager to vice president of U.S. strategy for McDonald's. While working in the regions, Karen was responsible for the performance of more than 500 McDonald's restaurants. Her perspective on strategy is based on real-world business situations in local, regional, and national situations. Her insights come from the day-to-day responsibility of working with multiple constituents to develop and implement a strategy that generates sustainable, profitable growth.

Coughlin: *Karen, what do you think makes a strategy effective in terms of achieving sustainable, profitable growth? What do you think makes a strategy ineffective?*

Wells: An effective strategy is focused, aligned with your core competencies, results-oriented, and quantifiable. Most importantly, an effective strategy must be supported by your management team. Ineffective strategies typically lack one or all of the above. The objective is too abstract or is not measurable. Or, it's completely unrealistic or not supported by senior management. Effective strategies increase clarity, and ineffective strategies increase confusion. Companies that are successful concentrate on just a few things and make sure those things connect to consumer needs and wants.

Coughlin: *How does a group develop an effective strategy?*

Wells: Know the customer, your core competencies, and how your products and/or services may fulfill the customer's unmet wants or needs. Assess your management team's vision for the future and gain their support. Our job is to crystallize this input into a clearly defined, consumer-focused strategy.

Coughlin: *How does a group of decision makers gain buy-in for the strategy from the people who will be responsible for implementing the tactics that fall under the strategy?*

Wells: The key is to engage stakeholders early in the process. While you're developing a strategy, there are times when you need to look at it from a tactical perspective. You might say, "Here's the big picture. Now, here's an example of what that might look like in the field. What do you think?" Or we might say, "If we went this route, here's what it might look like in the future. What are your thoughts?" This method facilitates understanding and visualization of the strategy and gains support, as well.

There is also a level of stakeholder engagement necessary in order gain buy-in to the final decisions. This does not mean that the entire organization is involved, but utilizing key stakeholders as sounding boards closest to the customer creates an even better strategy, notwithstanding consumer insights as your starting point.

Coughlin: *In your experience, what have you seen that makes for the successful implementation of a strategic plan, and what have you seen that gets in the way of the successful implementation of a strategic plan?*

Wells: Key stakeholders need to understand and buy in so there is a seamless focus and execution on the strategic areas or buckets of growth. In other words, everyone knows the key strategic areas we're focused on and every stakeholder is working toward executing in those strategic areas.

The opposite is what makes a strategy ineffective in its implementation. When stakeholders are scattered in their endorsement and execution against the strategy, you are back to nice words on a sheet of paper. Their efforts are not aligned and do not intersect under a common theme or strategy. It's better to have some overlap and have people working on the same end goal than to have people working in silos and going down different paths toward different end goals.

Coughlin: *When you first stepped into your role as the VP of U.S. strategy, what did you learn?*

Wells: Because previous efforts to focus on long-term growth and innovation were not as successful as we wanted them to be, we wanted to take a very methodical approach. As part of my development in this role, I purposely worked on short-term projects that could be implemented in the first year or two. It was not immediately clear what I would gain by this approach. However, in hindsight, it was paramount for my matriculation into our corporate office. It allowed me to build relationships and coalitions with those who would later help our team develop and implement the long-range strategy. It's mission critical to gain momentum in terms of building relationships, achieving short-term wins, and learning what does and doesn't work in terms of developing a strategy.

Again, you must have a level of engagement with the people who are responsible for understanding and implementing the strategy. If you only stand up in front of the group and talk about strategy and don't engage the people throughout the organization or know what is really happening on the frontline, then you probably won't have credibility with your audience, resulting in a highly likely ineffective strategy.

On a final note, there are times as leaders (particularly in a crisis) when strategy must be decided very quickly and executed very rapidly to change the trajectory of the business. An effective leader with credibility with stakeholders can do this, with very little engagement, and be successful. A great example is when Jim Cantalupo, our former CEO, took the helm of the company in late 2002 and our stock was at an all-time low. He immediately changed McDonald's global strategy to be "Better, not just Bigger." This was focused and easy to understand throughout the organization. He then utilized consumer insights to help determine how we were to get better and the rest is history. It is now a textbook case of a major turnaround for a Fortune 500 company.

Acceleration Tips

Strategic planning is an important process in accelerating the achievement of your organization's most important business outcomes. Keep in mind a few points as you build your strategic plan:

- ✓ Before you establish a strategy for deciding what to do and what not to do, increase your awareness of your organization, your competition, the marketplace, and consumer trends.
- ✓ Make the strategy so clear that it slices through all the possible activities and clarifies what activities could support it and what activities would not support it.
- ✓ Select tactics and planned activities that support your strategy.
- ✓ Do less in order to achieve more.

Chapter

14

USE TALENT MANAGEMENT

"Where Do We Find the Right People?"

About three months after I started recommending Jim Collins's book *Good to Great* to all my clients, the Question started coming at me.

In a chapter called "First Who, Then What," Jim Collins does a magnificent job explaining that the most important role of management is to get the right people in the right positions within your organization and to get the wrong people out of your organization.

Everywhere I went I heard people quote Collins by saying, "We have to get the right people on the bus, put them in the right seats, and get the wrong people off the bus." They were as excited as if they had solved the Da Vinci code. Once the importance of the idea began to sink in, a far more complex reality surfaced. That's when they started to ask the Question.

Clients from companies of all sizes would say to me, "Dan, I understand that we need to put the right people in the right positions, but where do we find the right people?" It was easy to say that getting the right people in the right positions and getting rid of the wrong people was the best way to move an organization forward, but it was an altogether different thing to know what a "best person" would look like for a given organization and to know where to find him or her.

Over the years, this topic simply wouldn't go away. And then I realized we were all discussing bits and pieces of the most important topic there is in terms of generating business acceleration. That topic is applying talent management.

The best organizations in the world are talent magnets. Places like Harvard University, the Walt Disney Company, Google, and GE are continually great because they continually attract and retain the type of specific talent they need to thrive as organizations. During the heyday of Microsoft, Bill Gates once said that if a competitor took his best 100 employees, then Microsoft would quickly fall to number two.

In August 2005 I heard Walt Jocketty, the general manager of the St. Louis Cardinals baseball team, give a luncheon presentation in St. Louis. He had just flown back to St. Louis from a game in Los Angeles the night before. He arrived around 6 AM. His voice was almost gone as he spoke to the audience.

His opening line was, "We're in the talent business." He went on to explain how every aspect of the Cardinals is focused on putting the best possible team on the field. He explained the Cardinals' approach to scouting, free agency, and following up on every lead.

He had an outfielder, So Taguchi, from Japan; an infielder who played poorly for years in the Pittsburgh Pirates organization, but whom blossomed with the Cardinals; another infielder he found through Dave Stewart, one of manager Tony LaRussa's former players; and an infielder, Scott Rolen, from a small town in Indiana. The team's best pitcher, Chris Carpenter, sat out the year before he joined the Cardinals with an injury. And they found their superstar, Albert Pujols, at a junior college in Kansas City. No one else went after him.

Jocketty gave the finest speech I've ever heard about finding talent. His point was that the most important job in any organization is to attract and retain talent. In clear and vivid terms, he explained how you have to look into every nook and cranny to find talent. He didn't say the player had to come from a certain geographic area or have a certain background. He said he simply looked for talent that could play together and compete for a championship. During the previous two seasons, the Cardinals had won more than 200 games. It quickly dawned on me that every organization is in the talent business.

Business talent is the capacity to help your organization add more value to customers and generate significant, sustainable, and profitable growth.

We live in a society obsessed with labels: men, women, blacks, whites, Hispanics, Asians, extroverts, introverts, tall people, short people, fat people, skinny people, number crunchers, touchy/feely people, gay, straight, liberal, conservative, atheist, Jewish, Protestant, Catholic, Christian, Baptist, Muslim, Buddhist, the Greatest Generation, Baby Boomers, Generation X, the Y Generation, and so on, and so on.

However, none of those labels mean anything relative to talent. I'll never forget the time when another consultant who wanted to work with me on a strategy project asked for my Myers-Briggs personality type so she could match me up with a corresponding personality type in her office. Yipes. I ran.

I encourage you to toss out the labels and search for talent. Now some people might read that and say, "Fine, let's go back to the 1950s and just have white males make up my entire organization. Since labels don't matter, let's not bother trying to have a diverse workforce." I would say just the opposite.

If you want to compete in the current world of digitization, globalization, outsourcing, insourcing, opensourcing, supply chain management, and informing that Tom Friedman talks about in his magnificent book *The World Is Flat,* you better learn to look for talent under every imaginable label. Personally, I have worked with or observed enormously talented people who had an endless list of different labels.

Thirty years ago an organization in the United States could thrive while not looking for talent regardless of the label, but folks, the world has changed. The all-white boys' club has given way to an explosion of diverse business talent, the American Century has become the Global Century, and the Information Economy has given way to the Creative Economy. What you need now is an army of talented people who can figure out how to add more value to your customers. That army should not depend on any label other than the label that says talent.

TEN KEYS TO TALENT MANAGEMENT

1. Define Talent

Identify the characteristics you want in your employees. Here are examples of characteristics I hear managers say they want in their employees: technically strong, honest, acts with integrity, stays customer-focused, can collaborate with others to generate a desired outcome, willing to search for best ideas in other industries, can stay focused long enough to get the job done well, can effectively influence others, and is open to improving as an individual and as a group member.

Notice that none of those characteristics has anything to do with age, gender, race, height, size, geographic area, culture, sexual orientation, or religious affiliation. The goal is to attract and retain as much talent as you possibly can. The organizations that do that will continue to thrive in the years to come.

Job one: define the talent you want in your organization. Make a list of what you want in terms of talent for a given position. Set your standards high and be as clear as possible. Just make sure your descriptions are not based on fixed labels such as gender, height, or size, but rather on intangibles such as the ability to work well with others, a desire to learn, possessing certain technical skills, and having a passion for adding value to other people.

2. Attract Talent

Once you know what you want in terms of values, technical skills, social skills, and experience, begin to get the word out in as many ways as you can. Let your entire management team know the types of people you are looking for in certain positions. That way they can be on the lookout at all times.

Describe the characteristics you're looking for in your organization's monthly newsletter for employees and in any publications you are putting out to the general public. Post the description for your desired new employees on your Web site. In your marketing budget for your organization's products and services, build in some money to market for the types of employees you want in your organization.

Create a massive radar system that gathers leads from as many different possible sources as you can. And then follow up on every lead. Amassing the right type of people in your organization can generate sustainable, profitable growth for many years to come.

Finding those right people is hard, hard work. A lot of organizations are fighting over the same few people. Just as Walt Jocketty had to turn over every rock to find his players, you need to look everywhere to find your best employees.

3. Select Talent

I love shopping at Nordstrom's. They give unbelievable customer service. One time I was there with my then three-year-old son, Ben. I was picking up five pairs of shoes that I had dropped off to be polished. After I paid for the shoes, I leaned over to pick up the bag, and the man behind the counter said, "Can I help you?" I thought he was going to put the bag under my arm so I could hold Ben's hand. Instead, he picked up the bag, walked through Nordstrom's, walked out into the parking lot, and put the bag of shoes in the trunk of my car, while I held Ben's hand. Now that's customer service.

The next week I went to the manager of Nordstrom's and said, "Where do you find so many friendly people?" She said, "Oh, it's our interview process." I looked at her incredulously and said, "What in the world do you ask?" She said, "We ask if the person is a compulsive smiler. If the person doesn't start smiling immediately, then we probably don't hire them."

Bingo. That's how you select the talent you want. First, know what you're looking for. Make a list of the characteristics you want for an employee in a given position. Then build interview questions, role plays, and case studies that you can use during an interview with a candidate.

Do this work *before* you meet with a prospective employee. Otherwise, you might end up falling for a person based on her or his charisma, charm, or good looks when in fact they have none of the talent you need for a certain position.

Take your time when hiring a new person. You will save yourself and your organization an enormous amount of time and effort by taking longer to hire the right person than by rushing to a decision and hiring the wrong person.

Have a few people interview the candidate, and then hold an open conversation so everyone gets to weigh in on the person who was interviewed. Remember Jim Collins's admonition: get the right people on the bus and get the wrong people off the bus. This mindset should be in place from the very first interview. If the candidate is not for your organization's bus, kick him off before the relationship goes any further.

4. Place Talent

Put people in a place where they will be challenged and where they can leverage their strengths and passions in a way that will help generate better sustainable results for your organization.

If you meet those simple requirements, you will enhancc thc individual's skills and produce better sustainable business results. It's this combination of meeting the needs of the organization and the individual that defines your success of getting the right people in the right positions. You have to meet both the needs of the organization and the individual, and not one or the other.

5. Develop Talent

Talent development means increasing an employee's capacity to help your organization add value to customers and generate sustainable, profitable growth. The most general form of talent development is to offer training courses on specific topics. A training course provides information and hands-on development of some specific technical skill whether it's selling, managing, or working in a manufacturing plant.

An in-house mentoring program is another approach to talent development. A more experienced member of a group pairs up with a less experienced member in order to provide insights that might otherwise take years for the less experienced person to develop.

Spending time with peers in other functions of your business can accelerate understanding of the business. The time invested may seem like a lot in the short term, but it really pays off over the long term.

In my role as an executive coach, I always tell my clients that my focus is on working with them to accelerate the achievement of high priority business outcomes for their organization. However, along the way to improving those desired outcomes, the individual will enhance certain aspects of his or her ability to add value to other people. This same thing occurs when a manager challenges an employee to achieve a meaningful business goal. Along the path to achievement, certain skills will be honed and new ones developed.

6. Evaluate Talent

When it comes to providing effective performance evaluations, I think most organizations could achieve a lot more by doing a lot less. Far too often I believe HR departments have, with the best of intentions, created performance development systems that are more complicated than college calculus.

They have managers fill out a seven- to eight-page performance evaluation for a single employee covering a mountain of core competencies, leadership competencies, advanced competencies, and who knows what else. The descriptions of performance include words like significant, outstanding, strategic leader, advanced, competent, and above average. More often than not, employees are left wondering why they received a certain word over another possible description and what the words really meant to start with.

Keep in mind the whole point of providing an evaluation is to help the employee do more of what she is good at, do less of what she is doing that gets in the way of achieving strong and sustainable results, and to start doing those things that will improve performance and results.

It's been my experience that performance evaluations tend to cause employees to miss the forest for the trees. They get so bummed out over a certain rating on an obscure competency that they lose sight of what they need to keep doing, stop doing, and start doing that would actually improve their impact on the desired business outcomes.

I suggest that managers can execute an effective performance evaluation with three questions:

- What does the employee do well in terms of improving sustainable business results and why do you feel that way?
- What does the employee do that gets in the way of improving sustainable business results and why do you feel that way?
- What could the employee do that would have an even greater impact on improving sustainable business results and why do you feel that way?

That's it. If you as the manager can clearly answer those three questions based on observed behavior, then the employee can decide what he will or will not do based on this input.

The advantage of this approach is it eliminates much of the confusion that is created by long and complicated performance evaluation forms. Invariably after a manager has filled out one of the seven-page forms, the employee still wants to know the answers to the three questions I just outlined.

7. Enhance Talent

Inertia is a real problem inside corporations. Isaac Newton's first law of motion, which is normally given as the definition of inertia, states that every object will remain at rest or in uniform motion in a straight line unless compelled to change its state by the action of an external force. I think this law applies in business, as well. Too often employees get the reputation of being good at some activity whether it's selling, strategic planning, organizing large meetings, or developing new hires. As a result, a person can end up doing the same basic job for years and years.

That creates two big problems. First, the organization suffers because it ends up paying the individual more to do the same job as the years go by. That's not a good return on investment. Second, it robs the individual from expanding his talent and being able to take on greater responsibilities.

Work to enhance the talent level of each employee. Notice what happens when a new person is hired. She is given substantial orientation, additional training, and a mentor to help guide her through her first six months.

Imagine if that same level of attention was paid to every employee at least every three years. For example, an employee with 15 years experience would take on a new responsibility, go through a full orientation, receive additional training when needed, and be provided with a mentor to help ease the transition. And she would have done that five times during those 15 years.

8. Promote Talent

Ripe apples need to be plucked from the tree or they fall and rot. Great employees need to be promoted in order to re-create the cycle of talent development. They need to be challenged and supported. They need to find new ways to apply their strengths and passions. Even if it's a lateral move, put your employees in positions that will provide them with a new perspective and new opportunities to develop and make a difference.

9. Retain Talent

You will lose some very talented people, and that's not all bad. If you're losing your top players because they are going on to run top business units, then you'll know you're doing something right and you'll attract more people who want that type of development.

However, if you lose too much talent, then you are essentially pouring a huge amount of money, time, and energy down the drain. Great players want to be around great players. By retaining your most talented employees, you will attract more talented employees. Money is certainly important to everyone, but that in and of itself will not help you keep the type of talent you need to accelerate as an organization.

In addition to rewarding people financially, I think the best way to retain your talent is to maintain ongoing communication with these individuals. Frequently ask for their opinion on what they think makes the organization successful, and what they think would make the organization more successful in the future. Beyond just getting them to do the daily work tasks, engage their minds and creativity in moving the business forward. People want to feel important. Make sure they know they are part of the solution, and not part of the problem.

Conversely, if you want to keep your best performers, then be willing to let go of poor performers. Poor performers are people who don't want to do their jobs and are not capable of doing their jobs. When a poor performer keeps his job no matter how incompetent he is or how much he doesn't care about his performance, then the top performers will likely want to leave the organization.

10. Diversify Talent

This is so much easier said than done. Creating a diverse workforce in terms of skills, knowledge, experience, race, culture, gender, big picture thinking, and the ability to execute well is one of the keys to accelerating as an organization. If you have 20 employees with the same strengths, passions, and background, then you really have one employee 20 times.

By hiring a widely diverse group of people, you plant new skills and perspectives into your organization. Other people can now learn those new skills and perspectives, and they can spread throughout the organization. If you never plant any diverse ideas, then no great new ideas ever flourish and grow.

Diversity does not equal minority hiring. Diversity means seeking out diverse types of people who can add a unique flair to your organization. Yes, minority hiring is very important and having various races, genders, and ethnic backgrounds does help to increase the diversity of perspective, but it is not the only way to create a diverse workforce.

You can diversify your current workforce by moving people into different functions every few years. Some of the most talented executives I've known have spent long periods of their careers in sales, marketing, operations, customer service, and market research. By seeing the business from multiple viewpoints, they developed diverse perspectives with which to approach any situation.

Acceleration Tips

- ✓ In sports, coaches know that if both teams work hard, the team with the greater talent will win more often. The same is true with symphonies, cruise ship staffs, and television programs. If you have more diverse talent, then more often than not you will win.
- ✓ The keys to successful talent management include knowing the type of talent you need, attracting and selecting that talent, developing and retaining that talent, and putting that talent in positions where it will constantly get stronger and will help move the organization forward.

Chapter

15

INCREASE INNOVATION

"We've Got to Find Ways to Grow the Business Now."

Alan was a fast-rising executive who had been promoted to regional vice president the year before. He was put in charge of the worst performing region in the country in terms of annual comp sales. After one year, he had fixed many of the problems in the region except that once again he had one of the worst regions in the country in terms of comp sales. Alan's boss delivered her annual performance review in a very succinct fashion. She explained what he had done well, and then closed with this advice for the following year: grow sales.

At our next coaching session, Alan said, "Dan, we've got to find ways to grow the business now. If my management team and I don't start growing sales pretty rapidly, we may not even be around next year to talk about anything else." And with that we began our crash course on organizational innovation. How could ideas be developed ultra fast and fed into a large system quick enough to show demonstrable improvement in sales? Not only that, but how could the momentum be sustained over a long period of time? These two questions ultimately led to the creation of the Cycle of Innovation.

The first thing Alan did was to send his director of marketing, Steve, on a nationwide search for proven ideas on growing sales. Steve got on the phone with the other regional directors of marketing, and asked each one of them if they were having dramatic success growing their sales in any part of their regions. From this nationwide search, Steve ultimately found four innovative ways to grow sales. And along the way, Alan and I began to develop certain insights into innovation.

Insight #1 on Innovation: Innovation doesn't mean you have to always come up with a brand new idea.

Microsoft didn't create their original software from scratch. Instead they built on what was already available. Look throughout your organization and into other organizations for ideas that you can build on that would add more value to your customers and help you to generate sustainable, profitable growth. Obviously don't do something illegal like stealing someone else's patented or copyrighted work, but do be on the lookout for ideas that could be combined together to generate more value for your customers.

At our next coaching session, Alan said, "Dan, I have great news. We found four ways to grow sales right away. I'm going to roll them out to all my retail stores next month." I paused. Alan had 500 retail stores in his region. Customers expected great service. If he rolled out all four changes at the same time, it could have a short-term boost on sales and a long-term devastating effect on customer relationships, operations, and, ultimately, sales.

I said, "Alan, here's my advice. Pick the one idea that you think could have the greatest impact on sales right now. Then move that idea toward a region-wide rollout. Take the other three ideas and test them on a few retail stores and see how they do."

I continued by saying, "That way you have a decent chance to achieve the sales comps your boss wants, and still not devastate the performance of the stores. Even if you could roll out all four ideas right now and do them all well and generate an explosion in sales, you won't be in a position next year to achieve decent comp sales.

You're not going to be able to roll out eight new ideas next year, are you? What you need is an ongoing series of innovations that get inserted at just the right time to steadily grow sales."

THE FOUR PHASES OF ORGANIZATIONAL INNOVATION

Alan took my advice and on our next phone call he told me about the region's new Cycle of Innovation. He explained there were four phases he wanted every innovation to go through: incubation phase, small test phase, large test phase, and regional rollout.

Phase One: The Incubation Phase

The incubation phase occurred at a monthly innovation meeting. This is where baby ideas could be tossed out and combined together. These meetings always had four parts. First, the director of marketing gave examples of innovations that were working well in terms of growing sales for their company from other parts of the country. These proven ideas were called "the low hanging fruit" because they were projects that could be replicated relatively easily.

The second part of the meeting was an update on consumer trends. These trends could be directly related to the business of the retail stores, or they could just be interesting bits of information about the customers who visited the stores or who wanted to visit the stores. The idea was to gain a stronger understanding of what people wanted. Sometimes these reports were based on statistical research, and sometimes they were based on conversations with small groups of customers.

The third part of the meeting was an opportunity for anyone in the room to toss out their business building ideas. Each person was given the opportunity to explain his or her idea to the group. These ideas were all recorded and saved. They may find an avenue to be used right away, to be implemented in the future, or to sit dormant.

In this manner, there was always a pile of ideas that could be reconsidered in the future.

The final part of the meeting was to determine which ideas, if any, should be implemented in the small test phase. This usually created a lively round of debate. The idea had to have potential for impacting region-wide sales, it had to be reasonably efficient to execute in terms of operations, and it had to be replicable in all the other stores if it turned out to be successful.

Phase Two: The Small Test Phase

If the innovation team decided to try an idea, it would then go into one to three retail stores for a test run. Since they couldn't put a lot of marketing behind such a small test, the sample size of customers who interfaced with the idea was fairly small. Therefore, the key was to talk with these customers in face-to-face conversations to gather their feedback. Sometimes the small test phase began with a focus group, but we determined that in most cases the ideas needed to be tested in the retail setting to see how actual customers reacted to the idea.

At this point, we were more interested in the reactions of a few customers rather than looking for huge sales of the item. We just wanted to know if customers liked the idea, would pay for the innovation, and had any recommendations on what would make it better. We also wanted to understand how this innovation would affect sales of the retail store's other products. If things went reasonably well through this phase, then we made adjustments and moved the idea to a larger test phase.

Insight #2 on Innovation: Innovation requires patience.

Phase Three: The Large Test Phase

At this point, a "successful" idea would be unveiled in a market of approximately 50 retail stores. In this way, the idea could be advertised to a large audience to see how it was received.

The innovation was only going to be deemed successful if it positively affected the decisions and behaviors of actual customers. Did overall sales grow as a result of having this innovation in place? Did the innovation have a positive affect on other aspects of the retail store? Could the idea be ramped up quickly and executed well region-wide? It wasn't critical at this phase for the innovation to be profitable. Profitability would increase as the innovation was rolled out in more stores and cost efficiencies were incorporated.

Insight #3 on Innovation: Successful innovations don't have to make a profit from day one.

Phase Four: The Roll Out Phase

Whether you're rolling out a new innovation across a region or across the world, there are a few key points to keep in mind. First, be sure that customers know that something different is happening. Leverage as many different points of contact with your customers as you can. Make a big deal on your Web site, focus your advertising on the innovation, and have your employees discuss the change with every customer that walks in.

Second, sustain your focus on the innovation for at least three months. It will take at least that much time for customers to really catch on that something has changed and to give the innovation a try.

Third, in order to gain support from your employees and business partners, you may need to build in some incentives around promoting the innovation successfully. Cash generally works pretty effectively, but also use public forums to recognize great performances with the new innovation.

Fourth, be a good role model. Personally use the innovation and talk about it with everyone you encounter. Get all the members of your group to try the innovation and to discuss it at meetings, with their customers and suppliers, and with their friends. Word of mouth advertising does work, but those words have to start somewhere.

Within 12 months, Alan's region was number two in comp sales in the country, and stayed consistently in the top five. One of the driving forces was a continuous pipeline of innovations.

THE DIVERSITY OF INNOVATIONS

As the story about Alan demonstrates, innovation is about identifying ways to add more value to customers and then delivering solutions. Those solutions can come in many different formats. In 2006, *BusinessWeek* listed the most innovative companies in the world. Here are the top ten: Apple, Google, 3M, Toyota, Microsoft, GE, Procter & Gamble, Nokia, Starbucks, IBM. Let's see, that means innovations happen with cars, computers, digital music players, coffee, cell phones, shampoo containers, and tooth brushes.

THE SIMPLICITY OF INNOVATION

Innovations don't have to be complicated, but they do have to be created consistently over the long term. It's not enough to create one innovation. Your organization has to develop a steady stream of innovations to generate sustainable, profitable growth.

Developing these innovations does not have to be a complicated affair. Let me repeat. Innovation is not complicated. It's also not a buzzword or a fad or a trend. Innovation is the lifeblood of business growth. It's simply a matter of not being satisfied with always doing things the way they've always been done. The process of innovation is essentially the same in every industry. Here are four steps involved in developing and delivering innovation.

1. Identify Your Desired Customers' Wants and Needs

Who knew they needed an iPod? Well, actually, no one *needs* an iPod to survive, but a lot of people sure have figured out how to use those little things. No one knew they wanted or needed Bluetooth enabled cell phones, but people sure use those things as well.

The first time someone gave me a USB flash drive for my computer, I threw it away. I didn't know what to do with it. Now the little guy travels with me everywhere I go, and I no longer have to carry floppy disks around.

The first step in developing any innovation is to identify what outcome your potential customer wants to achieve, needs to achieve, or would be better off if they achieved it. Once you know that desired outcome, you are in a position to effectively innovate. If you don't have a clear customer outcome in mind, then you are likely to create something that has no value.

2. Establish Your Innovation Inventory

Once you have established the desired customer outcome you want to improve, then ask, "Are there any products, services, or processes in our organization that we could apply toward improving that customer outcome?"

Essentially, you want to look at your current resources to see if you can redeploy some of them toward the desired outcome. If you can't deliver a total solution with your current resources, could you at least use some of your current resources to serve as part of the solution?

3. Find the Missing Pieces

Unless your organization has the total solution already in house, you will have to develop some, if not all, of the missing pieces. As I mentioned in the story about Alan, Steve, and their retail stores, there are a variety of places to look for solutions.

First, study the competition. Are they delivering this particular customer outcome better than your organization? If so, how are they doing it? Even if they are only providing a partial solution, find out what they are doing. It might turn out that they have the missing element you need to really improve performance.

Second, study organizations outside of your industry. Is a "noncompetitor" helping the customer to achieve this particular desired outcome better than your organization? If so, is there a way your organization could do what this noncompeting organization is doing? Sometimes executives become so myopic in terms of only looking at their direct competition that they don't realize the answer is already in the marketplace.

Third, be a business anthropologist. Study the customers in their natural habitat. See if they are getting the solution from a competitor or a noncompetitor to your organization. If no one is providing the customer with what she needs to achieve the desired outcome, then really examine what's getting in the way of success. Is there an obstacle that needs to be removed? Is there a gap between what she is achieving and what she wants to achieve that could be closed by something that you could provide? Talk with the customer and walk through the scenario and identify where things break down.

Fourth, be the customer. Actually go through the experience of trying to purchase a product or service that is supposed to help achieve the desired outcome, and see for yourself what works well for the customer and what goes wrong for the customer.

Fifth, form an innovation team within your organization to focus on what could be done to improve the customer's desired outcome. Gather a group of people with diverse talents and perspectives to look at the customer's situation and brainstorm ways to increase the chances that the customer will achieve the desired outcome.

Notice that none of these five steps required an advanced degree in innovation. The steps are so simple and logical that you could argue that they're just common sense. I won't debate you on that because that's my whole point. Don't make innovation appear to be this wildly complicated thing that only a genius can accomplish. Instead, look at it as a series of steps that can be walked through just like any normal day-to-day business process.

4. Carry Through to Execution

One definition of innovation is that it is applied creativity. Yes, there is a degree of creativity involved, but as I mentioned in the first section of this book, we all have the ability to be creative. However, there is an equally important degree of application involved in innovation. If you don't execute the ideas you've developed, then you haven't added any new value to your customers. Consequently, you really haven't innovated at all.

ACCELERATION ADVICE

From an Interview with Kevin Wade, St. Louis Cardinals, Vice President of Ticket Sales, 1997–2002

I served as Kevin's executive coach in 1999 and 2000. His sales team managed to break the then all-time club record for preseason ticket sales sold with 2.4 million tickets sold before opening day in 2000. Here's his story:

Coughlin: *How did you create an effective sales team that consisted of full-time nonunion workers, union workers, and part-time workers?*

Wade: When you have such a large and diverse group as I had, you find that you spend as much time managing personalities as you do sales strategies. By nature, I believe sales people are competitive. My biggest challenge was keeping this competitive nature directed toward ticket sales and not each other. The other challenge I had was the "burnout" factor. The number of daily calls each sales rep received and placed from January to May was staggering. And the work associated with each phone call didn't end when they hung up the receiver. In our business, follow-up was key.

I knew from past experience in doing many of the same responsibilities as the team I supervised that you need to get away from your comfort zone and see what else is going on in the company. You'll be surprised at how much you learn and how it gets the creative juices flowing again. A major aspect to our success was promoting interaction between the sales staff and other departments. A lot of great ideas came from listening. Some of the most successful sales programs we implemented came from the people who answer the switchboard or from employees who dealt with the fans once they came to the stadium for a game. When I first started in the ticket office in 1991, we had five different ticket prices in our general seating bowl. When I retired in 2002, we had close to 20. It takes a lot of ingenuity to come up with plans to sell three million tickets year after year with so many prices.

Coughlin: *How was the group able to sustain its focus and improve results year after year even in the midst of rising ticket prices?*

Wade: Each year we always brought in six to eight new sales representatives. They primarily sold season and group tickets. These were recent college grads and for the most part were always motivated and eager to prove themselves. It takes quite a bit of training to learn all the different ticket options, policies, etc. We let the veteran sales representatives design and assist in the training. Everyone benefited from that. The new employees were tutored by veterans who had been selling for years and the veterans were able to do a self-refresher course in how to sell just by mentoring a new employee.

Coughlin: *What role did creativity play in finding new market niches to develop and increase the sale of tickets?*

Wade: Creativity was key in growing sales. Take a Tuesday night game in May against the Pirates. Dead for ticket sales. A couple of our sales reps came up with the idea to start a health care night. This allowed individuals in the health care field to purchase tickets at a discounted price. I believe we had two health care nights the first year and sold over five thousand tickets. From there we added teacher appreciation days, police officer and firefighters night, and several other theme nights. Another program was our outer market sales program. A few of the seasonal reps, the recent college grads, noticed that they were receiving quite a few calls from churches and youth groups within a 200-mile radius of St. Louis. We immediately began targeting churches, civic organizations, schools, and other community groups. This direct mail and personal visit approach sold volumes of tickets for us.

Many of our sales ideas came from sitting around a table having lunch or happy hour. And it wasn't just the sales department that was included. Switchboard operators deal with the public more than our sales staff and they had great ideas. People from the marketing department always added a different twist as did people from the usher operations. You have to be careful not to put yourself in a vacuum and only concentrate on your own area.

Coughlin: *How were you able to raise the bar in terms of the leadership you provided to the group?*

Wade: I had to make sure I adapted with them. I had to step back and reflect, remember what it was like to be in their shoes. And I always made myself available. I pretty much had an open door policy into my office. I also had a phenomenal administrative assistant.

I also brought in other successful sales contacts to give a different perspective on what they found to be great ways to deal with customers. Interacting with your peers in other industries can shed new light on ways to improve.

Coughlin: *You went through some tough times and some great times. What were they like?*

Wade: Nineteen ninety-six was the year after the strike and all the bad feelings about canceling the World Series in 1994 and using replacement players in '95. Selling tickets was like pulling teeth. We only sold 2.6 million tickets in 1996 and that was the year we won our division. Then McGwire and Sosa's home run race brought the fans back in 1998. Once it started to seriously look as if he might catch or break the record, it was like having a World Series game at the park every night. That is still one of my best memories of working for the Cardinals.

Coughlin: *What's it like selling a really hot property?*

Wade: One key thing I learned was you have to take care of your customers when you have a hot item. For example, we reprinted the tickets and the game programs for the night McGwire broke Maris's record and mailed them to all our season ticket holders so they had a copy whether they came to the game or not.

If you don't take care of your customers when you have a hot item, they may not come back when you're not on top anymore. Don't ever let a hot item cause you to take advantage of customer relationships. There's no guarantee they will come back. You have to make deposits in the goodwill bank because there will be times when you won't be hot. We've had at least three million tickets sold every year since then, and keep in mind there are only two million people living in St. Louis.

When a property is really, really hot you have to be careful that your salespeople don't just become complacent. You can't forget how to sell.

Acceleration Tips

✓ Business innovation is the process of identifying, developing, evaluating, and combining ways to add more value to customers and generate sustainable, profitable growth.

- ✓ Make innovation as much a part of your day-to-day work routine as calling customers, selling products and services, and following up on e-mail. Just as you attend sales meetings, attend innovation meetings. Don't make it seem funky or weird. Make it seem normal. At the sales meeting you're going to focus on increasing sales, and at the innovation meeting you're going to focus on how to improve a specific customer outcome.
- ✓ Be serious about innovation. Consistently have ideas in all four phases of innovation. Consistent sales growth happens because of great execution and consistent innovations. One without the other is insufficient. You can't roll out a major innovation on day one, at least not without a lot of costs and risks involved. Successful innovations are tested on a small basis, retested on a larger basis, and then launched as far as you can launch them.

Part Four

ACCELERATE YOUR IMPACT ON CONSUMERS

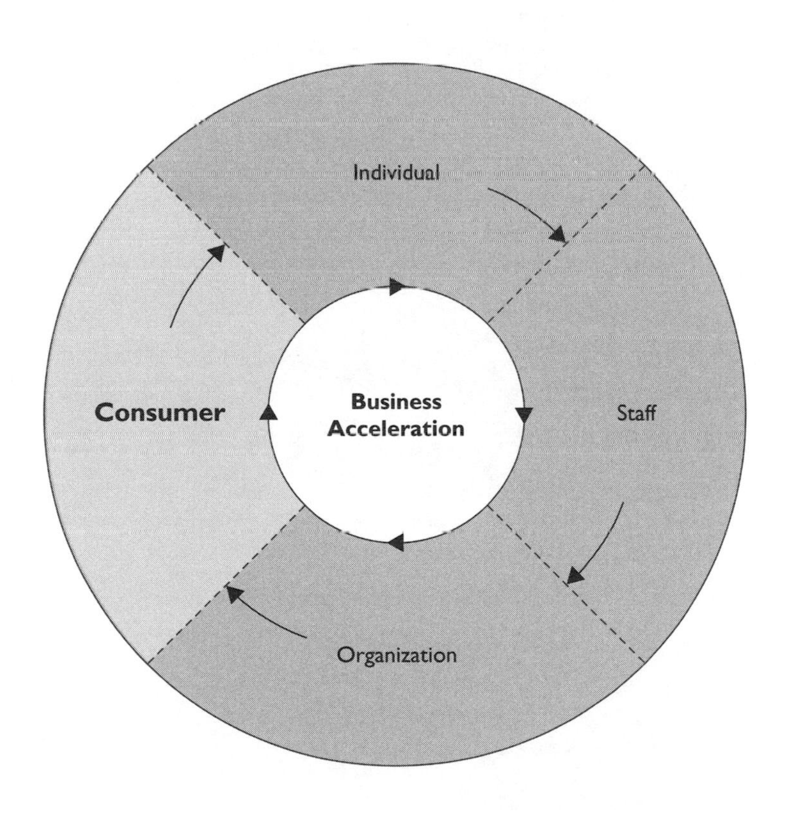

Chapter

16

STUDY BUSINESS RESEARCH

"Our Customers Just Didn't Do What They Were Supposed to Do."

A small group of us assembled in the conference room. I joined the top executive for the business unit, who was the person I was coaching, and the heads of operations, marketing, human resources, and finance to discuss the performance of the business unit over the previous quarter.

The head of marketing was relatively new in his position and clearly wanted to demonstrate that he was a hard-working team player. He went first and proceeded to praise the operations team and the marketing team for developing and executing a terrific set of initiatives during the previous quarter. Then the head of finance delivered the business results and explained that despite an influx of marketing dollars, the business unit's performance in the areas of sales and profit actually declined.

The new marketing director became somewhat embarrassed, and then said, "Look, we did a great job. The marketing ideas were clearly communicated and executed flawlessly by the operations team. The only problem was our customers just didn't do what they were supposed to do."

At that point, the vice president leaned forward and said, "Our customers did exactly what they wanted to do. That's what customers do. We just didn't figure out what they really wanted or needed." Shortly after this, the executive hired a full-time business research person to dig into the details of what was really happening.

THE FUNDAMENTAL PURPOSE OF BUSINESS RESEARCH

In a flash, the group's top executive explained to everyone the purpose of business research. The engine under the hood of effective decision-making is really good business research. All great relationships are based on understanding the other person, and then meeting the needs and wants of the other person. This is true in marriages, in boss-employee relationships, and in organization-consumer relationships.

No matter how sophisticated or simple your research is, the end-game is the same: to understand your customers. This understanding serves as the guide to developing your business strategy, marketing initiatives, operational areas of emphasis, the organization's brand, and talent management. The stronger your understanding of the outside of your business, which is where consumers reside, the better your chances are of serving them with the products, services, and experiences they want.

Consumers serve one enormously important purpose in the cycle of business acceleration. They are the ultimate teachers on what organizations should do and should not do in the future.

Rather than criticizing customers for what they did or did not do, remember that customers don't care about your organization or how hard everyone has worked. They only care about what they want to achieve. Leverage that mindset to your advantage. Remain emotionally detached from your actual results, and simply keep asking yourself why the customers are doing what they are doing.

After listening to one very lengthy presentation from a business research person at one of my larger clients, I raised my hand and asked, "I understand what you told us, but what does it mean? Are you recommending that we do more of the same activities, less of the same, or something altogether different?"

It doesn't do any good to simply know what happened as a result of a new initiative. The group has to dig deeper for understanding. Why did the customers react in the way they did? Was it because of something your organization did, or something the competition did? Or was it a trend outside of your organization that affected the success of your new project?

There's an art to conducting business research and an art to deciphering what the research means. Here are some of the keys I've witnessed in large and small organizations.

TEN KEYS TO EFFECTIVE BUSINESS RESEARCH

1. Search for Reliable Statistics and Trust the Facts

Find reliable sources of statistics that tell the actual story of what has transpired. If your company has grown sales by 14 percent, you might be elated. That is, until you find out that your industry has grown sales by 27 percent in your markets. Statistics allow you to base your decisions on facts.

There are three issues with gathering and analyzing statistics from outside your company.

First, you have to determine that the statistics are reliable. Find out how the information is gathered and test its validity. See if it can be backed up by another outside source.

Second, be certain that the interpretation of that data is accurate and consistent. Business researchers are human as well. They run into personal crises just like the rest of us. Don't just blindly assume that information is being analyzed and presented properly. I've sat in meetings where one PowerPoint slide didn't gel with the information on the next slide. Stay alert and make sure that the information and the analysis are flowing logically. Be willing to ask questions.

Third, once you've ensured that the statistics and the interpretation of that data are being done in a reliable and consistent manner, then trust what you are seeing and hearing. Blowing off the factual information and going with your gut is what causes customers to do what they are not supposed to do. Remember that you are not your customer. At the very least, examine the data and see if you can find any logical rationale for the decision that your gut is telling you to make. Statistics are not divine. Following them does not guarantee success, but they can help to increase your awareness of your desired customers.

2. Use Focus Groups

I have mixed feelings about focus groups. In my opinion, they are conducted in conference rooms with a see-through mirror and don't really match the reality of the actual customer's interface with the product or service. However, the upside is you can gather diverse opinions about a single product or service very quickly from people who are familiar with your organization.

As with all other research tools, conducting focus groups is just one more way to gain insights into your customers. Do what you can to understand as much as you can about your desired customers, but don't rely completely on any one method of research.

3. Be a Customer

As I mentioned earlier, one way to understand what customers go through when they use your product or service is to be a customer. Go to your organization's Web site and try to order a product online. Go to your own retail stores and be treated just like any other customer. If your organization provides a call center, then call in with a complaint and see how you are treated.

When Toyota wanted to improve the performance of its popular minivan, the Sienna, in the United States, the head engineer from Japan drove it through all 50 states and into Canada. He wanted to experience it the same way Americans did. He found that it needed more room in the back and more cup holders. Why more cup holders? Because Americans drive cars over much greater distances than drivers in Japan, and often they want access to two different types of drinks per person.

4. Sit and Observe

I've spent whole days with clients simply sitting in their establishments and watching customers walk in, study their options, make a purchase, and walk out. Many times we would stand outside of the building and just observe customers as they drove on to the parking lot. We wanted to see the same visual cues that customers saw, and watch how they responded. These insights could then be converted into specific improvements.

If it's possible, spend time with your customers in their homes, businesses, or offices to see how they use your products and services. Just sit and observe. Don't offer explanations on how something works or why things are done a certain way. You just want to take it all in visually and see what happens.

5. Talk to Customers

After customers interact with your organization, immediately follow up with them and ask them what the experience was like. What did they think of the price, service, responsiveness, courtesy, and overall experience? If you're testing a new product or service, ask the customer why they did or didn't buy it. Let them know you're going to do something for them to compensate for their time, and then just ask a few open-ended questions.

When I work with a client for the first time, I generally ask what went well, what didn't go well, and what would have made our exchange more useful for them. I repeat those three questions about every other month. I want the person to know that I'm interested in their specific situation. I prefer this method to a survey that people fill in with choices one to five.

Other people prefer some standards to shoot for in terms of customer satisfaction. That way they can measure whether or not they are making progress from quarter to quarter and year to year. Use whatever methods, formal or informal, that work best for your organization.

6. Know Your Industry

Attend local and national industry meetings. You'll learn more during the breaks in the hallways than from the general or breakout sessions. Find out what ideas other people are trying, and which ones are working and which ones are not working.

Find out which organizations are achieving extraordinary results, and why they stand out from the rest of the pack. These industry leaders can provide insights in a few minutes that you may not find out in a year's worth of trial and error. Keep an eye on the trends in the industry. You might just find a strategic advantage by going in a different direction.

7. Extend the Timeline Backward and Forward

Take the data you have compiled and stretch it back as many years as you can. You may find subtle but important clues from your organization's past performance that you can use to improve your decisions today and your results tomorrow.

For example, with one client we determined that their average positive comp sales cycle lasted three years. We then dug deeper to see what caused the cycle to stop. We found that the end of a traditional sales cycle was caused by a lack of consistent innovations.

Consequently, we made sure that each year, two to three innovations were introduced on top of a fanatical focus on improving operations and the customer experience. In doing so we were able to able to extend the streak of consecutive positive comp sales to nine years. What had seemed impossible in the past now seemed probable because we dug into the data and found the key factors that would allow positive comp sales to continue far longer than "normal."

8. Be an Expert on Your Competition

Don't work just to outdo your competition. That can actually lead to a diminishing of your industry. If your goal is profitable revenue growth, then hold to that as a priority over simply beating your competition. However, study your competition closely to try to gain insights into your customers. Is there something your competition is doing that is attracting customers or repelling customers?

Again the goal of business research is to gain a better understanding of your customers. If those insights come from watching the successes and failures of your competition, then so be it. Just keep compiling information on your customers and prospects.

9. Search for and Test Alternative Explanations

Business research is not infallible. While you thought you were gaining customers because you were providing faster service, it may turn out that they came to you because of rudeness on the part of your competition. Consequently, as you get faster and faster, you may actually lose customers. The solution they wanted was friendlier service, not faster service.

Be willing to hold all things constant except for one variable and see how customers react to it. That will give you some insights as to what really matters to your customers.

10. Explore Unexpected Successes and Failures

In his book *Innovation and Entrepreneurship*, Peter Drucker explains the sources of innovation. One such source was the unexpected successes and failures in your organization and in your competition. If you start to get great results with a wrinkle that you felt was unimportant, don't just cast it aside as luck. Dig deeper into the reasons why it's happening. If you can understand why customers are responding so well to a project you had barely focused on, you may gain insights into what else the customer might want.

Conversely, if you invested a lot of effort into a project with high expectations and it failed miserably, then dig deep into finding out why it failed. It may help you understand what other projects won't work.

EIGHT CUSTOMER INSIGHTS TO SEARCH FOR

While you spend a lot of time in business research looking for patterns and trends and subtle clues, what you are really searching for are insights into customer expectations and behaviors. Here are eight questions I believe you should try to find a reasonably strong answer to as you compile information about your desired customers.

1. What's the customer's desired outcome?
2. What's the customer's greatest need?
3. What's the customer's greatest obstacle to achieving his or her desired outcome?
4. What's the customer's best current option to purchase for helping to achieve the desired outcome, and what makes that option effective?
5. What would the customer be willing to pay more for?
6. What combination of outcomes would constitute more value for your customers?
7. What's working for your competition that's not working for your organization in terms of adding value to your customers?
8. What's the unique value you can add to your desired customer?

By knowing the answers to these questions, you're in a better position to provide creative solutions, deliver more convenience to your customers, meet what appear to be unrealistic customer demands, and build a strong brand. These are the topics of the remaining four chapters.

ACCELERATION ADVICE

From an Interview with Rene Huey-Lipton, GSD&M, VP/ Executive Managing Director, Marketplace Planning

Rene is responsible for conducting business research for clients of GSD&M, the national advertising agency. These clients include BMW, AT&T, Southwest Airlines, AARP, and many other national brands. She has five planning directors and 36 members of this department. I served as an executive coach for Rene in 2006. Rene is one of the true experts on business research that I've encountered.

Coughlin: *Why is business research important in making decisions on strategy, tactics, and branding?*

Huey-Lipton: Because timidity is the enemy of success—and a lack of knowledge makes for timid leaders. When you know the facts, you don't have to second-guess your decisions. Why not? Three reasons:

First, because it provides information you might not have and inspiration you'd never have guessed.

Second, because it provides a shared language for the team that's rooted in the customer's reality.

And finally because business research gives you a framework in which to make decisions. Of course, it doesn't make the decision for you, and should never determine in and of itself whether to move in any one direction.

Coughlin: *What makes for effective business research?*

Huey-Lipton: Knowing—and getting the team's agreement on—the objective upfront.

The objective is what you hope to get as a result of your research, articulated in actionable terms. A good objective will determine what kind of research is necessary and will ensure that the team gets its money's worth from the exercise.

An example of a bad objective is "I want to go do research to find out about brand awareness," because it doesn't provide a decision-making context. By contrast, an example of a good objective is "I want to find out the awareness of my brand so I can decide whether or not to spend more money to increase media." Another good example is "I'll do this research to determine whether I should change my targeted customer." Or, "I'll do this research to determine if I should change the company's name." In cases like these, it's important to set (or at least consider) action-standards right from the start so that everyone knows what degree of results should precipitate what kinds of actions. For example, "We'll change the company's name if less than 25 percent of customers feel positively about our current brand."

Many times the objective is less quantitative—rather than knowing the possible answers up front, you need some help getting the lay of the land. Your objective might then be something like "Identifying some possible themes that could lead to a new brand positioning." In either case, working with a client to determine the objective of the business research is where we spend most of our time.

Coughlin: *What should a company look for from business research?*

Huey-Lipton: Clarity, accuracy, and simplicity. At the end of all the research I do, I want clearly articulated, simple, actionable steps for the client to consider. I don't want to hand in an academic thesis. A good business researcher will make recommendations based on what they find. I call it "the push-off point." For example, let's say our objective is to understand the targeted customer's relationship to value. And say this targeted customer defines value as peace of mind. Then we can state in our report what we found that increases their peace of mind. Then the client can use that information to make decisions.

One thing a company should *not* look for from business research is rigidity. The whole point of doing research is that you don't know the answers yet—so it's entirely possible that something unexpected will come up along the way. You need a research design that is focused and flexible. Focused on the objective but flexible in how it gets there. Sometimes the most interesting thing is a tangent and you have to be willing to follow these tangents to see if there is anything valuable there.

Business researchers should have a strong POV (point of view) about their approach to business. It's another push-off point. And it means that perhaps the most important thing a company should look for is a level of trust in the researcher. Remember, numbers can be made to say anything you want them to say and focus groups are even more malleable. There's no such thing as unbiased research. You've got to trust that the researcher has your best interests at heart.

Coughlin: *What do you think about focus groups?*

Huey-Lipton: There are no bad focus groups, only bad moderators. A good moderator knows how to listen with her eyes and her ears, pushes back on consumers to really articulate their feedback, and has an honest discourse with the consumer. They make you believe they want to know what you think about things. They know how to "go with the flow" of the conversation and when to take charge. Good moderators also know how to signal key findings to the clients in the back room so that they know which comments to pay attention to and which to overlook.

The second worst thing after a bad moderator is a bad discussion guide. We spend a lot of time designing a discussion guide for the moderator, because you're basically choreographing a two-hour dance.

The moderator has to do something up front to set the stage. They have to make everyone comfortable so that they'll really speak their minds. But they've also got to get people thinking about the subject. For example, if you're researching for the safety of a car, a bad warm-up exercise is to say, "Tell me your favorite pet's name." A good exercise is, "Tell me your name, who is in your household, and a time when you felt the safest." Later in the focus group, the moderator could say, "You told me you felt safest when you were six years old with your mom. Can you ever imagine feeling that sense of safety in a car? Yes? How would that have to happen in a car? No? Why not?"

It's all about finding a way to link your brand or product with a real and powerful emotion. Make sure your brand or product has a legitimate link to that emotion. But don't push it—you've got two hours to discover something great!

Another way to gather information is to use ethnographies. That's when the business researchers go into people's lives and follow consumers around while they are shopping and driving and in their house. It's cultural anthropology. It's done one on one with consumers, and it helps distinguish what people *say* is important from what really matters in their lives.

Focus groups and enthnographies are examples of qualitative research in which you're focusing on small numbers of people and you're conducting really in-depth research. That's different from quantitative research, where you're looking at groups of people as opposed to the individual. This is data you can slice and look at. The difference between these two types is that qualitative research helps you understand what the possible answers might be, while quantitative research determines how many people agree with each possibility. You can conduct quantitative research through primary research, which is what happens when you design the tools and gather the input, and secondary research, which is information that has already been gathered by existing sources.

Coughlin: *How do you determine if information is useful or not?*

Huey-Lipton: Technically, it should be useful if it answers the objective you set up front—which is why that first step is so important. In practice, assuming a good objective, information is useful if it clarifies an issue or illuminates a possibility. That's why following tangents can be such a good idea. Good information tends to raise as many questions as it answers.

One sure-fire sign of usefulness is when you discover consumers' passions. I'm not looking for patterns; I'm more interested in what people strongly believe. If 65 percent of people are neutral about the client's brand, then that's useless information. We need to elicit a strong opinion or feeling in order to do something with it. We want to know what strong emotions people have so we can determine how to extend it if it's positive or eliminate it if it's negative. Then we can determine what to do.

Acceleration Tips

✓ Many times, I've seen managers who want to skip over the mundane work of business research in order to jump into the excitement of executing ideas. They have a thirst to find out how customers will respond to their new ideas. Unfortunately, this is not an effective way to generate business acceleration. It's like jumping into a conversation with a person you've never met only to find out that the topics you selected to talk about are of no interest to the other person.

✓ Effective business research creates a foundation of understanding the customer. Then you can try ideas that are rooted on this foundation to see what works and what doesn't work for the customer. Just as planting grass seed in the fall seems unattractive because the results won't happen until the spring, you need to invest in understanding your customer before jumping into action if your desire is to improve long-term business results in a sustainable manner.

Chapter

17

DELIVER CONVENIENCE

"You Can Do What with Your iPod?"

My long-time great friend Jeff Hutchison had suddenly become a technophile. I sat next to Hutch in our high school computer class back in 1980, and he didn't know computers any better than I did. Twenty-six years later, he explained to me how he downloaded all his favorite songs to his iPod, ran the system through his car, and set up another device in his house where he can play the music from the iPod throughout his house. He carried his entire music library in his pocket, and could play it while he jogged, drove, or sat at home. After he explained this to me, I said, "You can do what with your iPod?"

The iPod wasn't just a new device. It was a solution. When the iPod first came out in October 2001, consumers wanted all things digital. They were very familiar with e-mail, Web sites, digital cameras, and DVRs. Digital music players were the next obvious consumer demand. Consumers were already downloading music, although they were doing it illegally. And above all else, consumers wanted convenience and were willing to pay for it. The iPod and iTunes provided a comprehensive solution to these diverse consumer needs.

The original iPod had 5 Gigabytes, held 1,000 songs, and cost $400. The critics said that the letters I-P-O-D must stand for "Idiots Price Our Devices." They said no one would pay $400 for a device and then pay to download each song. As usual, the critics were wrong. The iPod became wildly popular, and Apple fueled that growth by continually providing more options for consumers.

By March 2006, there was a new iPod that cost $400. It had 60 Gigabytes and held 15,000 songs. In a little more than four years, Apple had increased the capacity of the iPod 15 times while keeping the price the same. Now that's an innovation that increased convenience dramatically.

The moral of the story is consumers today want convenience. They want companies to remove complexity and clutter and make their lives as convenient as possible, and they are willing to pay for the time and energy that this convenience saves them.

Consumers today don't mind paying for a dating service that helps them meet someone rather than having to find a good match on their own. They'll gladly pay someone to do their grocery shopping, prepare a dozen meals, and put the finished meals in the freezer for them. Just as Americans once thought having a new car was a valuable investment, Americans today think buying convenience is a good investment.

What does all this talk about convenience have to do with your organization? I think you need to factor in a commitment to improve customer convenience into every customer initiative. The fundamental question is "What would make this product, service, or customer experience more convenient for our customers?"

CONVENIENCE CREATORS

Here are ten simple examples of ways that businesses have increased convenience. As you read these examples, think of ten ways that you can make things easier for your customers or desired customers.

1. Express Lines

Visiting Disney World with my wife, Barb, in 1997 was a great experience except for standing in those incredibly long lines. Visiting Disney World in 2006 with our two children, Sarah and Ben, was an even better experience because they created an express line. You can go to the ride, get a ticket to come back in two hours, and then stand in a much shorter line.

2. Dinner and a Movie

McDonald's developed a new twist on an old concept. They created the modern version of "dinner and a movie" by putting Red Box in their restaurants. A customer can buy dinner, rent a DVD for $1, and take both home with them. Customers no longer have to stop by a video store in addition to visiting McDonald's.

3. Information on Homes at Your Fingertips

There was a day when home realtors literally held all the information on available homes. Today realtors serve more as advisers than information providers because buyers can pull up all the information they need from the Internet. The realtor who truly adds value is providing advice on pricing and information on local schools, religious organizations, and community groups.

4. Avoiding Commercials

Between digital recorders and TiVo you can watch your favorite television shows without ever seeing a commercial. Or you can watch your favorite commercials. What used to be a nuisance to viewers can now be avoided.

5. Toys, Groceries, and a Nurse

Wal-Mart continues to be a one-stop shop of convenience. Considering you can buy power tools, groceries, shampoo, and a get physical checkup all at the same location, you can now see convenience in action on a huge level.

6. Is That a Cell Phone or an Entertainment Center?

Pull out your cell phone, make a call, jump on the Internet, listen to your favorite music, watch a television show, and check e-mail. Now if we could just get our cell phones to drive our cars and put our kids to bed then we would really have something.

7. Pay Any Time of the Day, Anywhere You Want to Go

With 24-hour quick service restaurants, gasoline stations, and retail centers taking credit cards, you can eat on the run and shop at anytime anywhere in the country. Seems so obvious, but this is just another subtlety in the world of convenience. How about 24-hour dental service, school options, and car maintenance?

8. Advertising Agencies and Orchestra Conductors

This idea of delivering convenience applies in business-to-business relationships, as well. Here's one example. As the world of advertising continues to expand into nontraditional advertising, big corporations want ad agencies that not only can provide great advertising but can also integrate seamlessly with other ad agencies to develop a more complete advertising approach. These big corporations don't want to have to deal with multiple outside groups. They want one of the organizations to be strong enough at orchestrating the collective efforts of everyone that the client only has to deal with one point of contact.

9. Recognition Awards with a Personal Touch

By leveraging technology, small firms can now compete with huge companies in the very competitive field of service recognition awards. A service recognition company, regardless of its size, can now combine software and the Internet to ensure that on her employment anniversary date an employee receives a personalized letter of congratulation from her boss, special recognition on her company's Web site, and the ability to select from hundreds of items by going online. Then it's up to her boss to really inject the human touch with a handwritten note to the employee, but an automatic e-mail reminder can ensure that her boss does not forget. Bosses, and their admin counterparts, no longer need to run out and buy presents for everyone on their anniversary date or keep a supply of gifts in their offices.

10. Massages and Airports

As a road-weary traveler, this one is near and dear to my heart. Lacking the time to get to an outside facility, I welcome the convenience of getting a back massage before I jump on the next annoying airplane ride. Speaking of convenience, what was American Airlines thinking when they took away those pillows?

Acceleration Tips

✓ Americans have shifted from wearing the red badge of courage for embracing inconvenience to demanding convenience in everything they do. Understand how that shift impacts your industry, and work to constantly create greater convenience for your customers. These convenient innovations can separate you from your competition.

Chapter

18

OPERATE IN THE CREATIVITY AGE

"You Haven't Lived until You've Been Googled."

Twenty-five years after I had last seen my great friend Ginger Luke, she was in search of a speaker for her organization. Ginger and I had gone to grade school together, and then we lost track of each other. Through the grapevine she heard I was a professional speaker, but she didn't know how to reach me. So she did the only logical thing to do in that situation: she Googled me. When I picked myself up off of the floor after reading her e-mail, I gladly accepted the invitation.

We hit it off immediately again as though no time had elapsed. We went to lunch and talked about the old days. Then we decided to set up a day to go back to our old grade school. Ginger Googled a few more classmates, and so there were four of us. Wow, was that a magical day. We all wanted to get together again, and we all wanted to find some more classmates.

More Googling, more classmates.

At the next gathering, there were eight people from our fifth grade class, which was the grade we were in when the school closed down. A few months later, we were up to 12 members of our class. We located teachers we hadn't seen in 30 years who lived halfway across the country. At one gathering I leaned back, laughed, and said, "You haven't lived until you've been Googled by Ginger."

That confirmed it for me. Google truly has changed the world. It has become the great connector. Malcolm Gladwell wrote about connectors in his magnificent book *The Tipping Point*. However, he was referring to people who can connect you to key resources and contacts. Google became the ultimate connector. With a good search engine, you can literally find almost anything or anyone you want.

The world has shifted from the Information Age to the Creativity Age. No longer is having information a competitive edge because now large corporations and one-person businesses have virtually the same access to all the information they could ever want. Any competitive edge now has to be driven through creativity, which is the organized combination of ideas, assets, resources, information, and partnerships that adds more value to customers.

In Chapter 5, I talked about personal creativity. This chapter focuses on organizational creativity. One way to manage business acceleration is to challenge your business unit to look for combinations of available elements that can provide additional value for customers and prospects. In doing so, consumers will associate value with your organization's name. This means you have to build in time throughout your organization for people to step away from the day-to-day responsibilities of executing tactics and think about how they can create value-added combinations.

These combinations don't even have to produce revenue. You could start out by just getting your organization to focus on what it can give away for free that would be of real value to consumers. My children are consumers. Sometimes they're really big consumers. And they are huge fans of the Disney Company. One way that Disney adds value is through its Web site, *disney.com*. Ben and Sarah play the games on that site as much as they can. Disney isn't drawing any additional revenue through this Web site, but they are reinforcing their brand and strengthening their connection with my children.

Here are some ways different types of organizations can combine information to create stronger relationships with consumers. After you read this, I want you to work with your groups to come up with seven ways your organization can create free value for consumers.

SEVEN FREE VALUE-ADDED COMBINATIONS

1. Hotels

If a hotel has those fabulous beds with the cushy pillows and the unbelievable bed covers, they could provide their guests with the names and contact information of the mattress manufacturer, the pillow manufacturer, the sheet manufacturer, and the distributor who sells those items. They could just put a note on the pillow that says, "If you would like to sleep like this at home, here are some places to call . . ." That's free value.

The hotel could put its logo and contact info on the card. Every time the consumer slept at home with a great pillow he purchased using the information, he would remember that hotel.

2. Restaurants

The idea of eating healthy has affected restaurants of all types and sizes. A restaurant could put together a free laminated card on "How to Eat Healthy at Home and on the Road" that is packed with practical tips and offer it to every customer who orders a salad.

The restaurant could put its logo in the corner of the card with its contact info. Every time the consumer pulled out the card for tips on how to eat healthy, she would think about that restaurant. Remember, the goal is to associate your organization with value in the mind of the consumer.

3. Medical Tools Company

Medicated stents that can reduce the reoccurrence of heart attacks have been in the news a lot lately. What could the companies that produce those stents do to add value to the doctors who order the stents and the consumers who pay for the stents? Why not create a laminated card on "What to do if your loved one has a heart attack"? It could be packed with step-by-step advice on who to call, what to do, what not to do, and what to be aware of.

Doctors could give this to patients and their family members to reduce the stress of not knowing what to do in the midst of an emergency. And, of course, the stent manufacturer would put its logo on the card just to remind doctors and patients who it is that is giving away this great, free value.

4. Automobile Dealerships

When consumers come in looking at minivans, salespeople could give out information about where to find baby car seats, where to find car carriers, and where to sign up for satellite radio. They would just give away this information whether the customer bought from them or not. All this information could go into a really nice folder with the dealership's logo and contact info on it with a business card from the salesperson.

5. Realtors

Realtors could create a "Community at Your Fingertips" with every imaginable piece of information for the surrounding area for a given house or group of houses. They could have the names of schools, religious organizations, grocery stores, restaurants, youth organizations, adult groups, hot spots, famous places, not-so-famous places, and on and on. They would give this information to every person they drove around with. They would include their contact information on the last page of the information packet, and they would have different information packets for each community.

They could gather this information from Google and from the local chamber of commerce. Consumers could get to this information as well, but by being creative, the realtor could save the consumer time and effort. Remember the importance of convenience? Perhaps the realtor could have a variety of white papers on relevant topics for consumers looking for homes, and post the white papers on their Web site. Give away as much value as you can so people will always remember you.

6. Video Stores

Competition is very tough for video stores. People can get content from so many different sources. So how can stores make themselves unique? One of the hardest things for consumers to do in a video store is to make a decision in a reasonable amount of time.

Why not create a free kiosk in the video stores with in-depth information on films from a variety of angles? Consumers could type in "Favorite movies made in the 1960s for people under 30." Then a list would pop up of movies ranked by customers under 30 that were made in the 1960s. Each movie would have comments associated with it about why people liked the movie.

The consumer would have to come into the video store to get this additional free value-added service. Or the video store could provide this same service on their Web site. In that way, consumers would have to visit their Web site to get the free value-added service.

7. Retail Stores

Use the approach of the Santa Claus at Macy's from the film *Miracle on 34th Street.* This is an early example of combining information to provide a free, value-added service. In the film, when Kris Kringle meets with children and their parents at Macy's, he tells the parents the names of competitor stores where they can get the toys that the children want.

If you're in the retail industry, you can do the same thing. Have a list of other stores and phone numbers to give out to customers for free, letting them know where they can get the items they are looking for. You could even include competitors who sell the same things that the customer is looking for from you. You know customers shop around, so why not add more value to their experience in your store by just letting them know where else to go to look for the items? In doing so, you would give consumers a reason to always come to your store first.

Okay, now get groups throughout your organization to come up with seven creative ideas for your organization on what value you could give away for free that would strengthen your relationship with customers and prospects.

Acceleration Tips

✓ Creating new value for customers is not a rare skill. It's actually a very practical skill that many people can develop. It is simply the product of actively looking for new combinations of ideas, assets, available resources, and partnerships that will add new value to customers. The key once again is the work of stepping off of the train of daily activity, looking for ways to combine what is already available to your organization or within your organization, creating truly new value for your customers and prospects, and positioning it as an added value.

Chapter

19

CLARIFY CONSUMER DEMANDS

"I Want It Now at a Lower Price with Better Service."

Okay, that quote is not from an actual real-life experience, but it certainly captures the mindset of customers today. With each innovation, customers see more of what is possible to expect from businesses around the world. With the impact of the iPod, Google, the Internet, global competition, extraordinary call centers, and constantly improving products and processes, corporations can generate extraordinary value for consumers. That's the good news.

The bad news for businesses around the world is that customers now know what they can reasonably expect. As has happened throughout human history, customers' desire for more value continues to be the driving force for innovations, creativity, and enhancements in the market place. Rather than being frustrated by the ever-increasing demands of consumers, I encourage my clients to look at every customer request and complaint as the insight they needed to take their organization to the next level.

It's the tension created from consumer requests that causes you to reexamine your business continually, so that it adds value, and fills the gaps between what it offers and what is desired. Knowing where those gaps are is like finding where the pirate's treasure is hidden on a map. With these new insights into consumers, you can now move forward creatively, and provide the value that customers will pay for. Essentially, you need to believe customer complaints are positives rather than negatives.

TEN WAYS TO UNDERSTAND CONSUMER DEMANDS

1. View Consumers as Teachers

Consumers do not exist to please you, nor do they exist to anger you. Their job is to teach you what they do and do not like. If you're in the fashion industry and you come out with a new style that bombs in the marketplace, realize the consumer is teaching you something very valuable. Don't be frustrated or angry. Simply learn what is being taught.

Conversely, if a new style sells incredibly well, don't think consumers love you. They are teaching you what is of value to them. By storing every piece of input and leveraging it in future decisions, you may get closer to hitting the mark with what consumers really want and need.

2. Treasure Customer Complaints

Don't just accept complaints, treasure them. Get excited when a customer complains about your product or service. Know that the complaint contains a key insight you can use to improve their future, and yours. Too often people view complaints as an interruption to their day rather than seeing the complaint as a learning experience. Change the way you view complaints and you may very well accelerate the achievement of your desired business outcomes.

3. Follow Up after Every Complaint

Don't use the "random sampling" approach to dealing with complaints. The random sampling approach says that you will look into one out of every ten or every 50 complaints to see if you can find the underlying reasons why customers are unhappy.

Forget that. Customers are people, not statistics. Would you only listen to your children one in 50 times that they came to you with a concern? Would you only keep one-fiftieth of the money you earned this year? Realize that *every* complaint gives you more insight into how consumers view your organization.

Call each customer who complains and ask a variety of follow-up questions to better understand why he or she is unhappy. Not only will you gain a better understanding of your organization from the perspective of the customer, but you are also likely to strengthen your relationship with customers.

4. Set Aside Your Ego

It's not about you. Let me repeat. It's not about you. Consumers don't care about you. They don't even know you. All they know is whether they believe a product or service will be of value to them. That's the basis of their buying decision. So set aside your ego, and look at consumer behaviors in objective, logical, and rational terms.

By taking your ego out of the equation, you can now base your future decisions on facts, trends, and actual buying patterns. When Toyota first sold cars in the United States in 1957, they failed. They only sold 300 cars. The tires melted on the American highways, the engines overheated, and the cars guzzled gasoline. What did Toyota do? They made adjustments, and quickly began their ascent up the ladder of success.

5. Deficiencies Lead to Value Creation

A deficiency from the consumer's perspective is really an opportunity to create value from your perspective. In early 2001, people wanted a legally viable method to download music. The deficiency in the marketplace was a true opportunity for someone to create value. Apple Inc. inserted itself and created the wildly successful iPod.

What deficiencies are there in the marketplace that complaints from consumers are indicating? These complaints don't even have to be coming from your desired customers. For example, there is a huge deficiency right now in terms of low-cost energy that can transport people from one location to another. Oil supplies are limited, and oil is getting much more expensive as reserves become depleted. What value can your organization create for consumers in this changing scenario?

6. Reach Out Beyond Your Comfort Zone

Walt Disney was great at making animated films, but he had never done TV shows or theme parks or live action films or licensed products. When he took his daughters to amusement parks, he noticed how dirty they had become. He turned his complaint from a consumer's perspective into a business opportunity. When Disneyland opened in 1955, a number of things went wrong and customers complained, but he simply leveraged those complaints into improvements. Because he continually reached out beyond what he was comfortable with and looked at what people were complaining about, he was able to build the Walt Disney Company into a massive entertainment company.

What is beyond your comfort zone that would be of true value for your customers? Look at the ten biggest complaints you hear from your customers and from consumers in general, and see if there isn't a way to reach out beyond your organization's current comfort zone and deliver additional value.

7. Leverage the Loudest Crank

You know who I'm talking about. Who is the person you try to run away from whenever you see them coming into your store or calling you on the phone? Instead of running away from this person, embrace them. Yes, these people can be annoying, and, yes, they may have low self-esteem and just want to feel important by eating up your time, but they can also teach you valuable information.

The "loudest crank" may provide you with insights that no other consumer is willing to share with you. Give this person a reasonable amount of time, seriously consider the input, and thank him or her for taking the time to share his or her insights with you.

8. Experience the Worst Your Company Has to Offer

If you're in the retail industry, then go to the worst store you have and be a customer. Or if everyone knows you, send your spouse or a friend in to be a customer. Gain insights into the worst situations that your customers experience.

If you're in the hotel industry, then go stay at the worst hotel. If you're in the software industry, then buy the software that generates the most complaints and see what happens with it. By diving into the worst possible customer experiences, you may gain insights that can improve a host of other customer situations.

9. View Customer Rejection as Growth Opportunities

Business acceleration means continually increasing the rate of sustainable, profitable growth. If you think your company walks on water and never makes a mistake and gives consumers everything they could ever want or need, then your business unit might be in for a world of hurt. It can be terribly frustrating to think there is no way you can grow your business.

Actively look for products and services that are being rejected by consumers. These could be products and services from your organization, from your competition, or from the marketplace in general. There is a reason why those products and services are being rejected. Delve underneath the actual consumer decisions and find out why certain offerings are being rejected.

By consistently looking at what is being rejected, you can continually feed the pipeline of sustainable, profitable growth. Remember: rejection equals growth opportunity.

10. Search for Faults

Search for what is wrong with your products and services. Don't wait for a customer to complain. Actively look for errors on your Web site, poor service at your call centers, mistakes in your responses, and so on. Make it part of your regular routine to find what is wrong with your products and services. In doing so, you become your best customer because great customers are willing to be honest about what is good and what is not so good.

ACCELERATION ADVICE

From an Interview with Ted Carlson, McDonald's Corporation, Regional Business Research Manager

I never coached Ted directly, but I saw him present his business research at more than two dozen meetings. He is one of the very best business research people I've ever seen in terms of explaining complicated data in ways that other people can understand it and do something with it.

Coughlin: *Why is business research important in making decisions on strategy, tactics, and branding?*

Carlson: I started out as a marketing guy, and I would sit in meetings and hear people say, "We know that . . ." and I would think to myself, "How do we know that for sure?" And what worried me was that we sometimes made decisions based on those kinds of pronouncements. What was frustrating is that I knew we had the data necessary to prove or disprove many of the opinions being shared, but we didn't have anyone dedicated to the task.

When I got into business research, I found out that a lot of "conventional wisdom" just didn't hold up after close scrutiny of the facts. And sometimes what once had been true was no longer still true. Research is essential in order to base decisions on reality. We all screen things through our own biases and experiences, but good research will establish a foundation of facts that will reduce the tendency to rely on "conventional wisdom."

Coughlin: *What makes for effective business research?*

Carlson: Start by asking good questions, ones that will make a difference in the decision making process. It's important to be relentlessly curious, and to dig through any available information that can explain customer behavior.

Then it is critical to turn the numbers into English. There are relatively few people who are really comfortable with a bunch of numbers, and consequently research sometimes has the unfortunate reputation of being dry and boring.

I have found that research is really compelling when it is put together into a logical progression and it tells a story that leads to conclusions. We get to talk with people about something that they should be very passionate about—their business. We are coming to them with facts, insight, and a look into the future of an activity that consumes most of their waking hours. That should be something that grabs their attention. I know my audience is tracking with me when someone asks a question that is answered by the next side or states the conclusion before I can get to it.

Coughlin: *What do you look for?*

Carlson: I'll use anything that will help us understand customer behavior. I'm especially looking for an action-reaction relationship where we did something and customers reacted to it. It's like a scientific experiment where you change one variable to see what happens.

Coughlin: *How do you gather useful information?*

Carlson: We gather so much information, and we store it in so many places that it's often more a matter of digging than creating. There's usually no shortage of information. I start with this question, "What do we really need to know to make good decisions?" And then I ask, "Where can I find that information?"

Keep in mind that some of that information may be outside of our business. For example, right now the price of gas is a variable we need to get our hands around. How is it affecting our business?

Another outside variable that popped up for us happened when much of Indiana went to Daylight Savings Time for the first time. Our early morning sales were dramatically down from the previous year and our late evening sales shot up, and at first I didn't see the reason for it. We hadn't made any changes to our business, but our business changed anyway.

The change was so dramatic that I thought maybe we had forgotten to reset the clocks on our register systems, but that wasn't the reason. In the end, the facts showed that having an hour less of sunlight or an hour more of sunlight at different times of the day caused significant behavior changes among our customers. You always have to look at the impact of outside variables. We almost blamed a marketing initiative for the decrease in morning sales, which could have ended a program that really wasn't the root cause at all.

It's important to go beyond just the facts I'm given to determine what's actually happening and why it's happening. We need to fill in the blanks or connect the dots so that an accurate picture emerges from the chaos of numbers.

My dad was a surveyor, and much of what he did was based on the idea of triangulation. He needed two or three fixed points or known distances, and then he could locate anything through trigonometry. He worked from the known to the unknown using angles and distances. I use that mindset a lot in my work. If I have two or three known facts, then I can move into the unknown. Good surveyors always check their work by comparing actual field measurements to their mathematical calculations, and I try to do the same thing. Whenever possible, I will take a couple of extra steps and tie my calculated outcome back into another established fact to make sure my math or reasoning is accurate.

Coughlin: *What patterns should you look for?*

Carlson: I'm into trends because trends provide perspective. I want to see what is happening over time and identify factors that are having an impact on the trends. Business is all about controlled change. What factors under our control can we change to generate the outcome that we want? Looking at the trends is the best way to identify and measure that controlled change.

Keep in mind, two points are not a trend. Two points are a line, and sometimes the hardest thing is to be patient and wait until the trend has really developed instead of jumping to conclusions.

Coughlin: *How do you integrate business research into effective strategic planning?*

Carlson: My job is to look at the facts and then put them into a context that others will understand. I love to look at detail and to dig into some pretty obscure areas to try to find answers. But I don't want to inundate others with too much of that stuff. I want to explain key insights drawn from the research in a way that people can visualize it and understand it and use it to make better decisions.

Business research should diagnose a situation and that diagnosis should lead to a prescription. Determining and implementing that prescription is usually the primary responsibility of someone else in the organization, but the researcher needs to stay involved and keep the solution grounded in the facts. The research person needs to make the handoff in terms of recommended solutions as smooth as possible so the lead executive can see what needs to happen and can explain it to others.

Researchers should stand by the facts like a rock. A good business research person will steer the discussion back to the facts even in the middle of an emotional debate. That's our job and it doesn't ever need to become personal or defensive. The facts are the facts. We can agree to disagree with others about the interpretation of the facts and the decisions that are made, but we should not allow the facts to be ignored.

Coughlin: *What role should business research play in making adjustments throughout the course of a year?*

Carlson: Every year we establish a few ultimate measures of success for our organization along with intermediary milestones or performance indicators that we believe will get us to that destination. Throughout the year I'm going to look at both sides, the ultimate business measures and the performance indicators, to see if our plan is really playing out the way we thought it would.

The old adage about not confusing activity with achievement comes into play here. It's not enough to just report the numbers. It's about explaining what the numbers mean and how they relate to each other. Why are we getting these results and what are the implications? Are we on the right track or do we need to change our activities so that we will achieve our goals?

Research that just reports the numbers is simply a stat sheet. A good researcher should be like a coach who uses a stat sheet to help his team understand why the score is what it is and how to change it.

Acceleration Tips

- ✓ Realize that complaints and rejection have nothing to do with you personally.
- ✓ Complaints and rejections from consumers provide enormously valuable insights into how they view the value your organization is putting into the marketplace. Treasure every complaint and every rejection, convert them into learning experiences, and implement what you have learned to improve the value consumers receive.

Chapter

20

BUILD THE BRAND

"Will This Be Good for Our Brand?"

In the past ten years I've worked with five major consumer brands: Toyota, McDonald's, Marriott, Coca-Cola, and the St. Louis Cardinals. I've attended well over 100 meetings at those five companies during which I observed executives in action. When any new initiative was being seriously considered, the most common question that came up was "Will this idea be good for our brand?" The executives at these great companies understood that maintaining and strengthening a brand is far more important than any effort that just improves short-term results.

Are these companies infallible when it comes to brand building? Of course not. No company is. But by keeping the importance of their brands at the forefront of their decision making, they have done far more good in terms of protecting and strengthening their brands than they would have done if they just went after every idea that could produce good short-term results.

Here's my definition of a brand:

A brand is the perception of value that a customer thinks he gets from an organization or a prospect thinks he would get if he did buy from that organization.

Every organization in the world, regardless of size or industry, has a brand because a brand is merely how people outside the organization perceive the value that the organization provides. Disney World has a brand, and so does your local dry cleaning business. Organizations don't "own" their brands because brands reside in the minds of people outside of their organizations.

Why is it worth it to build a great brand? Considering how much conscious effort it takes to build, protect, and strengthen a great brand, you might want to stop working for a moment and think about the benefits of having a great brand, regardless of the size of your organization or the industry you're in.

SIX BENEFITS OF BUILDING A GREAT BRAND

1. Puts the "Sustainable" in Sustainable, Profitable Growth

One of my favorite lines about branding that I've learned from working with some of the world's greatest brands is "A great brand is the gift that keeps on giving."

If the perception of value that customers have of your organization is incredibly high, they will keep coming back to you over and over and over. This allows you to attract new customers and move forward. I define business acceleration as continually increasing the rate of *sustainable,* profitable growth. A great brand keeps the sustainable part going and growing.

If your organization doesn't have a strong brand, then you are starting from scratch after every sale. The next time your customer wants to purchase the same type of item, they won't think of your organization first. Without a strong brand, you are living in that horrible place known as commodity hell.

2. Allows You to Make a Mistake

Organizations with great brands are run by human beings. Human beings make mistakes. However, if people believe your organization is associated with great value, they will hang in there with you until you correct the mistake. My sister-in-law, Sue, loves Starbucks. When she comes to visit from Chicago she always makes a trip or two or three to Starbucks. If Starbucks were to come out with a new music feature that she didn't like, my hunch is she would ignore it and still buy the coffee.

Notice I said "mistake." If you lie to your customers, then that's another story. I believe it's in the section of books about Enron.

3. Creates the Launching Pad for New Ideas

Steve Jobs defined the Apple brand not as a computer company but as a technology company that makes cool stuff. That is the value people believe they receive when they buy from Apple. With that foundation in mind, the iPod made perfect sense.

When you understand the value that people perceive from your organization, then you can build on that value. Don't go off on a wild idea that has no relationship to that perceived value.

4. Provides a Filter for Saying No

You can't follow through on every good idea available. You have to say no to a lot of them. One big knife that can slice away a lot of ideas is your brand. If the idea doesn't fit well with the value you want customers and prospects to associate with your organization, then don't do it.

The PGA has a great brand in terms of providing the highest level of golf available, extraordinary human-interest stories, and competition between well-known individuals for all to see. They have no value in terms of providing education on cars. If the members of the PGA gave educational seminars on automobiles, it wouldn't make any sense to consumers.

Understand what your brand is and then use that understanding to make decisions on what to do and on what not to do.

5. Allows an Organization to Survive the Passing of a Great Executive

The biggest problem with having a domineering, superstar executive is that eventually the executive leaves the organization. If everyone depended on that person to make every decision, then you have a temporary brand. When that person goes away, the perceived value goes away as well.

When you have a great brand like Toyota, Coca-Cola, or McDonald's, the founder can leave the organization and the organization can still thrive. Why? Because the decisions made throughout the organization are related to whether or not they protect and strengthen the brand, not whether or not the founder would have done it that way.

6. Carves out Space in the Consumer's Mind

A great brand is really about positioning. Whenever your desired customer wants the certain type of value you provide, you want them to think of your organization first. If you have a great brand, that's what happens.

In your desired customer's mind, you want a space reserved with your organization's name on it. When I think of great hospitality, I think of Marriott hotels. When I think of a good, fast, hot meal, I think of McDonald's. When I think of a refreshing drink, I think of Coca-Cola. When I think of unbelievably well-made automobiles at reasonable prices, I think of Toyota. When I think of great professional baseball, I think of the St. Louis Cardinals.

You will know your organization is in the rarefied air of a great brand when it pops into your desired customer's mind when that person is searching for the value you offer.

FIVE STEPS TO BUILDING A GREAT BRAND

The most surprising thing to me about working with companies that have extraordinary brands is the simplicity involved in building a great brand. Regardless of the size of your organization or the industry you're in, there are five basic steps to building a great brand. These five steps are not hard to explain, but they can be complicated to execute.

As you will quickly notice, the really hard part in building a great brand consists of intangible characteristics such as courage, perseverance, and sacrifice. Building a great brand requires making decisions on what to do and what not to do. And you never know whether or not you made the right choice until your desired customers respond with their buying decisions. Having said that, following are the five steps to building a great brand.

1. Understand What Your Desired Customers Want to Achieve, Have, or Experience

That's code for "do your homework." Conduct the business research necessary to really understand what constitutes value for your customer. Continually gather insights into your desired customers so you have a panoramic view of their desired outcomes.

2. Identify the Three Most Important Desired Customer Outcomes Your Organization Can Impact

Of all the outcomes your desired customers want to achieve, and there are going to be a ton of them, what are the three most important ones that your organization can positively impact?

If the outcome is not that important to your desired customers, then they won't be willing to pay you enough money for you to generate sustainable, profitable growth. If you can't have a great enough impact on the desired customer outcome, then it doesn't matter how important it is to your desired customer because your competition will eat you alive. You have to find the customer outcomes that are really important to your desired customers *and* that you can truly improve.

3. Gear Every Decision toward Improving High Priority, Desired Customer Outcomes

The ability to substantially improve high priority outcomes for your desired customers is the greatest value your organization delivers. You've made the hard choice in terms of who you want to serve and which of their desired outcomes you want to improve. While that work was enormously important, the vast majority of your efforts are still in front of you. You now need to integrate everything we've discussed in this book including your personal effectiveness and leadership, talent management, teamwork, strategy, and execution toward improving those three desired customer outcomes.

4. Be Boringly Consistent and Constantly Innovative

You need to consistently say no to ideas that don't support the value you want to deliver into the marketplace, but you also have to constantly find ways to increase the value that you deliver.

If you don't reach deep enough to increase the value you're delivering, the competition will sprint by you. If you reach too far beyond the value you want to be known for delivering, you may dilute your brand and endanger your sustainable, profitable growth as an organization. Now do you see why courage, perseverance, and sacrifice play a critically important role in building a brand?

5. Market to Resonate

Deciding what value you want to put in the marketplace doesn't mean anything if your desired customers don't know about it. Your marketing efforts need to clarify for your desired customers the value they will receive from buying from your organization.

That's it. Five simple steps. But don't confuse the simplicity of these five steps with the amount of conscious effort you need to continually deploy in order to build a great brand.

22 BRANDING CONSIDERATIONS

I've saved the topic of branding for the last chapter because all the ideas in this book ultimately lead to the concept of branding. Building a brand is a two-way street. Your customers and prospects have a perception of value they think they get or could get from your organization. You have to determine if that's the perception of value you want to reinforce or change. Once you determine the perceived customer value you want to be known for, you then have to make sure that all the combined individual, group, and organizational efforts within your business strengthen that desired perception of value.

The simple definition of a brand that I gave at the beginning of this chapter generates an enormous number of questions, issues, and decisions that need to be made. Here's a sample. I think they will help you better understand what adjustments need to be made in your organization or business unit in order to create a great brand.

Business Research Questions

Practical managers make sure that decisions are based on true understanding of their desired customers. Be certain your organization can really say yes to the following two questions.

1. Are we conducting business research that allows us to really understand what constitutes value for our desired customers?
2. Are we conducting business research that helps us to better understand whether or not we are providing the value we want to be known for in the marketplace?

Perceived Value Questions

In answering the following questions, you will clarify the business research and make the information more practical in terms of making decisions about what needs to be done.

3. What value do our customers think they receive from our organization?
4. What value do our prospects think they would receive from our organization if they bought from us?
5. Is this the type of value we want to be known for in the marketplace?
6. Is providing this value helping us continually increase the rate of sustainable, profitable growth?
7. What value do we want our customers to think they receive from our organization?
8. What value do we want our prospects to think they would receive from our organization if they bought from us?

Personal Effectiveness Questions

Now that you've clarified the value you want your organization to deliver to consumers, it's time to focus on yourself as an individual. Specifically, you need to focus your talents and your passions in a way that will help your organization deliver the value you want it to deliver.

9. Am I applying my strengths and passions in a way that helps my organization deliver the value it wants to be known for? If not, how can I redistribute my efforts so I am using my strengths and passions? If I am, how can I do an even better job of using my strengths and passions?
10. Am I putting my time and energy into the few things that will have the greatest positive impact on delivering the value we want to be known for? If I'm not, how can I tighten my focus

so I'm channeling my talents and passions on to fewer things that really matter?

11. Am I influencing the way other members of my organization think in ways that enhance the delivery of the value we want to be known for as an organization? If not, what can I do to improve my influence?

Teamwork Questions

The next level of impact is on your staff. Collaboration and teamwork can be tremendous business drivers, but they don't happen by accident. Use these questions to clarify in your mind what needs to be done with your staff.

12. Are people in our organization supporting one another toward delivering the kind of value we want to be known for in the marketplace? If not, what can I do to strengthen the teamwork?
13. Across our organization, are people saying no to projects and meetings that do not have a significant impact on improving the value we want to be known for in the marketplace? If their energy is being dissipated over too many items, what can I do to help them say no to the activities that don't make much of an impact?
14. Across our organization, are people investing their time and effort in doing things that support the value we want to be known for in the marketplace? If not, what can I do to help them focus on the few things that matter the most?

Talent Management Questions

Perhaps the best way to enhance the performance of a group is to get the right people in the group and the wrong people out of the group. That alone will greatly enhance your performance as a manager.

15. Do the people in our organization have the strengths and passions and behaviors necessary to deliver the kind of value we want to be known for in the marketplace?
16. When we hire a new employee, are we making sure that this person has the talent and passion we need to enhance the value we want to be known for in the marketplace?
17. Are we developing the talents of our employees in ways that will increase their chances of delivering the type of value we want to be known for as an organization?

Strategy Question

The purpose of a strategy is to clarify what an organization will do to gain and maintain a competitive advantage from the perspective of the customer and to move toward the achievement of the desired business outcomes. To clarify your strategy, answer the following question.

18. Is the strategy we've selected for our organization or business unit guiding our decisions in ways that support the value we want to put into the marketplace? If not, what strategy would provide us with a more effective direction?

Execution Question

Practical managers realize that getting the right things accomplished is what separates the great managers from the mediocre ones. Take this question to heart.

19. Are we accomplishing the items that truly deliver the value we want to produce for our desired customers? If not, what do we need to do to get the right things done?

Innovation Question

Practical managers also know that almost any truly value-added product or service can eventually be copied. Therefore, they focus on staying innovative and always searching for new ways to add more value to customers.

20. When we develop innovations with our products and services, are we making sure that these innovations increase the type of value we want to be known for in the marketplace? If not, what else can we do?

Marketing Questions

Of course, the best strategy, planning, execution, and innovation in the world won't help you generate sustainable, profitable growth if your desired end users don't know about the value you've created. Marketing is just as important as delivering the goods.

21. Do our desired customers know the kind of value they can receive from our organization?
22. Do our marketing messages reinforce that we deliver the kind of value we want to be known for?

If you answered no to either of those two questions, then you need to work on your marketing efforts.

After you go through these questions, map out a plan on what you can do on an individual, group, and organizational basis to enhance the delivery and marketing of the value you want to be known for in the marketplace. By implementing your plan, you will be managing the acceleration of your business.

ACCELERATION ADVICE

From an Interview with Roy Spence, GSD&M, Co-founder and President

I've coached a half dozen executives at the national advertising agency GSD&M. I never coached Roy Spence, but I have learned an enormous amount from him. He is the foremost expert on branding that I've ever known. I think you will enjoy this last interview as Roy shares his insights on branding, purpose, leadership, and collaboration.

Coughlin: *Roy, what does the word "brand" mean to you and why is it important to achieving sustainable, profitable growth?*

Spence: A brand is a sacred promise. I choose both of those words for a reason. A sacred promise is nonnegotiable. It's what the brand stands for. Consumers feel it and get attracted to it. The Southwest Airlines brand equals a symbol of freedom. Positions, products, and tactics can change, but the sacred promise, the brand, doesn't change.

Consumers don't have time for companies to be confused. Consumers think, "If a company doesn't know what it stands for, how the heck am I supposed to know what it stands for?"

There are two types of brands: affinity brands and enabler brands. Affinity brands are brands people like to be associated with because they like what the brand stands for. It doesn't matter whether the brand is for jeans, cars, or watches. These brands are built on image and performance.

Enabling brands help you to do something. You think to yourself, "If I buy this brand, it will enable me to _____." For example, Southwest Airlines democratized the skies, enabling people to go places and do things that they didn't think were possible before. AT&T enables people to create their own world.

Coughlin: *In his book* The World Is Flat, *Thomas Friedman talked about the extraordinary pace of change in the world's economy. As change accelerates, do you see branding as becoming more important or less important in the marketplace? Why do you feel that way?*

Spence: I feel branding will become more important. There is a great deal of debate on that question right now, but I feel branding will become much more important. As the world gets faster and flatter, prices and features become commodities. Within seconds, someone can match your price on the Internet. On a whim, people can see a popup on their computer screen and buy something. However, that's no way to stand out in a crowd. Great brands have staying power. When people make a considered purchase, they turn to brands they believe in.

Coughlin: *At GSD&M, there is a lot of work done for clients on the idea of purpose-based branding. What do you mean by that concept, and why is it important for all businesses to consider?*

Spence: Our definition of "purpose" is that it is a definitive statement about the difference you are trying to make. Southwest Airlines' purpose-based brand is "to democratize the skies." Their purpose drives everything they do. Their purpose keeps their focus on keeping costs down in order to keep fares low for customers. Jim Collins, author of *Good to Great,* said, "Visionary companies have a purpose beyond making money."

We see three important ingredients to building a purpose-based brand. First, answer the question, "What is your purpose?" Clarify your purpose as an organization. Second, you need purpose-based leaders in your organization. Purpose-based leaders always put consumers and customers ahead of their own individual good. When an organization doesn't have purpose-based leaders, they can change the purpose of the organization by making decisions that are only focused on short-term gains or for their own personal gain. Those leaders can ruin the brand because they've lost sight of the purpose of the organization. Third, brand on purpose. Make sure all of your branding efforts fit within the purpose of your organization. Purpose is a fragile thing. If someone changes the purpose, it can ruin the company.

Coughlin: *What do you see as the keys for any size business to build an effective brand, to sustain it through changing conditions, and to make it stronger as the business grows?*

Spence: You have to understand the fundamental difference between purpose, mission, and vision. Purpose is the difference you're trying to make. This is at the foundation of all great companies, both for-profit companies and not-for-profit organizations. Your mission represents the tactics you're going to do to fulfill the purpose. And vision is how you see the purpose playing out.

Let's use Southwest Airlines as our example. Their purpose is to democratize the skies. Their mission is to keep costs down in order to keep fares down. Their vision is, "I see a time where everybody can fly." When Southwest Airlines started, 15 percent of Americans flew. Today 86 percent of Americans fly.

So the key to sustaining profitable growth is to not change the purpose of your organization. The trap people fall into is they start to change their purpose. Sometimes they don't even realize that they are changing the purpose of their organization. They think they're making good decisions, but little by little they take their organization away from its purpose.

Coughlin: *What role should business research play in developing a brand and what role should an executive's gut feeling play in developing a brand?*

Spence: Great question. This is the absolute essence of our business. It's part science and part gut. Herb Kelleher says, "It's the German side and the Irish side."

The German side comes down to the Sam Walton quote, "Give the customers what they want, not what you want them to want." It's critical to be closer to the wants and needs of your customer than your competition or you won't win. You need a lot of research on your competition, but you also need a lot of research on yourself. In the book *The Art of War,* Sun Tzu says, "If you know thy self, thy enemy, and thy terrain, it's like a pound against an ounce. You will win before you fight. If you have two out of the three, you will win 50 percent of the time. If you only have one out of the three, you will lose before you fight." Sun Tzu says you should pay the most to the scouts because the person armed with enlightenment will win.

Now the Irish side. You can have all those facts in front of you, but if you don't have a strong instinct, you won't know how to deploy the information. Your gut has to figure out how to bring the research to life.

Coughlin: *Like what GSD&M did with BMW?*

Spence: Yes. With BMW, we found that a great deal of the marketplace only knew BMW as a great performance car. We worked with them to clarify their purpose from a great performance car to a company of great ideas.

I think great leaders in all organizations reach a point where they use a combination of guts and research, and they realize they don't want to be right if they are wrong. Great leaders mature to a point where they don't stick with a position that they thought was right if they find out they were wrong.

Coughlin: *GSD&M has worked with some of the world's best-known brands for more than 20 years. What do you think are the keys for a brand to stay relevant over an extended period of time?*

Spence: That is always the question. If you've anchored your purpose in a universal truth, it will always be relevant. Then you have to always work to know the consumer because you can lose your relevancy overnight. We talk about the three stages businesses go through: built to survive, built to thrive, and built to last.

In today's flatter and faster world, the power of true collaboration is more important than in the past. As Thomas Friedman said, the best companies in the world believe they don't have the corner on smarts. The true collaborators will be the winners in the middle of the 21st-century world. It comes down to what Sam Walton used to say when he got down on one knee to talk with his associates. He said, "Okay, I know what I know. I want to know what you know." That's collaboration. This is the model everyone will have to practice.

Acceleration Tips

✓ A brand is the perception of value that a customer thinks he gets when he buys from an organization or a prospect thinks he would get if he did buy from that organization.

✓ Branding includes marketing, but it includes much more than just marketing. It integrates the role of the individual, staff, organization, and consumer.

✓ Building a great brand is the key to continually increasing the rate of sustainable, profitable growth.

Appendix

TOOLS TO ACCELERATE

I had the privilege of working with one particular executive for seven years. Each year he would identify one or two areas that he wanted to focus on that would make him a more effective executive. After we spent a few months working to improve a particular facet of his approach to management, we would then convert what we had developed into a repeatable process. In this manner, we turned each concept into a practical tool he could use in his day-to-day activities.

Each year, we would add the new tools to a card that he would carry with him to meetings. Eventually he came to call this set of tools the *Coach's Card.*

I'm sharing the processes we developed with you for two reasons. One, you may find these tools useful in your own work. Two, I encourage you to use a similar approach to creating repeatable processes specific to your desired approach to management.

Identify areas that would make you a more effective manager. After you've spent a reasonable amount of time developing ways to improve in that area, write down the steps that worked the best for you. Then carry those processes around with you so you can easily refer back to them.

Following is the final Coach's Card that my client and I developed to improve particular aspects of his approach to management.

THE CREATIVE PROCESS

My client used this practical approach to generate new ideas for achieving sustainable, profitable growth. He used this approach both in group brainstorming sessions and during his own scheduled thinking time.

- Identify and include the decision maker(s)
- Establish creative spaces
- Select one issue that is critically important to achieving sustainable, profitable growth
- Remove the doubts (Identify why this issue can't be resolved and then take the biggest doubt and make *that* the issue.)
- Turn it into a clear, specific, and value-driven question
- Clear the mental clutter (Mentally step away from the issue for a few moments.)
- Rotate the crops (Answer the question from a variety of perspectives.)
- Combine answers
- Select the best idea
- Clarify positive consequences for using the idea and negative consequences for not using it
- Develop an action plan
- Implement on a small scale
- Apply the Bar-Raising Process

THE BAR-RAISING PROCESS

My client applied this Bar-Raising Process at the end or the middle of each initiative. In this manner, he was able to work with his team to identify what would make the initiative more successful in the future.

- What was the goal?
- What is the current result of my efforts?
- What did I do to achieve these results?
- What worked well?
- What did not work well?
- What was the short-term impact?
- What could be the long-term impact?
- What lessons did I learn?
- How can I apply these lessons?

PREPARATION PROCESS

We created this tool to enhance the preparation before a meeting or event agenda was established. In doing so, my client held fewer meetings, which, in turn, were far more productive.

- Clarify purpose of the meeting or event
- Identify key people to turn to for insights
- Get on their schedule with specific questions to enhance the meeting/event
- Prepare in order to craft your position on key issues (Provide information that presents the impact to the business plan from the customer's perspective.)
- Pull back and craft your message in terms of value to the other person
- Practice your message
- Identify key people who will assist you
- Clarify plan of communication
- Move into action
- Review progress by using the Bar Raising Process

EFFECTIVE MEETING PROCESS

This tool was used to make sure meetings stayed practical and collaborative rather than becoming a series of reports with no interaction.

- Clarify key topics
- Break topic into specific issues
- Turn each issue into a clear, specific, value-driven question
- Give these questions to the members two weeks prior to the meeting
- At the meeting, break into small discussion groups to answer the questions one at a time
- Each small group combines ideas to generate better answers
- Small groups report best ideas to large group
- Large group looks to combine best ideas
- A decision is made on selecting an idea
- Action plan developed, communicated, and implemented (close the loop)
- Review progress by using the Bar-Raising Process

THE COACHING PROCESS

We developed this approach to provide my client with a step-by-step reminder on how to draw out ideas from other people and then work collaboratively with them to establish a plan of action. As with all the other tools, this is just a simple, practical approach to management. However, because he played a role in developing this process and he kept it in front of him during important meetings, my client was able to shift his behaviors from giving answers to employees to drawing out answers from employees. This is a subtle but powerful shift in terms of providing leadership.

- Ask a clear, specific, and value-driven question
- Pause while the other person is thinking
- Listen while they are talking
- Write down their input
- Offer feedback and suggestions
- Discuss ideas to develop a tailored solution
- Capture a commitment to action
- Schedule the next coaching session
- At the next meeting, review progress by applying the Bar-Raising Process

SOLUTION LEADERSHIP PROCESS

The term "solution leader" refers to "a person who provides leadership by drawing out the best solution from the group." We developed the following set of questions as a further reminder to my client to try not to solve the group's problems by himself, but rather to work with the members of the group to develop solutions that would generate the desired business outcomes. These questions served as a checklist for him to go through to make sure he was being a solution leader.

Be Less Certain

- How did I or will I take time to think about the issue before I respond?
- How did I incorporate other people's ideas into the mix of possible options?
- What was the effect?

Identify the Why Behind the What

- Was the why behind the what? Explain.
- Was it obvious what needed to be done?
- What was the result?

Focus on the Long-Term Impact

- Describe the long-term impact in terms of facts.
- What would other points of view be?
- What are the other options?
- Repeat the process.

Continually Improve

- What would be a better way to approach this situation in the future?

THE BIG THREE

We developed the "Big Three" to help this executive clarify his focus on the fewest things that would have the greatest positive impact on the business unit's achievement of the desired business outcomes.

Stay Focused on the Plan

- How does this issue affect our business plan?
- Does this issue keep us from achieving the business objectives on our plan?
- What will I do with this issue (Do I resolve it, assign it, or give it back?)

Unify the Approach

- What are the approaches that we are using throughout the business unit to achieve the desired objectives?
- Is it important that we're consistent? Why?
- If it is important that we're consistent, how can we ensure the consistency of the approach by everyone in the group?
- How will we know if it is consistent?
- When should we expect to be consistent by?

On Message

- Guideline: The "message" must help us stay focused on achieving the plan.
- What is the message I want delivered?
- What audience do I want to receive the message?
- How do I want to send the message—personalized letter, e-mail, voicemail, live conversation?
- What real-life example can we share to make the message more meaningful?
- When will I know the message is received?

STAY FOCUSED ON THE BIG THREE

We developed these questions to help maintain this executive's focus on the fewest things that really mattered.

Before an event:

- What will I do to influence people to work on achieving the plan and park their side issues, unify their approach, and communicate the same message?
- What will I stop doing so that I spend 90 percent of my time and energy influencing other people to do these three things?

At the end of a given day (or week, month, quarter), ask yourself these questions:

- What did I do?
- What did I stop doing?
- What else do I need to stop doing?
- What percentage of my time, discussions, and activities are focused on the Big Three?
- How can my calendar be better designed so I can spend more time on the Big Three?

DEVELOPING SOLUTION LEADERS

Once this executive began to strengthen his skills as a solution leader, we then focused on how he could develop the skills of solution leadership in other members of his staff.

Opening

- What are you trying to achieve?
- How does it fit with our business plan?

Coaching

- Who are you influencing to do that?
- Tell me about that.
- How does that approach fit with our values and behaviors?
- Have you thought about ______?
- Discuss with the other person a variety of approaches.

Commitment

- How will you know when it's working?
- What are you going to do now?

Support

- What do you need from me?
- Give me a shout in a week and let me know how it's going.

INTELLECT/ACTION CONVERSION PROCESS

We developed this tool so the executive could have a practical mechanism in place for converting ideas he gathered from books, magazines, newspapers, and conversations into useful applications for improving his organization's business outcomes.

Feed new information into my mind, and ask:

- What did I learn?
- What was interesting?
- What's the connection to our business?
- How and when will I use this information?

OPPORTUNITY INTERCEPTION PROCESS

We developed this tool to have a practical way of identifying business opportunities as they arose, assess them quickly, make a decision whether or not to pursue them, and determine which group would be responsible for each opportunity.

- Is this a viable business opportunity for us?
- How will we grab it?
- What issues do we need to resolve?
- Which team gets the opportunity to resolve the issues?
- How do we implement their solution?

About the Author

As a business speaker, Dan Coughlin has made several hundred presentations on business acceleration to clients including Toyota, McDonald's, Marriott, Coca-Cola, Boeing, St. Louis Cardinals, and AT&T. As an executive coach, he has provided more than 1,500 executive coaching sessions for presidents, vice presidents, and senior directors in Fortune 500 companies. He has invested more than 3,000 hours on site, observing managers in over 20 industries. Dan lives in St. Louis with his wife, Barb, and their two children, Sarah and Ben.

Visit Dan at *businessacceleration.com.*

Index

A

Acceleration tips
- branding, 270
- business research, 229
- change management, 131
- collaboration, 113
- communication, 51
- consumer demands, 253
- convenience, 235
- creativity, 76, 242
- execution, 124
- innovation, 212–13
- leadership, 67
- Leadership Council, 146
- personal effectiveness, 26
- priority management, 40
- strategic planning, 156, 187
- talent management, 199
- teamwork, 88, 108

Administrative assistant, 37
Adventure, 95–96
Affinity brand, 266
Alternative explanations, 223
American Airlines, 42
Analogy, 62
Andy, Ashley, 105–8
Apology, 110
Apple Inc., 163, 176, 179, 246, 257
Arrogance, 47, 152
Art of War, The, 269
Ask method, 59–61
Aspirational strategy, 181
AT&T, 266
Automobile dealerships, 240
Average performers, 121–22
Awareness, 85–86

B

Bar-raising process tool, 272–73
Behavior clarification, 66
Best effort, 63
Best reputation strategy, 182
Beyond the Core, 176, 179
Big talkers, 44
"Big Three," 276–77
Blue Ocean Strategy, 176, 177
BMW, 105–8, 269
Bold statement, 64
Books, 62, 74
Boredom, 46, 150–51
Bossidy, Larry, 116, 176
Brainstorming, 112–13
Brand
- acceleration tips, 270
- benefits, 256–58
- building steps, 259–61
- business research questions, 261
- considerations, 261–65
- definition of, 256
- development, 268–69
- execution, 264
- filter, 257–58
- importance of, 267
- innovation, 265
- marketing questions, 265
- perceived value, 262
- personal effectiveness, 262–63
- positioning, 258
- relevancy, 269
- strategy, 264
- talent management, 263–64
- teamwork, 263
- types of, 266

Buckingham, Marcus, 67, 127
Budget Rent A Car, 180
Buffett, Warren, 20
Burnout factor, 209
Business driver, 93
Business outcome, 65
Business plan, 144–45
Business research
- acceleration tips, 229
- adjustments and, 252–53
- alternative explanations, 223
- brand building, 259, 261

brand development role, 268–69
competition, 223
customer, 220–21, 224
data interpretation, 219–20
effective, 225–26, 249
expectations, 226–27
focus groups, 220, 227–28
importance of, 225, 248–49
industry knowledge, 222
information gathering, 250–51
observation, 221
purpose of, 218–19
reliable statistics, 219–20
strategic planning and, 251–52
timeline, 222
trends, 251
useful information, 228–29
Business talent, 191
Business-to-business, 234

C

Calendar, 38–39
Candidness, 34–35
Candor, 63
Cantalupo, Jim, 187
Career acceleration, 14
Career transition, 129–30
Carlson, Ted, 248–53
Carpenter, Chris, 190
Carter, Jimmy, 47, 63
Carty, Don, 42
Case study
review past success, 12
say no, 20
teamwork, 82, 98
teamwork-by-crisis, 85
Cell phone, 234
Challenge, 63–65
Change management
acceleration tips, 131
change types, 126–30
observations, 125–26
questions, 145
strategic options, 171–75
Charan, Ram, 116, 176
Clarification, 65–66
Coach's Card, 271–79
Coaching process tool, 274–75
Coca-Cola
competition, 65
iconic status, 181
positioning, 258
strategic error, 150
Collaboration
acceleration tips, 113
with boss, 37–38
creation steps, 111–13
definition of, 111
embracing, 109–13
teamwork test, 87
Collins, Jim, 189, 194, 267
Combined strategy, 182
Comfort zone, 58, 246
Commercials, 233
Commitment
benefits, 21
clarification, 21
follow through, 19, 20
ignoring, 47
mental, 22
negative consequences, 21
successful execution, 22
Communication
acceleration tips, 51
big talkers, 44
destructive behaviors, 43–51
devil's advocate, 46–47
disasters, 41–43
discipline in, 16
empathic listeners, 45
incorrect statements, 48–49
nitpickers, 44
nonverbal, 46
positives, 46
rumors, 49–50
screamers, 45
throwaway comments, 47
Competition
collaboration and, 110–11
cooperation and, 111
expert, 223
leadership challenges, 64–65
Competitor strategy, 155
Complexity, 102, 153
Confidentiality, 16
Consequences
expectations and, 117
teamwork and, 99–104
unity and, 86
Consistency, 260
Constructive criticism, 103
Consultants, 155–56
Convenience

acceleration tips, 235
creators, 232–35
delivery, 231–32
Cooperation, 111
Core business, 179
Corporate strategy, 168, 170
Creative Memories, 181
Creative process tool, 272
Creativity
acceleration tips, 76
importance of, 70–72
increase, 72–76
role of, 210–11
Creativity Age, 237–42
Crisis, 84–85
Critical path, 118–19
Culture, 117, 149–50
Customer/consumer
acceleration tips, 253
business research, 220–21
complaints, 244–45
demands, 243–53
desired, 166–67
insights, 224
intimacy, 177
outcomes, 259–60
purpose of, 218
rejection, 247–48
retention, 92–93
strategic planning and, 150
viewpoint, 75, 244
wants/needs identification, 206–7

D

Decision making, 97, 170
Deficiencies, 246
Dell Inc., 178–79, 181
Democratization strategy, 180
Demonstration, 56–58
DePaul University, 8
Depth and breadth strategy, 180
Devil's advocate, 46–47
Diffusion, 58
Dinner and a movie concept, 233
Discipline, 15–22
Discipline of Market Leaders, The, 176
Disempowerment, 47–48
Dishonesty, 48
Disney, Walt, 71, 74, 246
Disney World, 233
Dissonance, 58
Diversification, 198–99
Diversity, 74–75, 199
Domineering executive, 86
Downtime, 29–30
Drucker, Peter, 10, 31–32, 40, 176, 223
Dual expectations, 80–81

E

eBay, 13, 180
Effective Executive, The, 10, 31–32, 40
Effective meeting process tool, 274
Efficiency evaluation, 123
Ego, 83–84, 245
Eisner, Michael, 13–14, 42
Elitism strategy, 180–81
Emotional issues, 36
Employee
burnout, 153–54
passions, 163
retention, 92
skills, 154, 163
Empowerment, 57–58
Enabler brands, 266
Energized person, 8
Ensemble approach, 98
Execution
brand building, 264
management, 115–24
strategic planning, 156
Execution and Confronting Reality, 116, 176
Executive loss, 258
Expectations, 117
Express line concept, 233
Extraordinary goal, 64

F

Failure, capacity for, 23–25, 26
Family tradition strategy, 182
Faults, 248
Feedback, 16–17
Film, 62
Financial continuous improvement, 182
Fiorina, Carly, 18
Flexibility, 124
Focus groups, 220, 227–28
Follow through, 19, 20, 21
Follow-up, 120
Forgiveness, 101–2, 103–4

Friedman, Thomas, 191, 270
Friendliness factor strategy, 180
Functional person, 7–8
Future success, 11–13

G

Gates, Bill, 14, 190
GE, 190
General Motors, 182
Gladwell, Malcolm, 238
Good to Great, 189, 267
Google, 181, 190, 237–38
Gossip, 49–50
Group discussions, 61
Group purpose, 83, 84
GSD&M, 105–8, 225–29, 266–70

H

Harvard University, 190
Health, 18–19
Heartland Dental Care, 151
Hewlett-Packard, 18
Holtz, Lou, 100
Home Depot, 177
Honesty, 56
Hotels, 239
Huey-Lipton, Rene, 225–29
Hutchison, Jeff, 231

I

Iconic strategy, 181
Ideas
    building on, 112–13
    filter, 257–58
    generation, 92
    launching pad, 257
    sharing, 43, 112, 113
IKEA, 180
Imagination process, 75–76
Imagineer, 71
Imagineering Way: Ideas to Ignite Your Creativity, The, 71, 72
Imitation, 151
Immelt, Jeff, 97
Incubation phase, 203–4
Individual success, 104
Industry knowledge, 222
Industry norms, 151
Inertia, 197
Information, 228–29, 233
In-house mentoring program, 195
Innovation
    acceleration tips, 212–13
    brand building, 265
    business anthropologist, 208
    competitors, 207
    constant, 260
    customer, 208
    cycle of, 201–3
    definition, 209
    development, 206
    diversity, 206
    execution, 209
    inventory, 207
    noncompetitors, 208
    phases of, 203–6
    process, 143–44
    roll out, 205–6
    simplicity, 206–9
    sources of, 223
    team, 208
Innovation and Entrepreneurship, 223
Insights, 43
Integrity, 22–23, 26, 56
Intel, 182
Intellect/action conversion process tool, 278–79
Intersection of greatness, 13–15
Interview process, 194
Invisible enemy, 45
iPod, 232, 246, 257
Issue/opportunity resolution process, 141–42

J

Jobs, Steve, 257
Jocketty, Walt, 190–91, 193
John Deere, 182

K

Katzenberg, Jeffrey, 42
Kelleher, Herb, 89, 268
Kim, W. Chan, 176, 177–78
King, Larry, 74
Knowledge, 75, 165

L

Labels, 191–92
La-la land, 90–91
Large test phase, 204–5
LaRussa, Tony, 190
LCEC (Leadership Council Executive Committee), 142
Leadership
  acceleration tips, 67
  approaches, 53–55
  behaviors, 56–58
  definition of, 54, 94
  lack of, 155
  methods of, 56, 57
  relationships, 55–56
Leadership Council
  acceleration tips, 146
  business research, 140
  diversity, 136–37
  effectiveness, 144–45
  establishment of, 132–33
  operation of, 138–42
  purpose of, 131–32
  resolution process, 141–42, 143–44
  roles/responsibilities, 139
  strategy/tactics, 140
Leverage, 247
Listening, 45
L'Oreal, 181
Loudest crank, 247
Louis Vuitton, 179, 180
Luke, Ginger, 237–38

M

Management, 36–37
Managing for Results, 176
Market conditions, 165–67
Marketing, 260–61, 265
Marketplace approach
  core business, 179
  defining, 176–77
  differentiate, 177–78
  modeling, 180–83
Marriott International, 12, 180, 258
Mary Kay Cosmetics, 181
Maslow, Abraham, 29
Maslow on Management, 29
Massage, 235
Mauborgne, Renee, 176, 177–78
McDonald's Corporation
  business research, 248–53
  combined strategy approach, 182
  dinner and a movie concept, 233
  marketplace approach, 177
  positioning, 258
  strategy, 184–87
Medical tools company, 239–40
Mental detachment, 101
Mentoring program, 195
Mercedes-Benz, 180
Meyers, Dr. Richard, 19
Micromanagement, 120
Microsoft, 181, 190, 202
Microwave mentality, 150
Million Dollar Consulting, 126
Miracle on 34th Street, 241
Mission, 268
Mistakes, 257
Model behavior, 57
Mood-ring leader, 53–54

N

Negative emotions, 101
Neighborhood brand strategy, 181
Newton, Isaac, 197
Nitpickers, 44
Nokia, 182
Nonverbal communication, 46
Nonwork situations, 74
Nordstrom, 180, 193–94
Notre Dame, 6

O

Objectives, 96–97
Observation, 221
One Thing You Need to Know, The, 67, 127
One-stop convenience, 234
Open-ended questions, 73
Operational excellence, 176–77
Opportunity interception process tool, 279
Organizational asset audit, 162–65
Organizational creativity, 237–42
Other Side of Me, The, 24
Other Side of Midnight, The, 24–25, 26
Outcomes, 168, 169–70

P

Pampered Chef, 181
Paranoia, 50
Party central, 91
Passion. See Strengths/passions
Passionate group, 91–92
Past
    power of, 12
    success, 11–13, 60
PepsiCo, 65, 179, 181
Performance evaluations, 195–96
Personal dignity, 29–40
Personal effectiveness
    acceleration exercise, 15
    acceleration tips, 26
    capacity to fail, 23–25, 26
    discipline, 15–22
    enhancing, 3–6
    integrity, 22–23, 26
    intersection of greatness, 13–15
    review/preview success, 11–13
    strengths/passions, 8–9
    understanding value, 6–13
    weaknesses, 9
Personal integrity, 50
Personal story, 61–62
PGA, 257–58
Pittsburgh Pirates, 190
Planned activities
    critical path, 118–19
    definition of, 183
    evaluation, 123
    expectations, 117
    filters for, 184
    follow-up, 120
    sacrifice of, 118
    schedule of, 119–20
    sequence of, 117–18
Planning process, 183–84
Politically incompetent, 48–49
Politics, 48
Poor performers, 18, 86, 122–23
Positioning, 258
Preparation process tool, 273
Price matters strategy, 180
Priorities, 66, 111–12
Priority management, 27–40
Product excellence, 176
Profit from the Core, 176, 179
Promotion, 197–98
Punctuality, 17
Purpose, 94–95, 268
Purpose-based branding, 267–68

Q

QuikTrip, 181

R

Ralph Lauren, 181
Random sampling approach, 245
Realtors, 240–41
Reasonableness, 34
Recognition/rewards
    personal touch, 235
    self, 39–40
    supporters, 104
    top performers, 121
Red Box, 233
Relationship builders, 50, 145
Relationships, 55, 98–99
Religion, 48
Repetition, 22
Resources, 163, 165
Respect, 16, 51
Responsibilities, 99–104, 121
Restaurants, 239
Results, 66
Retail stores, 241–42
Retention, 198
Review past success, 99
Rewards. *See* Recognition/rewards
Rework, 39
Rickover, Hyman, 63
Risk/rewards, 65–66
Road victim, 37
Rolen, Scott, 190
Role-play, 60–61
Roll out phase, 205–6
Rowland, Pleasant, 94
Rudeness, 46
Rumors, 49–50

S

Say no, 19, 20, 32–33
Schedule
    changes, 17
    flexibility, 36–37
    of planned activities, 119–20
    workday, 34
Schwimmer, David, 98
Screamers, 45

Self-awareness, 101
Self-discipline
  acceleration tips, 26
  behavior, 15–22
  essential areas for, 16–20
  and scheduling, 120
  strengthening, 20–22
Self-disclosure, 50
Self-esteem, 29
Shadowing, 73
Shared sacrifice, 42
Share method, 61–63
Sheldon, Sidney, 24–25, 36
Silos, 80
Skills, 163, 164
Small test phase, 204
Societal change, 127–28
Socratic approach, 60
Solution leader, 278
Solution leadership process tool, 275–76
Southern Living, 181
Southwest Airlines, 89, 151, 268
Speed strategy, 181
Spence, Roy, 266–70
Stakeholder buy-in, 185–86
Starbucks, 170, 181, 219–20, 257
Stewart, Dave, 190
Stewart, Martha, 14
St. Louis Cardinals, 190, 209–12, 258
Strategic options, 171–75
Strategic planning
  acceleration tips, 156, 187
  arrogant executive and, 152
  business research and, 251–52
  competitors, 155
  complexity, 153
  consultants, 155–56
  culture and, 149–50
  customers and, 150
  employee burnout and, 153–54
  enthusiasm and, 149
  execution, 147–48, 156
  financial strength, 154
  focus, 157–58
  frequent changes, 151–52
  imitation, 151
  implementation, 186
  industry norms and, 151
  leadership, 155
  long-term, 152–53
  process, 183–84
  skills, 154
  staying the course, 150–51
  sustainable results, 150
  timeframe, 160
Strategy
  brand building, 264
  components, 161–70
  current, 168, 170
  decision making, 170
  definition of, 183
  development, 176–83
  effectiveness of, 184–85
  operating within, 17–18
  purpose of, 158–59
  tactical perspective, 185
Strengths/passions
  identification of, 26
  leveraging, 11, 26
  list of, 9, 10
  personal effectiveness and, 8–9
  question, 59
  strategic focus, 163
Stretch goals, 64
Subcommittees, 139
Suggestions, 112
Sustainable growth, 256–57

T

Tactic, 183–84
Taguchi, So, 190
Talent management
  acceleration tips, 199
  application, 145–46, 189–92
  brand building, 263–64
  development, 195
  diversification, 198–99
  employee characteristics, 192–94
  enhancement, 197
  evaluation, 195–96
  interview process, 194
  placement, 194
  promotion, 197–98
  retention, 198
Talk shows, 74
Team mergers, 129
Teamwork
  acceleration tips, 88, 108
  barriers, 80–88
  brand building, 263
  case study, 98
  financial price of, 87

impact reality check, 99–100
importance of, 92–94
member responsibilities/consequences, 99–104
purpose, 94–98
relationships, 98–99
responsibilities/consequences, 99–104
strengthening, 89–92
unity, 79–80
Teamwork-by-crisis, 85
Technology, 35–36
Test phase, 204–5
Thinking time, 38, 72–73
Throwaway comments, 47
Timeframe, 32
Time management
priority, 30–31, 40
redistribution, 31–32
Tipping Point, The, 238
Top performers, 121
Toxic habits, 100–102
Toyota, 220–21, 245, 258
Tragic zone, 90
Training program, 195
Treacy, Michael, 176–77
Trends, 251
Trust, 16, 19, 102–3
Tupperware, 181
24-hour quick service concept, 234
Tzu, Sun, 269

U

Unexpected success, 223–24
University of Washington, 20
Urgency, 95

V

Value
added, 13–14, 239–42
definition of, 6, 117, 162
delivery of, 90
organizational, 162–63
perception of, 257, 262
review/preview success, 11–13
understanding, 6–13
Value-adder, 6, 14
Video stores, 241
Vision
lack of, 81–82
Southwest Airlines, 268
statement, 159–60
Visionary leadership, 12

W

Wade, Kevin, 209–12
Wal-Mart, 151, 177, 180, 234
Walt Disney Company
communication errors, 42
corporate strategy, 168, 180
employee orientation, 117
intersection of greatness, 13–14
talent, 190
understanding consumer demands, 246
Walton, Sam, 160, 268
Weaknesses, 62–63
Webster University, 19
Weiss, Alan, 126–27
Welch, Jack, 14, 63, 93, 97, 113
Wells, Karen, 184–87
Whitman, Meg, 13
Wiersema, Fred, 176–77
Winfrey, Oprah, 74
Wooden, John, 60
Work in Progress, 42
Work/life balance
boundaries, 32
calendar, 38–39
candidness, 34–35
daily schedule, 34
downtime, 29–30
emotional issues, 36
fallacy, 27–29
focus, 31
habits to break, 32
priority management, 30–31
reasonable, 34
rewards, 39–40
say no, 32–33
schedules, 36–37
technology, 35–36
time, 31–32
timeframe, 32
time review, 40
World Is Flat, The, 191

Z

Zook, Chris, 176, 179